# THE LIGHT
## OF
# THE SOUL

# BOOKS BY ALICE A. BAILEY

# THE
# LIGHT OF THE SOUL

## Its Science and Effect

A paraphrase of
**THE YOGA SUTRAS OF
PATANJALI**

with commentary
By
ALICE A. BAILEY

LUCIS PUBLISHING COMPANY
New York

LUCIS PRESS, Ltd.
London

**LUCIS PUBLISHING COMPANY**
**120 Wall Street**
**New York, NY 10005**

**LUCIS PRESS, Ltd.**
**Suite 54**
**3 Whitehall Court**
**London SW1A 2EF**

MANUFACTURED IN THE UNITED STATES OF AMERICA

Gratefully dedicated

to

FOSTER BAILEY

# EXTRACT FROM A STATEMENT BY THE TIBETAN

## PUBLISHED AUGUST 1934

Suffice it to say, that I am a Tibetan disciple of a certain degree, and this tells you but little, for all are disciples from the humblest aspirant up to, and beyond, the Christ Himself. I live in a physical body like other men, on the borders of Tibet, and at times (from the exoteric standpoint) preside over a large group of Tibetan lamas, when my other duties permit. It is this fact that has caused it to be reported that I am an abbot of this particular lamasery. Those associated with me in the work of the Hierarchy (and all true disciples are associated in this work) know me by still another name and office. A.A.B. knows who I am and recognises me by two of my names.

I am a brother of yours, who has travelled a little longer upon the Path than has the average student, and has therefore incurred greater responsibilities. I am one who has wrestled and fought his way into a greater measure of light than has the aspirant who will read this article, and I must therefore act as a transmitter of the light, no matter what the cost. I am not an old man, as age counts among the teachers, yet I am not young or inexperienced. My work is to teach and spread the knowledge of the Ageless Wisdom wherever I can find a response, and I have been doing this for many years. I seek also to help the Master M. and the Master K.H. whenever opportunity offers, for I have been long connected with Them and with Their work. In all the above I have told you much; yet at the same time I have told you nothing which would lead you to offer me that blind obedience and the foolish devotion which the emotional aspirant offers to the Guru and Master whom he is as yet unable to contact. Nor will he make that desired contact until he has transmuted emotional devotion into unselfish service to humanity —not to the Master.

The books that I have written are sent out with no claim for their acceptance. They may, or may not, be correct, true or useful. It is for you to ascertain their truth by right practice and by the exercise of the intuition. Neither I nor A.A.B. is the least interested in having them acclaimed as inspired writings, or in having anyone speak of them (with bated breath) as being the work of one of the Masters. If they present truth in such a way that it follows sequentially upon that already offered in the world teachings, if the information given raises the aspiration and the will-to-serve from the plane of the emotions to that of the mind (the plane whereon the Masters *can* be found) then they will have served their purpose. If the teaching conveyed calls forth a response from the illumined mind of the worker in the world, and brings a flashing forth of his intuition, then let that teaching be accepted. But not otherwise. If the statements meet with eventual corroboration, or are deemed true under the test of the Law of Correspondences, then that is well and good. But should this not be so, let not the student accept what is said.

*"Before the soul can see, the harmony within must be attained, and fleshly eyes be rendered blind to all illusion.*

*Before the soul can hear, the image (Man) has to become as deaf to roarings as to whispers, to cries of bellowing elephants as to the silvery buzzing of the golden fire-fly.*

*Before the soul can comprehend and may remember, she must unto the silent speaker be united, just as the form to which the clay is modelled is first united with the potter's mind.*

*For then the soul will hear, and will remember.*

*And then to the inner ear will speak the voice of the silence."*

*From* THE VOICE OF THE SILENCE.

# INTRODUCTORY REMARKS

The Science of Raja Yoga, or the "Kingly Science of the Soul," as laid down by its main exponent, Patanjali, will eventually find its greatest demonstration in the West. This is owing to the fact that—under cyclic law—the fifth root race (in its fifth subrace) must inevitably touch its highest point. That point, in the economy of the races, is seen exemplified in the right use of the mind and its utilisation by the soul for the achievement of group objectives and the development of group consciousness upon the physical plane.

Hitherto the mind has either been prostituted to material ends or has been deified. Through the science of Raja Yoga, the mind will be known as the instrument of the soul and the means whereby the brain of the aspirant becomes illuminated and knowledge gained of those matters which concern the realm of the soul.

Under the law of evolution likewise, the mind, being the fifth principle, the fifth root race must be intimately concerned with it, and its corresponding fifth subrace more intimately than any other. Students would do well to bear in mind the following correspondences:

1. The fifth root race............................ Aryan.
2. The fifth subrace .............................. Anglo-Saxon.
3. The fifth principle ........................... manas, or mind.
4. The fifth plane ................................. the mental.
5. The fifth ray ..................................... concrete knowledge.

## INTRODUCTORY REMARKS

All the various Yogas have had their place in the unfoldment of the human being. In the first purely physical race, which is called the Lemurian, the Yoga at that time imposed upon infant humanity was Hatha Yoga, the Yoga of the physical body, that Yoga which brings into conscious use and manipulation the various organs, muscles and parts of the physical frame. The problem before the adepts of that time was to teach human beings, who were then little more than animals, the purpose, significance and use of their various organs, so that they could consciously control them, and the meaning of the symbol of the human figure. Therefore, in those early days, through the practice of Hatha Yoga, the human being reached the portal of initiation. At that time the attainment of the third initiation, resulting in the transfiguration of the personality, was the highest initiation that man was capable of achieving.

In Atlantean days, the progress of the sons of men was procured through the imposition of two Yogas. First, the Yoga which is called by the name of Laya Yoga, the Yoga of the centres which produced a stabilizing of the etheric body and of the centres in man and the development of the astral and psychic nature. Later on, Bhakti Yoga, growing out of the development of the emotional or astral body, was incorporated with Laya Yoga and the foundation of that mysticism and devotion, which has been the underlying incentive during our particular Aryan root race, was laid. The fourth initiation was at that time the objective.  The subject of these great initiations has been discussed more at length in my previous volume, *"Initiation, Human and Solar."*

Now, in the Aryan race, the subjugation of the mental body and the control of the mind is brought about through the practice of Raja Yoga, and the fifth initiation, that of adept, is the goal for evolving humanity.  Thus, all the Yogas have had their place and served a useful purpose and it will become apparent that any return to Hatha Yoga practices or those practices which deal specifically with the development of the centres, brought about through various types of meditation practices and breathing exercises, is, from a certain aspect, a retrogression.  It will be found that through the practice of Raja Yoga, and through assuming that point of directional control which is to be found by the man who centers his consciousness in the soul, the other forms of Yoga are unnecessary, for the greater Yoga automatically includes all the lesser in its results, though not in its practices.

When these are studied, it will become apparent why the day of opportunity has only just arrived. The East has preserved rules for us since time immemorial.  Here and there orientals (with a few Western adepts) have availed themselves of those rules and have submitted to the discipline of this exacting science.  Thus has been preserved for the race the continuity of the Secret Doctrine, of the Ageless Wisdom, and thus has been gathered together the personnel of the Hierarchy of our planet.  In the time of the Buddha and through the stimulation He produced there was a great gathering in of Arhats. These were men who had achieved liberation through self-initiated effort. This period, in our Aryan race, marked a climax for the East. Since then the tide of spiritual life has steadily flowed westward, and we may now look for a corresponding climax in the West, which will reach its zenith between the years 1965 and 2025. Towards this end the adepts of the East and of the West are unitedly working, for they follow always the Law.

This coming impulse is (as was that in the time of the Buddha) a second Ray impulse, and has no relation to any first Ray impulse, such as that which brought forth H. P. Blavatsky. First Ray impulses rise in the first quarter of each century and reach their climax on the physical plane during the last quarter. The interest now shown in Raja Yoga and the study of this science and the rules it provides for man's unfoldment, is indicative of the general trend of this rising second Ray impulse. This interest will be increasingly shown. Thus comes the day of opportunity.

There are three books which should be in the hands of every student, the Bhagavad Gita, the New Testament, and the Yoga Sutras, for in these three is contained a complete picture of the soul and its unfoldment.

In the *Gita* we have given us (in its eighteen chapters) a description of the soul, of Krishna, the second aspect, in his true nature as God in manifestation, culminating in that marvellous chapter where he reveals himself to Arjuna, the aspirant, as the soul of all things, and the point of glory behind the veil of every form.

In the *New Testament* there is depicted for us the life of a Son of God in full manifestation, wherein, freed from every veil, the soul in its true nature walks the earth. It becomes apparent to us, as we study the life of Christ, what it means to develop the powers of the soul, to attain liberation, and become, in full glory, a God walking on earth.

In the *Yoga Sutras* there are embodied for us the laws of that becoming, and the rules, methods, and means which—when followed—make a man "perfect even as your Father in Heaven is perfect." Step by step there is unfolded for us a graded system of development, leading a man from the stage of average good man, through those of aspirant, initiate and master on to that exalted point in evolution at which the Christ now stands. John, the beloved disciple, has said that "we shall be like him, for we shall see him as he is" and the revelation of the soul to man in physical plane incarnation works ever the great transformation. Christ himself has said that "Greater works than I do shall ye do," holding out to us the promise of the "kingdom, the power and the glory" provided our aspiration and endurance suffice to carry us along the thorny way of the Cross, and enable us to tread that path which "leads up hill all the way" to the summit of the Mount of Transfiguration.

How is this great change brought about? How does man, the victim of his desires and lower nature become man, the victor, triumph over the world, the flesh and the devil? It is brought about when the physical brain of the incarnated man becomes aware of the self, the soul, and this conscious awareness only becomes possible when the true self can "reflect itself in the mind-stuff." The soul is inherently freed from objects and stands ever in the state of isolated unity. Man, however, in incarnation has to arrive, in his physical brain consciousness, at a realization of these two states of being; he has consciously to free himself from all objects of desire and stand as a unified whole, detached and liberated from all veils, from all forms in the three worlds. When the state of conscious being, as known by the spiritual man, becomes also the condition of awareness of the man in physical incarnation then the goal has been reached. The man is no longer what his physical body makes him, when identified with it, the victim of the *world*. He walks free, with shining face (I. Cor. 3) and the light of his countenance is shed abroad upon all he meets. No longer do his desires swing the *flesh* into activity, and no longer does his astral body subjugate him and overcome him.

Through dispassion and the balancing of the pairs of opposites he has freed himself from the moods, feelings, longings, desires, and emotional reactions which characterise the life of the average man and has arrived at the point of peace. The *devil* of pride, the personification of the misused mental nature and the distorted perceptions of the mind, are overcome and he stands liberated from the three worlds. The nature of the soul, the qualities and activities inherent in the love nature of the Son of God, and the wisdom which demonstrates when love and activity (the second and third aspects) are brought together, characterise his life on earth, and he can say as did the Christ, "It is finished."

The date of the birth of Patanjali is unknown and there is a good deal of controversy upon this matter. Most of the occidental authorities ascribe a date between the years 820 B. C. to 300 B. C., though one or two place him after Christ. The Hindu authorities themselves, however, who may be supposed to know something about the matter, ascribe a very much earlier date, even as far back as 10,000 B. C. Patanjali was a compiler of teaching which, up to the time of his advent, had been given orally for many centuries. He was the first to reduce the teaching to writing for the use of students and hence he is regarded as the founder of the Raja Yoga School. The system, however, has been in use since the very beginning of the Aryan race. The Yoga Sutras are the basic teaching of the Trans-Himalayan School to which many of the Masters of the Wisdom belong, and many students hold that the Essenes and other schools of mystical training and thought, closely connected with the founder of Christianity and the early Christians, are based upon the same system and that their teachers were trained in the great Trans-Himalayan School.

It should be stated here that the Sutras have

been dictated and paraphrased by the Tibetan Brother and the commentary upon them has been written by myself, and subjected to revision and comment by the Tibetan. It should be noted that the translation is not literal, and is not an exact definition of each original Sanskrit term. It is an attempt to put into clear and understandable English the exact meaning, insofar as it is possible to do so through the medium of that non-elastic and unimaginative tongue. The student may find it of use in the study of these sutras to compare the rendition here given, with the various other procurable translations.

ALICE A. BAILEY.

New York, May, 1927.

# BIBLIOGRAPHY

of the translations of and commentaries upon
## THE YOGA SUTRAS OF PATANJALI
used in the preparation of the present work.

The Yoga-Sutra of Patanjali...........*M. J. Dvivedi.*
The Yoga-Darsana.........................*Ganganatha Jha.*
The Yoga Sutras of Patanjali....*Charles Johnston.*
The Yoga Aphorisms of Patanjali....*W. Q. Judge.*
The Yoga Sutras of Patanjali........*Rama Prasada.*
Yoga Philosophy................................*Tookaram Tatya.*
A Compendium of Raja Yoga Philosophy,
      *Rajaram Tookaram.*
Raja Yoga.................................. ...*Swami Vivekananda.*
The Yoga System of Patanjali............*J. H. Woods.*

# TOPICAL OUTLINE

# BOOK I.

## THE PROBLEM OF UNION

a. The higher and lower natures defined.
b. The obstacles and their removal considered.
c. A summation of the Raja Yoga system.
   Topic: The versatile psychic nature.

# THE YOGA SUTRAS OF PATANJALI.

## BOOK I

### THE PROBLEM OF UNION

1. AUM. The following instruction concerneth the Science of Union.
2. This Union (or Yoga) is achieved through the subjugation of the psychic nature, and the restraint of the chitta (or mind).
3. When this has been accomplished, the Yogi knows himself as he is in reality.
4. Up till now the inner man has identified himself with his forms and with their active modifications.
5. The mind states are five, and are subject to pleasure or pain; they are painful or not painful.
6. These modifications (activities) are correct knowledge, incorrect knowledge, fancy, passivity (sleep) and memory.
7. The basis of correct knowledge is correct perception, correct deduction, and correct witness (or accurate evidence).
8. Incorrect knowledge is based upon perception of the form and not upon the state of being.
9. Fancy rests upon images which have no real existence.
10. Passivity (sleep) is based upon the quiescent state of the vrittis (or upon the non-perception of the senses.)
11. Memory is the holding on to that which has been known.
12. The control of these modifications of the internal organ, the mind, is to be brought about through tireless endeavour and through non-attachment.

[ 3 ]

13. Tireless endeavour is the constant effort to restrain the modifications of the mind.

14. When the object to be gained is sufficiently valued, and the efforts towards its attainment are persistently followed without intermission, then the steadiness of the mind (restraint of the vrittis) is secured.

15. Non-attachment is freedom from longing for all objects of desire, either earthly or traditional, either here or hereafter.

16. The consummation of this non-attachment results in an exact knowledge of the spiritual man when liberated from the qualities or gunas.

17. The consciousness of an object is attained by concentration upon its fourfold nature: the form, through examination; the quality (or guna), through discriminative participation; the purpose, through inspiration (or bliss); and the soul, through identification.

18. A further stage of samadhi is achieved when, through one pointed thought, the outer activity is quieted. In this stage, the chitta is responsive only to subjective impressions.

19. The samadhi just described passes not beyond the bound of the phenomenal world; it passes not beyond the Gods, and those concerned with the concrete world.

20. Other yogins achieve samadhi and arrive at a discrimination of pure Spirit through belief, followed by energy, memory, meditation and right perception.

21. The attainment of this state (spiritual consciousness) is rapid for those whose will is intensely alive.

22. Those who employ the will likewise differ, for its use may be intense, moderate, or gentle. In respect to the attainment of true spiritual consciousness there is yet another way.

23. By intense devotion to Ishvara, knowledge of Ishvara is gained.

24. This Ishvara is the soul, untouched by limitation, free from karma, and desire.

25. In Ishvara, the Gurudeva, the germ of all knowledge expands into infinity.

[ 4 ]

26. Ishvara, the Gurudeva, being unlimited by time conditions, is the teacher of the primeval Lords.

27. The Word of Ishvara is AUM (or OM). This is the Pranava.

28. Through the sounding of the Word and through reflection upon its meaning, the Way is found.

29. From this comes the realisation of the Self (the soul) and the removal of all obstacles.

30. The obstacles to soul cognition are bodily disability, mental inertia, wrong questioning, carelessness, laziness, lack of dispassion, erroneous perception, inability to achieve concentration, failure to hold the meditative attitude when achieved.

31. Pain, despair, misplaced bodily activity and wrong direction (or control) of the life currents are the results of the obstacles in the lower psychic nature.

32. To overcome the obstacles and their accompaniments, the intense application of the will to some one truth (or principle) is required.

33. The peace of the chitta (or mind stuff) can be brought about through the practice of sympathy, tenderness, steadiness of purpose, and dispassion in regard to pleasure or pain, or towards all forms of good or evil.

34. The peace of the chitta is also brought about by the regulation of the prana or life breath.

35. The mind can be trained to steadiness through those forms of concentration which have relation to the sense perceptions.

36. By meditation upon Light and upon Radiance, knowledge of the Spirit can be reached and thus peace can be achieved.

37. The chitta is stabilized and rendered free from illusion as the lower nature is purified and no longer indulged.

38. Peace (steadiness of the chitta) can be reached through meditation on the knowledge which dreams give.

39. Peace can also be reached through concentration upon that which is dearest to the heart.

40. Thus his realization extends from the infinitely small to the infinitely great, and from annu (the atom or speck) to atma (or spirit) his knowledge is perfected.

41. To him whose vrittis (modifications of the substance of the mind) are entirely controlled, there eventuates a state of identity with, and similarity to that which is realized. The knower, knowledge and the field of knowledge become one, just as the crystal takes to itself the colours of that which is reflected in it.

42. When the perceiver blends the word, the idea (or meaning) and the object, this is called the mental condition of judicial reasoning.

43. Perception without judicial reasoning is arrived at when the memory no longer holds control, the word and the object are transcended and only the idea is present.

44. The same two processes of concentration, with and without judicial action of the mind, can be applied also to things subtle.

45. The gross leads into the subtle and the subtle leads in progressive stages to that state of pure spiritual being called Pradhana.

46. All this constitutes meditation with seed.

47. When this super-contemplative state is reached, the Yogi acquires pure spiritual realisation through the balanced quiet of the chitta (or mind stuff).

48. His perception is now unfailingly exact (or his mind reveals only the Truth).

49. This particular perception is unique and reveals that which the rational mind (using testimony, inference and deduction) cannot reveal.

50. It is hostile to, or supersedes all other impressions.

51. When this state of perception is itself also restrained (or superseded), then is pure Samadhi achieved.

# THE YOGA SUTRAS OF PATANJALI

## BOOK I

### THE PROBLEM OF UNION

**1. AUM. (OM)   The following instruction concerns the Science of Union.**

AUM. is the Word of Glory; it signifies the Word made flesh and the manifestation upon the plane of matter of the second aspect of divinity. This blazing forth of the sons of righteousness before the world is achieved by following the rules herein contained.  When all the sons of men have demonstrated that they are also Sons of God, the cosmic Son of God will likewise shine forth with increased intensity of glory.  The great initiate, Paul, had a vision of this when he said that "the whole creation groaneth and travaileth in pain  .  .  .  waiting for the manifestation of the sons of God."  (Rom. VIII.)

Raja Yoga, or the science of Union, gives the rules and the means whereby:

1.   Conscious contact can be made with the soul, the second aspect, the Christ within,

2.   Knowledge of the self can be achieved and its control over the not-self maintained,

3. The power of the ego or soul can be felt in the daily life and soul powers manifested,

4. The lower psychic nature can be subdued, and the higher psychic faculties demonstrated,

5. The brain can be brought en rapport with the soul and its messages received,

6. The "light in the head" can be increased, so that a man becomes a living Flame,

7. The Path can be found and man himself become that Path.

The following triplicities may be found of value to the student, especially if he remembers that it is the central column which contains the terms applicable to the soul or second aspect. The union to be achieved is that of the third and second aspects. This is consummated at the third initiation (in Christian terminology, the Transfiguration). A later synthesis is then effected between the united third and second aspects and the first:

| 1st Aspect | 2nd Aspect | 3rd Aspect |
|---|---|---|
| Spirit | Soul | Body |
| Father | Son (Christ) | Holy Ghost |
| Monad | Ego | Personality |
| Divine self | Higher self | Lower self |
| Life | Consciousness | Form |
| Energy | Force | Matter |
| The Presence | The Angel of the Presence | The human being |

A clear distinction should be made between the Christ Principle as indicated above, which is a high spiritual aspect to which each member of humanity must attain, and the same term applied to a personage of exalted rank representing that

[ 8 ]

Principle, whether in the historical reference to the Man of Nazareth or otherwise.

**2. This Union (or Yoga) is achieved through the subjugation of the psychic nature and the restraint of the chitta (or mind).**

The follower after union has two things to do:

1. To gain control of the "versatile psychic nature,"

2. To prevent the mind from assuming the many forms it so easily does. These are frequently called "modifications of the thinking principle."

These two produce control of the emotional body and therefore of desire, and control of the mental body, and therefore of lower manas or mind. The student should remember that uncontrolled desire and an unregulated mind shut off the light of the soul and negate spiritual consciousness. Union is impossible as long as the barriers exist, and the Master therefore directs the attention of the student (at the beginning of his instruction) to the practical work to be done in liberating this light so that it may "shine forth in a dark place;" *i. e.*, on the physical plane. It should be borne in mind that, occultly speaking, when the lower nature is controlled it can manifest the higher. When the second aspect of the lower personal self, the emotional body, is subjugated or transmuted then the Christ light (the second aspect egoic) can be seen. Later, in its light, the Monad, the Father, the One, will stand revealed. Equally, when the first aspect of the lower personal self, the mental body, is restrained, then the Will aspect of the ego can be known, and through its activities, the purpose of the Logos Himself will be cognized.

There are certain lines of least resistance in the spiritual life and along them certain forces or energies are released.

a. Emotional..intuitional ......monadic ..........to the heart of
   or buddhic                              the aspirant.

b. Mental ......spiritual..........logoic ..............to the head of
   or atmic                              the aspirant.

The student is therefore given the WORD of restraint or control as a key to all his endeavors.

The *chitta* is the mind, or mind-stuff, the mental body, the faculty of thought and of thought-form making, the sum total of the mental processes; it is the material governed by the ego or soul out of which thought forms are made.

The *"psychic nature"* is kama-manas (desire-mind), the emotional or astral body, tinged faintly with mind, and is the material clothing all our desires and feelings. Thereby they are expressed.

These two types of substance have their own line of evolution to follow and they do so. Under the logoic plan, the spirits or divine sparks are imprisoned by them, being first attracted to them through the mutual interplay of spirit and matter. By the control of these substances and the restraint of their instinctual activities, these spirits gain experience and eventually liberation. Thus union with the soul is brought about. It is

[ 10 ]

a union known and experienced in the physical body upon the plane of densest manifestation through the conscious intelligent control of the lower nature.

**3. When this has been accomplished, the Yogi knows himself as he is in reality.**

This might be described in the following way: The man who knows the conditions and has fulfilled them as indicated in the preceding sutra,
1. Sees the self,
2. Realises the true nature of the soul,
3. Identifies himself with the inner Reality, and no longer with the concealing forms,
4. Dwells in the centre and no longer upon the periphery,
5. Achieves spiritual consciousness,
6. Awakes to recognition of the God within.
In these three verses, the method and the goal are described in clear and certain terms and the way prepared for the more detailed instruction to follow. The aspirant faces his problem, the clue to its solution is given to him, and the reward— union with the soul—is held before his seeking eye.
The past is briefly covered in the next verse.

**4. Up till now the inner man has identified himself with his forms and with their active modifications.**

These forms are the modifications mentioned in the various translations, conveying the subtle truth concerning the infinite divisibility of the atom; these are the veiling sheaths and rapidly changing transformations which prevent the true nature of the soul becoming manifest. These are the externalities which hinder the light of the inner God from shining forth, and which are occultly spoken of as "casting a shadow before the face of the sun."

The inherent nature of the lives which constitute these active versatile forms has hitherto proved too strong for the soul (the Christ within, as the Christian puts it) and the soul-powers have been prevented full expression. The instinctual powers of the "animal soul," or the capacities of the aggregate of lives which form the sheaths or bodies, imprison the real man and limit his powers. These lives are intelligent units on the involutionary arc of evolution, working towards self-expression. Their objective is, however, different from that of the Inner Man and they hinder his progress and self-realization. He becomes "enmeshed in their activities" and must free himself before he comes into his heritage of power and peace and bliss. He cannot attain "unto the measure of the stature of the fullness of the Christ" (Eph. 4:13) until there are no modifications to be felt, until the forms are transformed, their activities quieted, and their restlessness stilled.

The student is urged to bear in mind the nature of this aspect of evolution which is proceeding concurrently with his own. In his right apprehension of this problem comes realization of the practical work to be done, and the embryo yogi can begin his work.

The lower forms are constantly and ceaselessly active, endlessly assuming the forms of impulsive desires or dynamic mental thought forms, and it is only as this "form-taking" is controlled and the tumult of the lower nature stilled that it becomes possible for the inner ruling entity to liberate himself from thraldom and impose *his* vibration upon the lower modifications.

This is achieved through concentration—the concentrated effort of the soul to hold steadily the position of observer, or perceiver and of seer. When he can do this the lower "spectacle" of the rapidly changing forms of thought and desire fades away, and the realm of the soul, the true field of soul knowledge, can be seen and contacted.

**5. The mind states are five, and are subject to pleasure or pain; they are painful or not painful.**

In the original the word "pleasure" does not occur; the thought conveyed is more technical, and is usually translated as "not painful." Nevertheless, the underlying thought is the hindrance to realization caused by the pairs of opposites. The student must remember that in this sutra it is the chitta or mind-stuff which is under consideration, with the modifications it undergoes as long as its versatility and activity are controlling factors. He must not lose sight of the fact that we are

dealing with the lower psychic nature, which is
the term occultly applied to the lower mind processes as well as to the astral or emotional reactions. All activity in the lower nature is the result of kama-manas, or of mind tinged with feeling, of the desire-will of the lower man. The goal
of the Raja Yoga system is that these impulses
should be replaced by the considered intelligent
action of the soul or spiritual man, whose nature
is love, whose acts are wise (occultly understood)
and whose motive is group development. Therefore that reaction called pain must be transcended
and likewise that termed pleasure, for both of
these are dependent upon identification with form.
Non-attachment must supersede them.

It is interesting to note that the modifications
of the internal organ, the mind, are five in number. Manas, or mind, the actuating principle of
the chitta, or mind-stuff, is the fifth principle, and
like all else in nature, manifests as a duality.
This duality is:

1. Lower concrete mind, demonstrating as the
activity of the mental body.

2. Abstract mind, demonstrating as the lowest
aspect of the ego.

In the microcosm, man, this duality becomes a
triple modification upon the mental plane, and in
these three we have in miniature a picture of the
macrocosmic manifestation. These three are:

1. The mental permanent atom, the lowest aspect of the spiritual Triad or of the soul,

2. The egoic body, the causal body, or the
karana sarira,

**3.** The mental body, the highest aspect of the lower personal self.

The mental body itself has five modifications or activities, and thus is a reflection, or correspondence of the fifth principle, as it manifests upon the fifth plane, the mental. The modifications are the lower shadow of manas (or mind in the microcosmic manifestation), and this mind is a reflection of mahat (the universal mind), or mind manifesting in the macrocosm. This is a great mystery but will reveal itself to the man who overcomes the five modifications of the lower mind, who through non-attachment to the lower, identifies himself with the higher, and who thus solves the mystery of the "Makara" and treads the Way of the Kumaras. Herein lies a hint to the more advanced students of this science as to the esoteric problem of the Makara, hinted at in the *"Secret Doctrine"* by H. P. Blavatsky.

**6. These modifications (activities) are correct knowledge, incorrect knowledge, fancy, passivity (sleep) and memory.**

There exists a vast field of knowledge which the seer must cognise at some time or another. It is generally conceded among occult psychologists, that there are three modes of apprehension:

1. *Direct cognition* through the avenue of the senses, each sense, when in use, putting its user into contact with a distinct range of vibrations, demonstrating as form manifestations.

2. *Deduction or inference*, the use by the cogniser of the reasoning powers of the mind in re-

lation to that not directly perceived. This is, for
the occult student, the use of the Law of Correspondences or of Analogy.

3. *The direct cognition of the yogi or seer,*
centered in the consciousness of the self, the ego
on its own plane. This is achieved through the
right use of the mind as an organ of vision and
transmission. Patanjali says:

"The seer is pure knowledge (gnosis). Though
pure he looks upon the presented idea through the
medium of the mind." Book II. Sutra 20.

Deduction is not a sure method of ascertaining
knowledge and the other modifications refer primarily to the wrong use of the image making faculty (imagination), to the self-induced passivity
of the mind, a condition of semi-trance, and to
the retention of thought forms within the mental
aura, through the use of the memory. Each of
these is now dealt with in a separate sutra by
Patanjali.

**7. The basis of correct knowledge is correct
perception, correct deduction and correct witness (or accurate evidence).**

One of the most revolutionary realizations to
which the occult student has to adjust himself
is the appreciation that the mind is a means
whereby knowledge is to be gained. In the west
the idea has mostly been held that the mind is
that part of the human mechanism which utilizes
knowledge. The "process of turning things over
in the mind," of striving to solve problems by
hard mental labor has no part ultimately in the

unfoldment of the soul. It is only a preliminary stage and has to be superseded by a different method.

The student of Raja Yoga has to realise that the mind is intended to be an organ of perception; only thus will he arrive at a right understanding of this science. The process to be followed in relation to the mind might be described somewhat as follows:

1. Right control of the modifications (or activities) of the thinking principle.

2. Stabilization of the mind and its subsequent use by the soul as an organ of vision, a sixth sense, and the synthesis of all the five other senses.

Result: Correct knowledge.

3. Right use of the perceiving faculty, so that the new field of knowledge which is now contacted is seen as it is.

4. That which is perceived is rightly interpreted through the subsequent assent of the intuition and the reason.

5. Right transmission to the physical brain of that which has been perceived; the testimony of the sixth sense is correctly interpreted, and the evidence is transmitted with occult accuracy.

Result: Correct reaction of the physical brain to the transmitted knowledge.

When the process is studied and followed, the man on the physical plane becomes increasingly aware of the things of the soul, and the mysteries of the soul realm—or the "Kingdom of God." All group concerns and the nature of group consciousness are revealed to him. It will be noted that these rules are even now regarded somewhat as essential premises where all accurate testimony is under consideration in world affairs. When these same rules are carried forward into the world of psychic endeavor (both lower and higher) then we shall have a simplification of the present confusion. In an old book written for disciples of a certain degree these words occur and are of value to all probationary and accepted disciples. The translation gives the sense, and is not literal.

"Let the one who looks out take care that the window through which he gazes transmits the light of the sun. If he use it in the early dawn (of his endeavor. A. B.) let him remember that the orb is not yet risen. The clear cut outlines cannot be perceived, and wraiths and shadows, gloomy spaces and areas full of darkness as yet confuse his vision."

At the close of this sentence is found a curious symbol, which conveys to the disciple's mind the thought of "Keep silent and reserve your opinion."

**8. Incorrect knowledge is based upon perception of the form and not upon the state of being.**

This sutra is somewhat difficult to paraphrase. Its significance consists in this: Knowledge, deduction and a decision which is based upon externals, and upon the form through which any life in any kingdom of nature is expressing itself, is (to the occultist) false and untrue knowledge.

At this stage in the evolutionary process no form of any kind measures up to, or is an adequate expression of, the indwelling life. No true adept judges any expression of divinity through its third aspect. Raja Yoga trains a man to function in his second aspect and through that second aspect to put himself en rapport with the "true nature" latent in any form. It is the "being" that is the essential reality, and all beings are struggling toward true expression. All knowledge therefore which is acquired through the medium of the lower faculties and which is based upon the form aspect is incorrect knowledge.

The soul alone perceives correctly; the soul alone has the power to contact the germ or the principle of Buddhi (in the Christian phraseology, the Christ principle) to be found at the heart of every atom, whether it is the atom of matter as studied in the laboratory of the scientist, whether it is the human atom in the crucible of daily experience, whether it is the planetary atom, within whose ring-pass-not all our kingdoms of nature are found, or the solar atom, God in manifestation through the medium of a solar system. Christ "knew what was in man" and therefore could be a Saviour.

**9. Fancy rests upon images which have no real existence.**

This means that these images have no real existence in so far as they are conjured up by men themselves, constructed within their own mental auras, energized by their will or desire and are consequently dissipated when attention is directed elsewhere.

"Energy follows thought" is a basic tenet of the Raja Yoga system and is true even where these images of fancy are concerned. These fancied images fall primarily into three groups, which the student would do well to consider.

1.  Those thought forms which he constructs himself, which have an evanescent life and which are dependent upon the quality of his desires; being therefore neither good nor evil, low nor high, can be vitalized by low tendencies or idealistic aspirations, with all the intermediate stages to be found between these extremes. The aspirant has to guard himself in order that he may not mistake these for reality. An illustration might well be given here, in respect to the facility with which people judge they have seen one of the Brothers (or Masters of the Wisdom), whereas all they have perceived is a thought form of one of Them; the wish being father to the thought they are the victim of that form of incorrect perception called by Patanjali, fancy.

2.  Those thought forms which are created by the race, the nation, the group or the organization. Group thought forms of any kind (from the planetary form to that constructed by any band of thinkers) form the sum total of the "great illusion." Herein lies a hint to the earnest aspirant.

3.  That thought form created by a man since his first appearance in physical form, and called the "Dweller on the Threshold." Being created

by the lower personal self and not by the soul, it is impermanent and is simply held together by the man's lower energy. When the man begins to function as the soul this "image" he has created, through his "fancy" or his reaction to delusion, is dissipated by a supreme exertion. It has no real existence once there is nothing in the aspirant to feed it, and the realization of this enables him to free himself from its thraldom.

This is one of the sutras which, though apparently short and simple, is of the most profound significance; it is studied by high initiates who are learning the nature of the creative process of the planet, and who are concerned with the dissipation of planetary maya.

**10. Passivity (sleep) is based upon the quiescent state of the vrittis (or upon the non-perception of the senses).**

Some explanation as to the nature of the vrittis is perhaps necessary here. The vrittis are those activities of the mind which eventuate in the conscious relation between the sense employed and that which is sensed. Apart from a certain modification of the mental process or an assertion of the I-am-I realization, the senses might be active yet the man be unaware of them. The man is aware that *he* sees, tastes or hears; he says, "I see, I taste, I hear," and it is the activity of the vrittis (or those mental perceptions which have relation to the five senses) which enables him to recognize the fact. By withdrawing himself from active sense perception, by no longer utilising the "outward-going" consciousness, and by abstracting that consciousness from the periphery to the centre, he can bring on a condition of passivity,—a lack of awareness, which is not the samadhi of the yogi, nor the achievement of one-pointedness such as the student of yoga aspires to, but which is a form of trance. This self-imposed quieting is not only a detriment to the achievement of the highest yoga but is excessively dangerous in many cases.

Students will do well to remember that right activity of the mind and its correct use is the goal of yoga, and that the state called "a blank mind" and a condition of passive receptivity, with the sense relations cut off or atrophied, is not part of the process. The sleep here referred to is not the passing of the body into the state of slumber, but the putting to sleep of the vrittis. It is the negation of the contacts of the senses without the sixth sense, the mind, superseding their activities. In this condition of sleep, a man is open to hallucination, to delusion, to wrong impressions and to obsessions.

Sleep is of several kinds, and only a short tabulation is possible in such a commentary as this is.

1. The ordinary sleep of the physical body, where the brain does not respond to any sense contacts;

2. Sleep of the vrittis, or of those modifications of the mental processes which correlate the man with his environment, through the medium of the senses and the mind;

3. The sleep of the soul, which, occultly speaking, covers that part of human experience which dates from a man's first human incarnation until he "awakens" to a knowledge of the plan, and endeavors to bring the lower man into line with the nature and will of the inner spiritual man;

4. The sleep of the ordinary medium, wherein the etheric body is partially extruded from the physical body, and is likewise separated from the astral body, bringing in a condition of very real danger;

5. Samadhi, or the sleep of the yogi, the result of the conscious scientific withdrawal of the real man from his lower threefold sheath in order to work on high levels, preparatory to some active service upon the lower;

6. The sleep of the Nirmanakayas, which is a condition of such intense spiritual concentration and focussing in the spiritual or atmic body that the outward going consciousness is withdrawn not only from the three planes of human endeavor but likewise from the two lower expressions of the spiritual Triad. For purposes of his peculiar and specific work the Nirmanakaya "sleeps" to all states save that of the third, or atmic plane.

**11. Memory is the holding on to that which has been known.**

This memory concerns several groups of realizations, either active or latent; it deals with certain congeries of known factors, and these might be enumerated as follows:

1. The thought images of that which is tan-

[ 23 ]

gible, objective and which has been known by the thinker upon the physical plane.

2. Kama-manasic (or desire-lower mind) images of past desires and their gratification. The "picture making faculty" of the average man is based upon his desires (high or low desires, aspirational or degrading, in its sense of pulling down) and their known gratification. This remains equally true of the memory of a gluttonous man, for instance, and his latent image of a satisfactory dinner, and the memory of the orthodox saint, based upon his picture making of a joyous heaven.

3. That memory activity which is the result of mental training, the accumulation of acquired facts, the consequence of reading or of teaching, and which is not purely based upon desire, but which has its basis in intellectual interest.

4. All the various contacts which the memory holds and recognises as emanating from the five lower sense perceptions.

5. Those mental images, latent in the memory making faculty, which are the total of the knowledge contacted and the realisations evoked by the right use of the mind as a sixth sense.

All these forms of the memory faculty have to be dropped and no longer held; they must be recognised as modifications of the mind, of the thinking principle, and therefore as part of that versatile psychic nature which has to be dominated before the yogi can hope to attain liberation from limitation and from all lower activity. This is the goal.

6. Finally (for it is not necessary to enumerate more intricate subdivisions) memory includes also the accumulated experiences gained by the soul through the many incarnations, and stored up in the true consciousness of the soul.

**12. The control of these modifications of the internal organ, the mind, is to be brought about through tireless endeavour and through non-attachment.**

A few brief explanations are all that is necessary with a sutra as easy to apprehend as this one; intellectually its meaning is clear; in practice, however, it is difficult to carry out.

1. The *internal organ* is of course the mind. Occidental thinkers should remember that the Eastern occultist does not consider the organs to be the physical organs. The reason for this is that the physical body in its dense or concrete form is not regarded as a principle, but simply as the tangible outcome of the activity of the real principles. The organs, occultly speaking, are such centres of activity as the mind, the various permanent atoms, and the centres of force in the various sheaths. These all have their objective "shadows" or results, and these resultant emanations are the external physical organs. The brain, for instance, is the "shadow" or the external organ of the mind, and it will be found by the investigator that the contents of the brain cavity have a correspondence to the aspects of the human mechanism found upon the mental plane. This latter sentence should be emphasised;

it conveys a hint to those capable of taking advantage of it.

2. *Tireless endeavour* means literally constant practice, ceaseless repetition and the reiterated effort to impose the new rhythm upon the old, and to efface deep seated habits and modifications by the institution of soul impression. The yogi or Master is the result of patient endurance; his achievement is the fruit of a steady effort which is based upon intelligent appreciation of the work to be done and the goal to be reached, and not upon spasmodic enthusiasm.

3. *Non-attachment* is the one thing that eventually brings all sense perceptions to perform their legitimate functions. Through non-attachment to those forms of knowledge with which the senses put a man in contact, they continuously lose their hold over him; the time eventually comes when he is liberated, and is the master of his senses and of all sense contacts. This does not involve a state wherein they are atrophied and useless, but is one in which they are useful to the yogi when and as he chooses and in so far as he chooses; they are utilized by him in increasing his efficiency in group service and in group endeavour.

**13. Tireless endeavour is the constant effort to restrain the modifications of the mind.**

This is one of the most difficult sutras to translate so as to give its real significance. The idea involved is that of the constant effort made by the spiritual man to restrain the modifications or the fluctuations of the mind and to control the lower psychic versatile nature in order fully to express his own spiritual nature. Thus, and only thus, can the spiritual man live the life of the soul each day upon the physical plane. Charles Johnston in his translation seeks to give this meaning in the words "the right use of the will is the steady effort to stand in spiritual being."

The idea involved is that of applying to the mind (regarded as a sixth sense) the same restraint that the five lower senses are subjected to: their outward going activities are stopped and they are held from responding to the pull or attraction of their particular field of knowledge.

**14. When the object to be gained is sufficiently valued, and the efforts towards its attainment are persistently followed without intermission, then the steadiness of the mind (restraint of the vrittis) is secured.**

All followers of Raja Yoga must first be devotees. Only intense love of the soul and of all that knowledge of the soul entails will carry the aspirant with sufficient steadiness toward his goal. The objective in view—union with the soul, and consequently with the Oversoul and with all souls —must be justly appraised; the reasons for its achievement correctly judged, and the results to be gained most earnestly desired (or loved) before the aspirant will make that sufficiently strong effort which will give him his hold upon the modifications of the mind and consequently upon his

[ 27 ]

entire lower nature. When this appreciation is true enough and his ability to go forward with the work of subjugation and control is *without intermission,* then the time will come when the student will know consciously and increasingly what is the meaning of restraint of the modifications.

**15. Non-attachment is freedom from longing for all objects of desire, either earthly or traditional, either here or hereafter.**

Non-attachment can also be described as thirstlessness. This is the most correct occult term to use as it involves the dual idea of water, the symbol of material existence, and desire, the quality of the astral plane, whose symbol is also water. The idea of man being the "fish" is curiously complete here. This symbol (as is the case with all symbols) has seven meanings; two are of use in this place:

1. The fish is the symbol of the Vishnu aspect, the Christ principle, the second aspect of divinity, the Christ in incarnation, whether it is the cosmic Christ (expressing Himself through a solar system) or the individual Christ the potential saviour within each human being. This is the "Christ in you, the hope of glory." (Col. I:27) If the student will also study the fish Avatar of Vishnu he will learn still more.

2. The fish swimming in the waters of matter, an extension of the same idea only carried down to its more obvious present expression, man as the personality.

Where there is no longing for any object whatsoever, and where there is no desire for rebirth
(ever the outcome of longing for "form-expres-
sion" or material manifestation) then the true
thirstlessness is attained, and the liberated man
turns his back upon all the forms in the lower
three worlds and becomes a true saviour.

In the *Bhagavad Gita* the following illuminating words are found:—

"For the possessors of wisdom, united in soul-
vision, giving up the fruit of works, freed from
the bondage of rebirth, reach the home where no
sorrow dwells.

"When thy soul shall pass beyond the forest of
delusion, thou shalt no more regard what shall
be taught or what has been taught.

"When withdrawn from traditional teaching,
thy soul shall stand steadfast, firm in soul-vision,
then shalt thou gain union with the Soul." (Gita
II, 51, 52 and 53.)

J. H. Woods makes this clear in his translation
of the comment by Veda Vyasa which is here
appended:

"Passionless is the consciousness of being Master on the
part of one who has rid himself of thirst for either seen
or revealed objects."

"The mind stuff (chitta)—if it be rid of thirst for objects that are seen, such as women, or food or drink or
power, if it be rid of thirst for the object revealed (in the
Vedas) such as the attainment of Heaven or of the discarnate state or of resolution into primary matter—if even
when in contact with objects either supernormal or not it
be, by virtue of elevation, aware of the inadequateness of
objects—will have a consciousness of being Master . . ."

## BOOK I

The word "traditional" carries the student's thought away from that which is usually regarded as the object of sensuous perception into the world of thought forms, into that "forest of delusion" which is constructed of men's ideas about God, heaven or hell. The sublimation of all this and its highest expression in the three worlds is that "devachan" which is the goal of the majority of the sons of men. Devachanic experience must, however, be transformed eventually into nirvanic realization. It may be of value to the student to remember that heaven, the object of aspirational desire, which is the outcome of traditional teaching, and of all formulations of doctrinal faiths has several meanings to the occultist. For the purpose of a clearer understanding the following may be found to be of use:

1. *Heaven,* that state of consciousness upon the astral plane which is the concretion of the longing and desire of the aspirant for rest, peace and happiness. It is based upon the "forms of joy." It is a condition of sensuous enjoyment, and being constructed for himself by each individual is as varied as there are people participating in it. Non-attachment has to be achieved with respect to heaven. It is realized as enjoyed by the lower self, and by the man when bereft only of his physical body, prior to passing out of the astral body on to the mental plane.

2. *Devachan,* that state of consciousness upon the mental plane into which the soul passes when deprived of its astral body and functioning in, or limited by, its mental body. It is of a higher

order than the ordinary heaven and the bliss enjoyed is more mental than we ordinarily understand by the word, yet nevertheless it is still
within the lower world of form and will be transcended when non-attachment is known.

3. *Nirvana,* that condition into which the
adept passes when the three lower worlds are no
longer "attached" to him through his inclinations
or karma, and which he experiences after he has:

a. Taken certain initiations,
b. Freed himself from the three worlds,
c. Organized his Christ body.

Strictly speaking those adepts who have
achieved non-attachment but who have chosen to
sacrifice themselves and abide with the sons of
men in order to serve and help them are not technically Nirvanis. They are Lords of Compassion
pledged to "suffer" with, and to be governed by,
certain conditions analogous to (though not identical with) the conditions governing men who are
still attached to the world of form.

**16. The consummation of this non-attach-
ment results in an exact knowledge of the
spiritual man when liberated from the qualities
or gunas.**

Certain points should be remembered by the
student when considering this sutra:

1. That the spiritual man is the monad,
2. That the evolutionary process when carried to its climax produces not only the freeing
of the soul from the limitations of the three
worlds, but the freeing of the spiritual man from

[ 31 ]

all limitations, even that of the soul itself. The goal is formlessness or freedom from objective and tangible manifestation, and the true significance of this becomes apparent as the student remembers the oneness of spirit and matter when in manifestation; *i. e.* our seven planes are the seven subplanes of the lowest cosmic plane, the physical. Consequently only "the time of the end" and the dissolution of a solar system will reveal the true meaning of formlessness.

3. The gunas are the three qualities of matter, the three effects produced when macrocosmic energy, the life of God which persists independently of form-taking, actuates or energizes substance. The three gunas are:

| | | | | |
|---|---|---|---|---|
| 1. | Sattva...Energy of Spirit..Father | ........rhythm or harmonious vibration |
| | Monad | |
| 2. | Rajas.....Energy of Soul... Son | ...........mobility or activity |
| | Ego | |
| 3. | Tamas...Energy of Matter.Holy | ........inertia. |
| | Personality Ghost | |

These three correspond to the quality of each of the three aspects which express the one Life.

In such a brief commentary as this perforce must be it is not possible to enlarge to any extent upon this subject, but some idea can be gained as to what is meant by the consummation of nonattachment when applied to the macrocosm or the microcosm. The three gunas have all been used, full experience through the use of form has been acquired, consciousness, perception or awareness through attachment to an object or to a form has been developed, all resources have been utilised, and the spiritual man (logoic or human) has no further use or need for them. He is therefore freed from the gunas, released from form taking as the result of attachment, and enters into a new state of consciousness upon which it is useless for us to speculate.

**17. The consciousness of an object is attained by concentration on its fourfold nature: the form, through examination; the quality (or guna), through discriminative participation; the purpose, through inspiration (or bliss) and the soul, through identification.**

It will be apparent therefore that the statement "as a man thinketh so is he" (Prov. 23:7) is based on occult facts. Every form of any kind has a soul, and that soul or conscious principle is identical with that in the human form; identical in its nature though not in its scope of development, or its degree. This is equally true of the great Lives or superhuman Existences in which man himself "lives and moves and has his being" (Acts 17: 28) and to Whose state of development he aspires.

As the aspirant chooses with care the "objects" upon which he will meditate, he through these objects, builds himself a ladder by means of which he arrives eventually at the objectless. As his mind assumes increasingly the meditative attitude of the soul, the brain becomes also increasingly subjugated to the mind as the mind is to the soul. Thus is the lower man gradually identified with the spiritual man who is omniscient and omnipresent. This meditative attitude is assumed through a fourfold process:—

1. *Meditation on the nature of a particular form,* realising, as the form is pondered upon, that it is but a symbol of an inner reality, our whole tangible objective world being built up of form, of some kind (human, subhuman and superhuman), which expresses the life of hosts of sentient beings.

2. *Meditation upon the quality of any particular form,* so that an appreciation of its subjective energy may be gained. It should be borne in mind that the energy of an object may be regarded as the colour of that object, and hence the words of Patanjali IV, 17 become illuminating in this connection and serve as a commentary upon this second point. This is called "discriminative participation," and through it the student arrives at that knowledge of energy in himself which is one with the object of his meditation.

3. *Meditation upon the purpose of any particular form.* This involves consideration of the idea back of or underlying any form manifestation and its display of energy. This realisation carries the aspirant onward to a knowledge of that part in the plan or purpose of the All which is the motivating factor in the form's activity. Thus through the part, the Whole is contacted and an expansion of consciousness takes place, involving bliss or joy. Beatitude always follows upon realisation of the unity of the part with the Whole. From meditation upon the tattvas, the energies or principles, or upon the tanmatras or

elements composing spirit-matter, a knowledge of the purpose or plan for the microcosmic or macrocosmic manifestations eventuates and with this knowledge comes bliss.

In these three are to be found correspondences to the three aspects, spirit, soul and body, and an illuminating study for the earnest student.

4. *Meditation upon the soul,* upon the One who uses the form, who energises it into activity and who is working in line with the plan. This soul, being one with all souls and with the Oversoul subserves the one plan and is group-conscious.

Thus through these four stages of meditation upon an object, the aspirant arrives at his goal, knowledge of the soul, and of the soul powers. He becomes consciously identified with the one reality, and this in his physical brain. He finds that truth which is himself and which is the truth hidden in every form and in every kingdom of nature. Thus he will eventually arrive (when knowledge of the soul itself is gained) at a knowledge of the All-Soul and become one with it.

**18. A further stage of samadhi is achieved when through one-pointed thought, the outer activity is quieted. In this stage the chitta is responsive only to subjective impressions.**

The word "samadhi" is subject to various interpretations, and is applied to different stages of yogi achievement. This makes it somewhat difficult for the average student when studying the various commentaries. Perhaps one of the easiest ways to realise its meaning is to remember that the word "Sama" has reference to the faculty of the mind-stuff (or chitta) to take form or to modify itself according to the external impressions. These external impressions reach the mind via the senses. When the aspirant to yoga can control his organs of sense-perception so that they no longer telegraph to the mind their reactions to that which is perceived, two things are brought about:

a. The physical brain becomes quiet and still,

b. The mind stuff or the mental body, the chitta, ceases to assume the various modifications and becomes equally still.

This is one of the early stages of samadhi but is not the samadhi of the adept. It is a condition of intense internal activity instead of external; it is an attitude of one-pointed concentration. The aspirant is, however, responsive to impressions from the subtler realms and to modifications arising from those perceptions which are still more subjective. He becomes aware of a new field of knowledge, though as yet he knows not what it is. He ascertains that there is a world which cannot be known through the medium of the five senses but which the right use of the organ of the mind will reveal. He gets a perception of what may lie back of the words found in a later sutra as translated by Charles Johnston, which expresses this thought in particularly clear terms:

"The seer is pure vision . . . he looks out through the vesture of the mind." (Book II. Sutra 20.)

The preceding sutra dealt with what may be

called meditation with seed or with an object; this sutra suggests the next stage, meditation without seed or without that which the physical brain would recognise as an object.

It might be of value here if the six stages of meditation dealt with by Patanjali are mentioned as they give a clue to the entire process of unfoldment dealt with in this book:

1. Aspiration,
2. Concentration,
3. Meditation,
4. Contemplation,
5. Illumination,
6. Inspiration.

It is of value here to note that the student begins by *aspiring* to that which lies beyond his ken and ends by being *inspired* by that which he has sought to know. Concentration (or intense focussing) results in meditation and meditation flowers forth as contemplation.

**19. The samadhi just described passes not beyond the bounds of the phenomenal world; it passes not beyond the Gods and those concerned with the concrete world.**

It should be noted here that the results achieved in the processes dealt with in sutras seventeen and eighteen only carry the aspirant to the edge of the realm of the soul, to the new field of knowledge of which he has become aware. He is still confined to the three worlds. All that he has succeeded in doing is stilling the modifications of the mental body so that for the first time the man (on the physical plane and in his physical brain) becomes cognisant of what lies beyond those three worlds—that is, the soul, its range of vision and its knowledge. He has yet to strengthen his link with the soul (dealt with in sutras twenty-three to twenty-eight) and then having transferred his consciousness into that of the real or spiritual man, he must begin working from that new standpoint or vantage point.

The idea has been expressed by some translators as the condition in which the aspirant becomes aware "of the rain cloud of knowable things." The raincloud has not precipitated sufficiently for the rain to fall from heavenly heights onto the physical plane or for the "knowable things" to become known to the physical brain. The cloud is perceived as the result of intense concentration and the stilling of the lower modifications, but until the soul or Master has assumed control the knowledge of the soul cannot be poured into the physical brain via the sixth sense, the mind.

The science of yoga is a real science and only as students approach it by the correct stages and employ the scientific methods, will the true samadhi or realization be achieved.

20. **Other yogins achieve samadhi and arrive at a discrimination of pure spirit through belief, followed by energy, memory, meditation and right perception.**

In the previous groups of yogins dealt with, perception was limited to the phenomenal world, though we must understand by that only the three worlds of mental perception, astral perception and of the physical senses. The energies producing concretion and the motive power of thought as it produces effects on the physical plane are contacted and known. Here however the yogin translates himself into more spiritual and subtler realms and becomes aware of that which the self (in its true nature) perceives and knows. He enters into the world of causes. The first group might be regarded as comprising all who are treading the path of discipleship, and covers the time from their entrance upon the Probationary Path until they have taken the second Initiation. The second group is comprised of those higher disciples who—having controlled and transmuted the entire lower nature—make a contact with their monad, spirit or "Father in Heaven" and discern what that monad perceives.

The first form of realisation comes to those who are in process of synthesising the six lower centres into the head centre, through the transmutation of the lower four into the higher three, and then of the heart and throat into the head. The second group—through a knowledge of the law—works with all the transmuted and purified centres. They know how to achieve the real samadhi or state of occult abstraction through their ability to withdraw the energies into the thousand petalled lotus of the head, and from thence to abstract them through the other two subtler bodies until all is centred and focussed in the causal vehicle, the karana sarira, the egoic lotus. We are told by

Patanjali that this is produced by the following five stages. Students should bear in mind that these stages relate to soul activities, to egoic realisation and not to the reactions of the lower man and the physical brain.

1. *Belief.* On his own plane the soul rehearses a condition analogous to the belief of the aspirant in the soul or Christ aspect, only in this case the objective is the realisation of that which the Christ or soul is seeking to reveal, the spirit or Father in Heaven. First the disciple arrives at a realisation of the angel of His Presence, the solar angel, ego or soul. This is the achievement of the previous group. Then the Presence itself is later contacted and that Presence is pure spirit, the absolute, the Father of Being. The self and the not-self have been known by this group of initiates. Now the vision of the not-self dims and passes away and only spirit is known. Belief must ever be the first stage. First the theory, then the experiment, and lastly realisation.

2. *Energy.* When the theory is grasped, when the goal is perceived, then activity ensues—that right activity and that correct use of force which will bring the goal nearer and make theory fact.

3. *Memory,* or right mindfulness. This is an interesting factor in the process as it involves right forgetfulness, or the elimination out of the consciousness of the ego of all those forms which have hitherto veiled the Real. These forms are either self-chosen or self-created. This leads to a condition of true apprehension or the ability to register correctly that which the soul has per-

ceived, and the power to transfer that correct perception to the brain of the physical man. This is the memory referred to here. It does not refer so specifically to recollection of the things of the past, but covers the point of realisation and the transference of that realisation to the brain where it must be registered and eventually recollected at will.

4. *Meditation.* That which has been seen and registered in the brain and which has emanated from the soul must be meditated upon and thus woven into the fabric of the life. It is through this meditation that the soul-perceptions become real to the man upon the physical plane. This meditation therefore is of a very high order as it follows upon the contemplative stage and is soul-meditation with the object of illuminating the vehicle upon the physical plane.

5. *Right perception.* The experience of the soul, and the knowledge of the spirit or Father aspect begins to form part of the brain content of the Adept or Master. He knows the plan as it is to be found on the highest levels and is in touch with the Archetype. It is, if I might illustrate in this way, that this class of yogins have reached the point where they can perceive the plan as it exists in the mind of the "Grand Architect of the Universe." They are now en rapport with Him. In the other class of Yogins, the point reached is that in which they are able to study the blue-prints of the great plan and thus can intelligently co-operate in the building of the Temple of the Lord. The perception referred to here is of such a high

order as to be almost inconceivable to any but advanced disciples, but in an appreciation of the stages and grades there comes to the aspirant, not only an understanding of what is his immediate problem and of where he stands, but also an appreciation of the beauty of the entire scheme.

**21. The attainment of this stage (spiritual consciousness) is rapid for those whose will is intensely alive.**

This would naturally be so. As the will, reflected in the mind, becomes dominant in the disciple, he has awakened that aspect of himself which is en rapport with the will aspect of the Logos, the first or Father aspect. The lines of contact are as follows:

1.  Monad or the Father in Heaven, the will aspect,
2.  Atma or spiritual will, the highest aspect of the soul,
3.  The mental body or intelligent Will, the highest aspect of the personality,
4.  The head centre.

This is the line followed by the raja-yogins and it brings them to a realisation of the spirit and to adeptship. There is yet another line:

1.  Monad,
2.  The Son or Christ aspect,
3.  The love aspect, or wisdom aspect,
4.  Buddhi or spiritual love, the second aspect of the soul,
5.  The emotional body, the second aspect of the personality,

6. The heart centre.

This is the line followed by the bhakti, the devotee and the saint and brings him to a knowledge of the soul and of sainthood. The former line is that to be followed by our Aryan race. This second line was the path of attainment for the Atlanteans.

If students would follow these tabulations with care much light would come. The necessity for a strong energetic will becomes apparent if the path of Initiation is studied. Only an iron will, and a steady, strong, unswerving endurance will carry the aspirant along this path and out into the clear light of day.

**22. Those who employ the will likewise differ, for its use may be intense, moderate or gentle. In respect to the attainment of true spiritual consciousness there is yet another way.**

It would be wise here to make clear the two ways whereby men reach the goal,—knowledge of the spiritual life, and emancipation. There is the *way of Yoga* as outlined by Patanjali whereby, through the use of the will, discrimination between the self and the not-self is achieved and pure spirit is arrived at. This is the way for the fifth or Aryan race, for those whose function it is to develop the fifth principle or mind and thus become true sons of mind. It is their part to become the five-pointed star, the star of the perfected man, in all his glory. Through following this way the five planes of human and superhuman evolution are dominated and atma (or the will of God, the Father aspect) stands revealed through the medium of buddhi (or the Christ consciousness), having for its vehicle, manas or higher mind.

The other way is the way of pure devotion. Through intense adoration and entire consecration the aspirant arrives at a knowledge of the reality of spirit. This is the way of least resistance for many; it was the method of attainment for the race preceding the Aryan. It largely ignores the fifth principle and is the sublimation of sensuous perception, being the way of intense feeling. Through following this method the four planes are dominated and buddhi (or the Christ) stands revealed. Students should differentiate clearly between these two ways, remembering that the white occultist blends the two and if in this life he follows the way of Raja Yoga with fervour and love it will be because in other lives he set his foot upon the way of devotion and found the Christ, the Buddhi within. In this life he will recapitulate his experience, plus the intense exercise of the will and control of the mind which will eventually reveal to him his Father in Heaven, the point of pure spirit.

Commentators upon this sutra point out that those who follow the method of Raja Yoga and use the will are divided into three main groups. These can correspondingly be divided into nine. There are those who use the will with such intensity that exceedingly rapid results are achieved, attended however with certain dangers and risks. There is the risk of uneven development, of a negation of the heart side of nature, and of certain destructions which will later have to be remedied. Then there are those aspirants whose progress is less rapid, and who are exponents of the middle path. They proceed steadily and moderately and are called the "discriminative adepts" as they permit no excesses of any kind. Their method is to be recommended to men in this particular cycle. Again there are those gentle souls whose will may be regarded as characterised by an imperturbable pertinacity and who go steadily, undeviatingly forward, eventually arriving at their goal. They are distinguished by intense tenacity. Their progress is slow. They are the "tortoises" of the Path just as the first group are the "hares."

In some of the old books there are detailed accounts of these three groups of aspirants and they are portrayed under three symbols:

1. The intense group are depicted as *goats*, and aspirants of this type are frequently found in incarnation under the sign Capricorn,

2. The moderate group are depicted by a *fish*, and many born under the sign Pisces are found in this category,

3. The gentle or slow group are pictured as *crabs* and often come into incarnation under the sign Cancer.

In these three groups are to be found various subdivisions and it is interesting to note that in the archives of the Lords of Karma, the majority of these three groups pass into the sign of Libra (or the balances) towards the close of their en-

deavour. When in incarnation under this sign
they balance the pairs of opposites with care, they
equalise their one-sided development, modifying
the unevenness of their efforts hitherto, and begin
to "set an even pace." They frequently then
enter the sign of Aquarius and become bearers of
water, having to carry "on their heads the bowl of
living water." Thus the rapidity of their climb
up the mount of initiation has to be modified, or
"the water will be spilt and the bowl be shat-
tered." Because the water is intended to slake
the thirst of the masses, they must hasten their
progress for the need is great. Thus the "first
shall be last and the last shall be first" and the
hare and the tortoise meet at the goal.

**23. By intense devotion to Ishvara, know-
ledge of Ishvara is gained.**

Ishvara is the son in manifestation through the
sun. This is the macrocosmic aspect. Ishvara is
the son of God, the cosmic Christ, resplendent in
the heart of each of us. The word "heart" is here
used in its occult connotation. The following correspondences may be found illuminating and
should be studied with care.

| | Aspect | | Quality | Centre | Macrocosm |
|---|---|---|---|---|---|
| Spirit | Father | Monad | Will | Head | Central spir-itual sun. |
| Soul | Son | Ego | Love | Heart | Heart of the sun. |
| Body | Holy Spirit | Person-ality | Active Intelli-gence | Throat | Physical sun. |

Ishvara is the second aspect, and therefore the

real meaning of this sutra is that through intense devotion to, and love of Ishvara, the Christ in manifestation, that Christ or soul may be contacted or known. Ishvara is God in the heart of every child of God; He is to be found in the cave of the heart; He is to be reached through pure love and devoted service, and when reached He will be seen seated upon the twelve petalled lotus of the heart, holding in his hands the "jewel in the lotus." Thus the devotee finds Ishvara. When the devotee becomes the raja yogin then Ishvara will reveal to him the secret of the jewel. When Christ is known as king upon the throne of the heart, then He will reveal the Father to His devotee. But the devotee has to tread the Path of Raja Yoga, and combine intellectual knowledge, mental control and discipline before the revelation can be truly made. The mystic must eventually become the occultist: the head qualities and the heart qualities must be equally developed, for both are equally divine.

24. **This Ishvara is the Soul, untouched by limitation, free from karma and desire.**

Here we have the picture of the spiritual man as he is in reality. His relation to the three worlds is shown. This is the state of the master or the adept, of the soul who has come into its birthright, and is no longer under control of the forces and energies of the lower nature. There is given in this and the following three sutras, a picture of the liberated man who has passed through the cycle of incarnation and through struggle and experience has found the true self. Here is depicted the nature of the solar angel, the son of God, the ego or the higher self. He is stated to be

1. *Untouched by limitation.* He is no longer "cribbed, cabined and confined" by the lower quaternary. He is no longer crucified upon the cross of matter. The four lower sheaths—dense, etheric, emotional and mental—are no longer his prison. They are but instruments which he can use or vacate at will. His will functions freely and if he stays within the realm of the three worlds, it is of his own choice, and his self-imposed limitation can be terminated at will. He is master in the three worlds, a son of God dominating and controlling the lower creations.

2. *Free from Karma.* Through knowledge of the law he has adjusted all his karma, paid all his debts, cancelled all his obligations, settled all claims against him, and through his subjective realisation has entered consciously into the world of causes. The world of effects is left behind, in so far as the three worlds are concerned. Thus he no longer (blindly and through ignorance) sets in motion conditions which must produce evil effects. He works ever with the law and every demonstration of energy (the spoken word and the initiated action) is undertaken with a full knowledge of the result to be attained. Thus nothing he does produces evil results and no karma is thereby entailed. Average men deal with effects and blindly work their way through them. The Master deals with causes, and the effects He

produces, through the wielding of the law, do not limit or hold him.

3. *Free from desire.* No longer do the things of sensuous perception on any of the three planes attract or allure Him. His consciousness is inward and upward. It is no longer downward and outgoing. He is at the centre and the periphery no longer attracts him. The longing for experience, the craving for physical plane existence, and the desire for the form aspect in its many variations has for him no appeal. He has experienced, He knows, He has suffered, and He has been forced into incarnation through His longing for the not-self. Now all that is ended and He is the freed soul.

**25. In Ishvara, the Gurudeva, the germ of all knowledge expands into infinity.**

In the macrocosmic sense God is the Master of all and He is the sum total of omniscience, being (as is easily seen) the sum total of all states of consciousness. He is the soul of all things, and the soul of the atom of matter as well as the souls of men are a part of His infinite realisation. The soul of the human being is potentially the same, and as soon as the consciousness ceases to identify itself with its vehicles or organs, the germ of all knowledge begins to expand. In the disciple, the adept, Master or Mahatma, in the Christ, the Buddha, and in the Lord of the World, Who is mentioned in the Bible as the Ancient of Days, this "germ of all knowledge" can be seen at differing stages of unfoldment. God consciousness

is theirs, and they pass from one initiation to
another. At each stage a man is a master but
ever beyond the point attained another possible
expansion becomes apparent and ever the process
is the same. This process may be summed up in
the following statements:

1. An urge, or determination to achieve the
new knowledge,

2. The holding of the consciousness already
unfolded and its utilisation, and from the point
achieved working forward towards further realisation,

3. The overcoming of the difficulties incident
to the limitations of the vehicles of consciousness
and to karma,

4. The occult tests which are imposed upon
the pupil when he shows ability,

5. The triumph of the pupil,

6. The recognition of his triumph and attainment by the guides of the race, the planetary
Hierarchy,

7. The vision of what lies ahead.

Thus does the unfoldment proceed and in each
cycle of endeavor the evolving son of God comes
into his birthright and takes the position of a
knower, "One who has heard the tradition, experienced the dissolution of that hitherto held, seen
that which is hidden from those who abide by the
tradition, substituted that which is newly seen,
donated the acquired possession to those who hold
out empty hands, and passed on to inner halls of
learning."

Students would do well in studying these few

sutras relating to Ishvara to bear in mind that they have reference to the son of God, the second person of the Trinity as He manifests through the medium of the solar system, to the macrocosmic soul. The secondary meaning has reference also to the divine son of God, the second aspect monadic, as He manifests through the medium of a human being. This is the microcosmic soul. The following synonyms of the Ishvara aspect may be found of value.

### The Macrocosm

| | |
|---|---|
| Ishvara, the second aspect | Whose nature is love. |
| The Son of God | The revealer of the Father. |
| The cosmic Christ | God in incarnation. |
| Vishnu | Second person of the Hindu Trimurti. |
| The soul of all things | Atoms and souls are synonymous terms. |
| The All-Self | The sum total of all selves. |
| I am That | Group consciousness. |
| AUM | The Word of Revelation. |
| The Word | God in the Flesh. |
| The Gurudeva | The Master of all. |
| The light of the world | Shining in darkness. |

### The Microcosm.

| | |
|---|---|
| The second aspect | Love wisdom. |
| The son of the Father | The revealer of the Monad. |
| The Christ | Christ in you, the hope of glory. |
| The Soul | Consciousness. |
| The higher Self | The Lord of the bodies. |
| The Ego | The Self-realizing Identity. |
| The Word | God in incarnation. |
| AUM | The Word of revelation. |
| The Master | The self on the throne. |
| The radiant Augoeidas | The light within. |
| The spiritual Man | Utilizing the lower man. |

**26.  Ishvara (the Gurudeva), being unlimited
by time condition, is the teacher of the primeval
Lords.**

Since the conditions of time and space existed
there have been those who have achieved omniscience, those whose germ of knowledge has been
subjected to proper culture and thus developed,
until it flowered forth into the full glory of the
liberated soul.  This condition became possible
through certain factors:

1.  The identity of each individual soul with
the Oversoul.

2.  The attractive force of that Oversoul as it
drew the separated soul of all things gradually
back into Itself.  This is the force of evolution
itself, the great attractive agent which recalls the
outgoing points of divine Life, the units of consciousness, back to their source.  It involves the
response of the individual soul to cosmic soul
force.

3.  The intensive training given towards the
climax by the occult Hierarchy whereby souls receive a stimulation and vitalisation which enables
them to make more rapid progress.

The occult student must remember that this
process has gone on in the wheels and cycles preceding our planet Earth.  The primeval Lords,
or Sages, are those great Adepts Who—having
"tasted experience" under the Law of Rebirth,
were initiated into the mysteries by the one Ini-
tiator, the representative in our planet of the

Oversoul. They in their turn became teachers and initiators into the mysteries.

The one Master is found within; it is the soul, the inner ruler, the thinker on his own plane. This one Master is a corporate part of the Whole, of the All-Soul. Each expansion of consciousness which a man undergoes fits him to be a Master to those who have not taken a similar expansion. Therefore — mastery being achieved — there is nothing (speaking in terms of the human kingdom) to be found except Masters who are likewise disciples. All are learners and all are teachers, differing only in degree of realisation. For instance:

a. Aspirants to the Path are disciples of lesser disciples,

b. Probationers on the Path are disciples of higher ones,

c. Accepted disciples are the disciples of an adept and of a Master,

d. An adept is the disciple of a Master,

e. A Master is the disciple of a Mahatma,

f. The Mahatmas are the disciples of still higher initiates,

g. These in turn are the disciples of the Christ or of that official who is at the head of the teaching department,

h. The head of the teaching department is a disciple of the Lord of the World,

i. The Lord of the World is the disciple of one of the three planetary spirits who represent the three major aspects,

[ 53 ]

j.  These are again disciples of the solar Logos.
It will be apparent therefore to the careful
student how interdependent all are and how the
achievement of one will profoundly affect the entire body.  Discipleship can be regarded as a
generic term covering all those states or conditions of being in the fourth and fifth kingdoms
(human and spiritual) wherein certain expansions of consciousness are brought about through
specific training.

**27.  The Word of Ishvara is AUM (or OM).
This is the Pranava.**  (See Book I. Sutra 1.)

Students should remember that there are three
basic Words or sounds in manifestation.  This is
the case as far as the human kingdom is concerned.  They are:

I.  *The Word, or note of Nature.*  This is the
Word or the sound of all forms existing in physical plane substance, and as is usually known, it is
sounded on the fundamental note "FA."  It is a
note with which the white occultist has nothing to
do, for his work is concerned not with the increase
of tangibility but with the demonstration of the
subjective or the intangible.  This is the Word of
the third aspect, the Brahma or Holy Ghost
aspect.

II.  *The Sacred Word.*  This is the Word of
Glory, the AUM.  This is the Pranava, the sound
of conscious Life itself as It is breathed forth into
all forms.  It is the Word of the second aspect,
and just as the Word of Nature when rightly

emanated provides the forms which are intended to reveal the soul or second aspect, so the Pranava, when rightly expressed, demonstrates the Father or Spirit through the medium of the soul. It is the Word of the incarnated sons of God. In such a short commentary as this, it is not possible to write a treatise on this secret of secrets, and this great mystery of the ages. All that can be done is to collate certain facts about the AUM, and leave the student to extend the concept and grasp the significance of the brief statements made according to the state of his intuition.

III. *The Lost Word.* The idea of this Lost Word has been preserved for us in Masonry. It is the Word of the first aspect, the spirit aspect, and only the initiate of the third degree can truly begin the search for this word for only the freed soul can find it. This word concerns the highest initiations and it is profitless for us further to consider it.

The following statements about *the Sacred Word* can therefore be made and should be studied with care:

1. The AUM is the Word of glory, and is the Christ in us, the hope of glory.

2. The Word when rightly apprehended causes the second, or Christ aspect of divinity to shine forth resplendently.

3. It is the sound which brings into manifestation the incarnated soul (macrocosmic or microcosmic), the ego, the Christ, and causes the "radiant Augoeides" to be seen on earth.

4. It is the Word which is the releaser of consciousness and when correctly understood and used, releases the soul from the limitations of form in the three worlds.

5. The AUM is the synthesiser of the three aspects and therefore is primarily the Word of the human kingdom in which the three lines of divine life meet—spirit, soul and body.

6. It is also the Word of the fifth, the Aryan race, in a special sense. The work of that race is to reveal in a newer and fuller way the nature of the inner Identity, of the soul within the form, the son of mind, the solar angel, the fifth principle.

7. The significance of the Word only becomes apparent after the "light within" is realised. By its use the "spark" becomes a radiant light, the light becomes a flame, and the flame eventually becomes a sun. By its use the "sun of righteousness arises" in the life of every man.

8. Each of the three letters has relation to the three aspects, and each can be applied to any of the known triplicities.

9. The Master, the God within, is indeed the Word, the AUM, and of this Master (found at the heart of all beings) it is true that "in the beginning was the Word, and the Word was with God (thus duality) and the Word was God." Through its use man arrives at a realisation of:

    a. His own essential divinity,
    b. The purpose of the form-taking process,

    c.   The constitution and nature of those forms,

    d.   The reality of consciousness, or the relation of the divine self or spirit to the form, its polar opposite.

This relation, in its evolutionary working out, we call consciousness and the essential characteristic of this consciousness is love.

10.   The Guru or Master who leads a pupil up to the door of initiation and who watches over him in all the initial and subsequent tests and processes likewise represents the Word, and through the scientific use of this great sound He produces a certain stimulation and vitalisation in the centres of the disciple, thus rendering certain developments possible.

More about the Sacred Word is not advisable to add here. Enough has been given to indicate to the aspirant its purpose and potency. There will have to be communicated in other ways and at other times further information as the student—through study and self initiated effort—arrives at just conclusions. It might be added, that this great Word, when meditated upon, gives the clue to the true esoteric meaning of the words in the *Secret Doctrine* by H. P. Blavatsky:

"Life we look upon as the One Form of Existence, manifesting in what we call Matter; or what, incorrectly separating them, we name Spirit, Soul and Matter in man. Matter is the vehicle for the manifestation of Soul on this plane of existence, and Soul is the vehicle on a higher plane for the manifestation of Spirit, and these three are a Trinity synthesized by Life, which pervades them all."

28. **Through the sounding of the Word and through reflection upon its meaning, the Way is found.**

This is a very general paraphrase but conveys nevertheless the correct significance of the terms used in the Sanskrit. Only Vivekananda, among the many translators, gives this interpretation, putting it as follows:

"The repetition of the OM and meditating upon its meaning (is the Way)."

The other translators omit the final three words, though the inference is clear.

The expression "the sounding of the Word" must not be too literally interpreted; the esoteric "sounding forth" is based upon a study of the Law of Vibration, and the gradual tuning of the lower vibrations of the sheaths or vestures of consciousness so that they synchronise with the note or sound of the conscious indweller. Speaking correctly, the Word is to be sounded by the soul or the ego on its own plane, and the vibration will subsequently affect the various bodies or vehicles which house that soul. The process is therefore a mental one and can only really be done by those who—through meditation and discipline, coupled with service—have made a conscious at-one-ment with the soul. Aspirants to this condition have to utilise the potent factors of the imagination, visualisation and *perseverance in meditation* to reach this initial stage. It should be noted that this stage has to be reached, even if only in a relatively small degree, before the aspirant can become an accepted disciple.

The process of sounding the Word is dual, as is emphasized here.

There is, first of all, the act of the ego, solar angel, higher self or soul, as he sounds out the Word from his own place, on the abstract levels of the mental plane. He directs that sound, via the sutratma and the vestures of consciousness to the physical brain of the man in incarnation, the shadow or reflection. This "sounding forth" has to be constantly repeated. The Sutratma is that magnetic link, spoken of in the Christian Bible as the "silver cord," that thread of living light which connects the Monad, the Spirit in man, with the physical brain.

Secondly, there is the earnest reflection of the man in his physical brain upon that sound as he recognizes it. The two poles of being are hinted at here: the soul and the man in incarnation, and between these two is found the thread, along which the Pranava (or word) vibrates. Students of the esoteric science have to recognize the technique of the processes outlined. In the case of the sounding forth of the Word we have the following factors:

1. The soul who sends, or breathes it forth,
2. The sutratma or thread along which the sound vibrates, is carried or transmitted,

3. The vestures of consciousness, mental, emotional and etheric which vibrate in response to the vibration or breath and are stimulated thereby,

4. The brain which can be trained to recognize that sound and vibrate in unison with the breath,

5. The subsequent act of the man in meditation. He hears the sound (called sometimes the "still small Voice," or the "Voice of the Silence"), he recognizes it for what it is and in deep reflection he assimilates the results of his soul's activity.

Later when the aspirant has passed on into the mysteries and has learnt how to unify the soul and the lower man so that they function as a coordinated unit on earth, the man learns to sound the Word on the physical plane with the object of awakening the forces which are latent within him and thereby arouse the centres. Thus he participates increasingly in the creative, magical and psychical work of manifestation, with the object ever in view of benefiting his fellow men and thus furthering the plans of the planetary hierarchy.

**29. From this comes the realization of the Self (the Soul) and the removal of all obstacles.**

When the Master within is known, the assertion of his power becomes increasingly felt, and the aspirant submits his entire lower nature to the control of that new ruler.

It should be noted here that the eventual complete removal of all obstacles transpires *after* the initial flash of realization. The sequence of happenings is as follows:

1. Aspiration after knowledge of the soul,
2. Realization of the obstacles, or an understanding of the things which prevent true knowledge.
3. Intellectual comprehension as to the nature of those obstacles,
4. Determination to eliminate them,
5. A sudden flash or vision of the soul Reality,
6. Fresh aspiration and a strong determination to make that fleeting vision a permanent reality in the lower plane experience,
7. The battle of Kurukshetra, with Krishna, the soul, heartening Arjuna, the aspirant, on to steady and continuous effort. The same thought is to be found in the Old Testament, in the case of Joshua before the walls of Jericho.

It might be well here to conclude this comment with Sutras 31, 32, 33 and 34, of Book IV:

31. When, through the removal of the hindrances and the purification of all the sheaths, the totality of knowledge becomes available, naught further remains for the man to do.

32. The modifications of the mind-stuff (or qualities of matter) through the inherent nature of the three gunas come to an end, for they have served their purpose.

33. Time, which is the sequence of the modifications of the mind, likewise terminates, giving place to the Eternal Now.

34. The state of isolated Unity becomes possible when the three qualities of matter (the three gunas or potencies of Nature. A.B.) no longer exercise any hold over the Self. The pure Spiritual Consciousness withdraws into the One.

30. **The obstacles to soul cognition are bodily disability, mental inertia, wrong questioning, carelessness, laziness, lack of dispassion, erroneous perception, inability to achieve concentration, failure to hold the meditative attitude when achieved.**

*Obstacle I. Bodily disability.*

It is interesting to note that the first obstacle has relation to the physical body. Aspirants would do well to remember this and should seek to adjust the physical vehicle to the demands later to be made upon it. These adjustments will be great and they fall into four groups:

1. The rendering of the body immune to the attacks of disease or indisposition. This is in itself a triple process involving:

    a. The eradication of present disease,
    b. The refining and the purifying of the body so as to rebuild it eventually,
    c. The protection of the body from future attack and its utilization as a vehicle of the soul.

2. The strengthening and refining of the etheric body in order that it may be finally tuned up so that the work of force direction may be safely undertaken. The disciple has to pass the forces used in his work through his body.

3. The unfoldment and awakening of the centres in the etheric body, the centralization of the fires of the body and their just progression up the

spine, in order to make union with the fire of the soul.

4. The coordination of the physical body in its two divisions and its subsequent alignment with the soul via the sutratma or the thread, which is the magnetic link.

The third adjustment spoken of can only safely be undertaken after the first three means of yoga have been used and developed. These are:

1. The five commandments, (See: Book II. Sutras 28 and 29.)

2. The five rules, (See: Book II. Sutras 32 to 46.)

3. Right poise. (See: Book II. Sutras 46 to 48.)

This is a point often forgotten by aspirants to yoga, and hence the disasters and trouble so often seen amongst those who prematurely occupy themselves with the awakening of the centres and the arousing of the serpent fire. Only when the entire relation of the aspirant to the social economy (as dealt with in the commandments), only when the task of purifying and regulating the threefold lower nature has been worked at (as outlined in the rules), and only as a balanced and controlled condition of the emotional nature has been brought about and right poise achieved, can the aspirant to Raja Yoga safely proceed to the more esoteric and occult work connected with the fires of his little system. This point cannot be too strongly emphasized. Only at a very advanced stage of discipleship will it be safe for the man to deal consciously with the vital fires and direct

[ 63 ]

their right progression up the spine. Few there are as yet who have "kept the law and the commandments."

*Obstacle II. Mental inertia.*

The next great basic obstacle (for these obstacles are given in the order of their relative power over average man) is inability to think clearly about the problem of attainment. Unless clear thinking precedes action, insufficient momentum will be found coupled with failure to appreciate the magnitude of the problem. Mental inertia is due to the lethargic condition of the "vesture of consciousness" which we call the mental body and to the heavy rate of rhythm found in most people. That is the reason why Raja Yoga necessarily makes a greater appeal to mental types than to pure devotees, and it accounts for the fact that those whose mental bodies are well equipped and actively used can more quickly be trained in this sacred science. For the majority of people, the awakening of the mental body, the development of an intellectual interest, and the substitution of mind control in place of control by the emotions has to precede any later realisation of the need of soul culture. The apparatus of thought must be contacted and used before the nature of the thinker can be intelligently appreciated.

When this is realised, the contribution to human development by the great schools of thought we call Mental Science, Christian Science, New Thought and other groups which lay the emphasis upon the mental states will be more justly appraised. The human family is only now becoming aware of the "vesture of consciousness" which we call the mental body.

The majority of men have as yet to build that vesture which occult students call the mental body. From among those who are so doing, the true raja yogins will be gathered.

*Obstacle III. Wrong questioning.*

This is the next stage and is also dependent upon a certain amount of mental development. Some translators call this 'doubt.' This wrong questioning is that which is based upon lower perception and the identification of the real man with that illusory instrument, his mental body. This leads him to question the eternal verities, to doubt the existence of the fundamental realities and to seek for the solution of his problems in that which is ephemeral and transitory, and in the things of the senses.

There is a questioning which is right and proper. It is that "asking of questions" spoken of by the Christ in the words "Ask and ye shall receive." This faculty of enquiry is deliberately cultivated in their disciples by all true Masters in the Orient. They are taught to formulate questions about the inner realities and then to find the answer for themselves through a search for that source of all knowledge, latent at the heart of all beings. To ask intelligently and to find the answer, they must first free themselves from all outer imposed authority and from all tradition and from the imposition of every theological dogma, whether religious or scientific. Only thus can the reality be found and the truth be seen.

"When thy Soul shall pass beyond the forest of delusion, thou shalt no more regard what shall be taught, or what has been taught.

When withdrawn from traditional teaching thy Soul shall stand steadfast, firm in soul-vision, then thou shalt gain union with the Soul." Gita II.51.52.

*Obstacle IV. Carelessness.*

The attitude of mind dealt with here has been translated by some as "light-mindedness." It is really that versatile mental attitude which makes one-pointedness and attention so difficult to achieve. It is literally the thought-form-making tendency of the mind stuff which has also been described as the "mind's tendency to flit from one object to another." See Book III, Sutra 11.

*Obstacle V. Laziness.*

All the commentators agree as to this translation, employing the terms, sloth, languor or laziness. This refers not so much to mental inertia (for it may accompany acute mental perception) as to that slothfulness of the entire lower man which prevents him from measuring up to the intellectual recognition and the inner aspiration. The aspirant has been told what he has to do, the "means of yoga" have been clear to him. He has glimpsed the ideal and is aware of the obstacles; he knows theoretically just what steps he has to take but there is no correspondence between his activity and his knowledge. There is a gap between his aspiration and his performance.

Though he longs to achieve and to know, it is too hard work to fulfill the conditions. His will is not yet strong enough to force him forwards. He permits time to slip by and does nothing.

*Obstacle VI.   Lack of dispassion.*

This has been well translated by some as "addiction to objects." This is the desire for material and sensuous things. It is love of sense perceptions and attraction for all that brings a man back again and again into the condition of physical plane existence. The disciple has to cultivate "dispassion" or that attitude which never identifies itself with forms of any kind, but which is ever detached and aloof, freed from limitations imposed by possessions and belongings. This is covered in many places in the various sutras and need not be enlarged upon here.

*Obstacle VII.   Erroneous perception.*

This inability to perceive correctly and to vision things as they really are, is the natural outcome of the six previous obstacles. As long as the thinker identifies himself with form, as long as the lesser lives of the lower vestures of consciousness can hold him in thrall, and as long as he refuses to separate himself from the material aspect, just so long will his perceptions remain erroneous. Vision is of various kinds and these might be enumerated as follows:

1.   *Physical vision* reveals the nature of the physical plane, and is achieved through the medium of the eyes, photographing through the lens of the eye, the aspect of the tangible form, upon

the wonderful film which every man possesses.
It is circumscribed and limited.

2. *Etheric vision.* This is a rapidly developing faculty of the human eye which ultimately
will reveal the health aura of all forms in the four
kingdoms of nature, which will bring about recognition of the vital pranic emanations of all living centres and will make manifest the conditions
of the centres.

3. *Clairvoyance.* This is the faculty of sight
upon the astral plane and is one of the lower
"siddhis" or psychic powers. It is achieved
through a surface sensibility of the entire "body
of feeling," the emotional sheath, and is sensuous
perception carried to a very advanced condition.
It is misleading and, apart from its higher correspondence, which is spiritual perception, is the
very apotheosis of maya or illusion.

4. *Symbolic vision.* This is a faculty of the
mental body and the factor which produces the
seeing of colours, of geometrical symbols, fourth
dimensional sight, and those dreams and visions
which are the result of mental activity, and not of
astral sight. Frequently these visions have a
quality of prevision.

These four types of vision are the cause of
wrong perception and will only produce illusion
and error until that time when the higher forms
of vision, enumerated below, supersede them.
These higher forms of sight include the others.

5. *Pure vision.* This is spoken of by Patanjali in the words:

"The seer is pure Knowledge (gnosis). Though

pure, he looks upon the presented idea through the medium of the mind." (Book II, Sutra 20.)

The words "pure knowledge" have been translated "pure vision." This vision is the faculty of the soul which is pure knowledge, and is manifest when the soul uses the mind as its instrument of vision. Charles Johnston translates the same Sutra as follows: "The seer is pure vision. . . . He looks out through the vesture of the mind."

It is that clear apprehension of knowledge and a perfect comprehension of the things of the soul which is characteristic of the man who—through concentration and meditation—has achieved mind control. The mind then becomes the window of the soul, and through it the spiritual man can look out onto a new and higher realm of knowledge. Simultaneously with the development of this type of vision, the pineal gland becomes active, and the third eye (in etheric matter) develops with a paralleling activity.

6. *Spiritual vision or true perception.* This type of vision opens up the world of the intuitional or buddhic plane, and takes its possessor beyond the abstract levels of the mental plane. The things of pure spirit, and the basic purposes underlying all manifestation are thus realised, just as pure vision permitted its owner to tap the resources of pure wisdom. With the development of this vision the alta major centre becomes active, and the thousand-petalled lotus unfolded.

7. *Cosmic sight.* This is of a nature inconceivable to man and characterises the realisation of those Existences Who manifest through the

medium of a planetary scheme in a solar system just as a man manifests through his bodies.

By the study of these types of perception, the student will arrive at a just appreciation of the work he has to do. He is thus aided to place himself where he at present stands, and consequently to prepare intelligently for the next step forward.

*Obstacle VIII. Inability to achieve concentration.*

The two last obstacles indicate the way whereby "old things can pass away" and the new man come into his heritage. The method of the disciple must not only include self-discipline or the subjugation of the vestures or sheaths, nor must it only include service or identification with group consciousness, but it must also include the two stages of concentration, focussing or control of the mind, and meditation, the steady process of pondering upon what the soul has contacted and knows. These two will later be dealt with and will not be further touched upon here.

*Obstacle IX. Failure to hold the meditative attitude.*

It will be apparent therefore that the first six obstacles deal with wrong conditions and the last three with the results of those conditions. They contain a hint as to the method whereby liberation from the wrong states of consciousness can be effected.

The next sutra is most interesting as it deals with the effects produced in each of the four bodies of the lower nature, in the case of the man who has not overcome the obstacles.

**31. Pain, despair, misplaced bodily activity and wrong direction (or control) of the life currents are the results of the obstacles in the lower psychic nature.**

Each of these four results expresses the condition of the lower man; they deal with the effects of wrong centralisation or identification.

1. *Pain* is the effect produced when the astral or emotional body is wrongly polarised. Pain is the outcome of failure to balance correctly the pairs of opposites. It indicates lack of equilibrium.

2. *Despair* is an effect of remorse, produced in the mental body and is itself a characteristic of what may be called "the unregenerated mental" nature. The aspirant has a perception of what might be, though the obstacles as yet overcome him; he is ceaselessly conscious of failure, and this engenders in him a condition of remorse, of disgust, despair and of despondency.

3. *Misplaced bodily activity.* The inner condition works out on the physical plane as an intense activity, a violent seeking for solution or for solace, a constant running hither and thither in search of peace. It is the main characteristic at this time of our mental Aryan race and is the cause of the aggressive intensity of endeavour found in all walks of life. To this the educational processes (as they speed up the mental body) have been largely contributory factors. The

great contribution of education (in schools, colleges, universities and other allied activities) has been to stimulate the mental bodies of men. It is all part of the great plan, working ever towards the one objective—soul unfoldment.

4. *Wrong directions of the life currents.* This is the effect produced in the etheric body by the inner turmoil. These life currents (for the student of occultism) are two in number:

a. The life breath or prana,
b. The life force or the fires of the body.

It is the misuse of the life breath or wrong utilisation of prana that is the cause of eighty per cent of the present physical diseases. The other twenty per cent is produced through ill directed life force through the centres, and attacks primarily the twenty per cent of humanity which can be called mentally polarised. The clue for the student of occultism who aspires to liberation is not to be found in breathing exercises, however, nor in any work with the seven centres in the body. It will be found in an intense inner concentration upon rhythmic living and in the careful organisation of the life. As he does this, coordination of the subtler bodies with the physical body on the one hand, and with the soul on the other, will eventuate in the automatic subsequent adjustment of pranic and vital energies.

32. **To overcome the obstacles and their accompaniments, the intense application of the will to some one truth (or principle) is required.**

It would be wise here, if the aspirant to yoga

would note that there are seven ways whereby
peace may be achieved, and thus the goal be
reached. These seven are next dealt with, and
each has a distinct relation to the seven obstacles
earlier considered.

| Obstacle | Remedy |
|---|---|
| 1. Bodily disability | Wholesome, sane living. (1.33.) |
| 2. Mental inertia | Control of the life force. (1.34.) |
| 3. Wrong questioning | One pointed thought. (1.35.) |
| 4. Carelessness | Meditation. (1.36.) |
| 5. Laziness | Self discipline. (1.37.) |
| 6. Lack of dispassion | Correct analysis. (1.38.) |
| 7. Erroneous perception | Illumination. (1.39.) |

These corrections of wrong conditions are of
profound importance in the early stages of yoga
and hence their emphasis in Book I.

But a theoretical understanding of the obstacles
and their cure is of small avail as long as the
intense application of the will is omitted. Only
the constant, steady, enduring effort of the will,
functioning through the mind, will suffice to bring
the aspirant out of darkness into light and to lead
him from the condition of death into immortality.

Once the principle is understood, then the disciple can work intelligently and hence the necessity of a right understanding of the principles or
qualities where the truth regarding reality or God
can be known.

All forms exist in order to express truth. By
the steady application of God's will in the Whole
is truth revealed through the medium of matter.
When the truth or basic principle is known spirit
will then stand revealed. When the disciple real-

ises what principle his various forms, sheaths, or bodies are intended to express, then he will know how to direct his will with exactitude so as to bring about the desired conditions. The sheaths and vehicles are simply his bodies of manifestation on the various planes of the system, and those sheaths must express the principle which is the characteristic or quality underlying each plane. For instance, the seven principles with which man is concerned are:

1. Prana.........vital energy....etheric body.....physical plane.
2. Kama ........desire, feeling..astral body ....astral plane.
3. Lower
   Manas ........concrete mind..mental body....mental plane.
4. Higher
   Manas ........abstract mind..egoic body.......mental plane.
5. Buddhi ....Intuition ........buddhic body..buddhic plane.
6. Atma ........spiritual will....atmic body ......atmic plane.

And that which corresponds to the "boundless immutable principle" in the macrocosm, the Monad (on its own plane) constitutes the seventh principle. There are other ways of enumerating the principles, for Subba Rao is correct in one respect when he says there are only five principles. The two highest, atma and the life monadic, are not principles at all.

Through the conscious utilisation of the will on each plane, the vehicle is directed constantly into an increasingly accurate expression of the one truth. This is the true significance of the sutra under consideration and the clue to why the adepts are as yet still studying this treatise on yoga. Their understanding of truth in its entirety is not yet complete on all planes and the basic rules hold good throughout, though they are variously applied. Principles are applicable to all differentiations and to all states of being.

As a man studies the spheres in which his consciousness is functioning, as he comes to an understanding of the vehicles he must use in any particular sphere, as he awakens to a knowledge of the specific divine quality which the body is intended to express as a part or aspect of the one truth or reality, he becomes aware of the inadequacies present, of the obstacles which hinder and of the difficulties which must be surmounted. Then comes the application of the will and its concentration upon the principle, or upon the quality seeking expression. Thus the lower manifestation is brought into line with the higher for "as a man thinketh so is he."

**33. The peace of the chitta (or mind stuff) can be brought about through the practice of sympathy, tenderness, steadiness of purpose, and dispassion in regard to pleasure or pain, or towards all forms of good or evil.**

In this sutra we are dealing with the physical body, which undergoes experiences on the physical plane and which utilises the brain consciousness. The tendency of that body is towards all other objective forms, and it is apt (in its unregenerate state) to gravitate with facility towards material objects. The nature of those objects will be dependent upon the point in evolution of the experiencing ego. This must be carefully remembered when studying this sutra, otherwise there will be a misapprehension of the final clause. Discriminative action must ever be taken with reference to all demonstrations of good and evil force, and the law works in this connection, but emancipation from all the physical forms which that energy may take, eventuates when dispassion towards these objective forms is practiced. It might be useful if we note that the *sympathy* dealt with concerns our relation to all other pilgrims, or towards the fourth kingdom in nature; *tenderness* covers our relation to the animal or third kingdom; *steadiness of purpose* deals with our relation to the Hierarchy of the planet, and *dispassion* concerns our attitude to all the reactions of the lower personal self. The comprehensiveness of this sutra is therefore apparent and concerns all the brain vibrations of the disciple.

The physical body is consequently looked upon as a vehicle for the expression of:

a.   Helpfulness to our fellow men,

b.   Tender handling of the animal kingdom,

c.   Service on the physical plane in cooperation with the Hierarchy,

d.   Discipline of the physical appetites and dispassion in regard to all forms which appeal to the appetites and to the senses, whether called harmful or not. All alike must be transcended.

Thus peace is achieved, peace of the chitta or mind stuff, peace of the brain reactions and eventually complete quiet and calm. The idea is well covered by Charles Johnston in the words of his translation of this sutra, "The psychic nature moves to gracious peace," and the man expresses wholesomeness, a rounded out nature, and complete sanity of thought and act. All bodily disability is in this way overcome, and wholeness expresses the nature of the manifestation.

**34. The peace of the chitta is also brought about by the regulation of the prana or life breath.**

Students will do well to note that Patanjali includes Pranayama (or the science of the breath or of pranic energy) among other methods for arriving at the "peace of the chitta." He does not however lay any special emphasis upon it. As has been earlier pointed out, pranayama is a term which can be used to cover three processes, all interrelated and allied.

1. *The science of rhythmic living,* or the regulation of the acts of daily life through the organisation of time and the wise utilisation of space. Through this the man becomes adept, a creator on the physical plane and a cooperator in the plans of the hierarchy as they demonstrate in cyclic evolution.

2. *The science of the breath,* or the vitalisation of the lower man through inhalation and exhalation. Man knows himself occultly to be a "living soul," and utilizes the factor of the breath. Through this he becomes aware of the unity of life and the relationship existing between all forms wherein the life of God is found. He becomes a brother as well as an adept and knows

that brotherhood is a fact in nature and not a
sublime theory.

3. *The science of the centres,* or laya yoga;
this is the application of the law to the forces of
nature and the scientific utilisation of those forces
by the man. It involves the passing of certain
septenates of energy through the centres up the
spine and into the head by a certain specified
geometrical progression. This makes a man a
master psychic, and unfolds in him certain latent
powers which—when unfolded—put him in touch
with the soul of all things and with the subjective
side of nature.

It is significant to note that this mode of arriving at peace follows upon the method of sane
wholesome living and its consequent result—a
sound physical body. Later on, when Patanjali
again refers to the regulation of the breath and of
the energy currents, he places it as the fourth
means of yoga and states that only when right
poise has been achieved (the third Means) as a
result of keeping the Commandments and the
Rules (Means one and two) is this regulation to
be attempted. Students would do well to study
these means and note how interest in the centres
is only permissible *after* a man has so balanced
his life and purified his nature that danger is
no longer possible.

**35.  The mind can be trained to steadiness
through those forms of concentration which
have relation to the sense perceptions.**

We are dealing with those forms of unfoldment

and of control which eventuate in what has been called "gracious peace." We have seen that correct group relations and rhythmic living will produce that condition wherein stillness of the vehicles or of the sheaths is attained, and the lower man can then adequately reflect the higher or spiritual man. Now we touch upon certain aspects of the Raja Yoga philosophy and the key to the understanding of this sutra is found in the word *detachment*. The aspirant (as he makes his sense contacts and through the medium of the five senses comes into touch with the phenomenal world) will gradually assume more and more the position of onlooker. His consciousness therefore shifts slowly out of the realm of the sense vehicles into that of the "dweller in the body."

It is interesting to note here, the Hindu teaching upon the uses of the tongue and the entire region of the nose and the palate. The orthodox oriental teaching gives the following suggestions:

| Method | Sense | Result |
|---|---|---|
| 1. Concentration upon the tip of the nose | smell | perfumes. |
| 2. Concentration upon the root of the tongue | hearing | sounds. |
| 3. Concentration upon the tip of the tongue | taste | flames. |
| 4. Concentration upon the middle of the tongue | touch | vibration. |
| 5. Concentration upon the palate | sight | pictures, visions. |

The aspirant must not literalise these things nor seek blindly to meditate, for instance, upon

[ 79 ]

the tip of the tongue. The lesson to be learnt, under the law of analogy, is that the tongue typifies the creative faculty, the third aspect in its five fold nature. The relation of the five senses (as synthesised here in the region of the mouth) to the five rays forming the synthesis governed by the Mahachohan (director of the third ray aspect upon our planet), will be found illuminating. Students would find it valuable to work out the analogy between these five rays and the five senses and the mouth as the organ of speech. As the study is carried forward it will be seen that two other physical organs, the pituitary body and the pineal gland, correspond to the remaining two aspects, love wisdom and organising power, will or purpose. These seven points in the head (and all are found within a comparatively small area) are the symbols in physical matter of the three great aspects manifesting as the seven.

As the aspirant therefore assumes the position of the ruler of the senses and as the analyser of all his sense perceptions, he gradually becomes more mentally concentrated, and the advanced yogi can identify himself at any moment with any one of the ray energies to the exclusion—where desired—of the others.

The student is warned not to imagine that this "gracious peace" can be achieved through definite meditation upon any specific sense. Through an understanding of the laws of creation and of sound, through a consideration of the sounding board of the mouth and the method whereby speech becomes possible, a knowledge of the world creative processes can be arrived at, and the man can achieve an understanding of the laws whereby all forms come into being. The senses of all yogis are naturally abnormally acute and this fact should be remembered.

**36. By meditation upon Light and upon Radiance, knowledge of the Spirit can be reached and thus peace can be achieved.**

The student should here note that each of the methods outlined above concerns certain centres. There are seven methods of attainment mentioned and therefore we can infer that the seven centres are involved.

Method I.  Sutra 33.  Solar plexus centre.

The peace of the chitta (or mind stuff) can be brought about through the practice of sympathy, tenderness, steadiness of purpose, and dispassion in regard to pleasure or pain, or towards all forms of good or evil.

Method II.  Sutra 34.  Centre at the base of the spine.

The peace of the chitta is also brought about by the regulation of the prana.

Method III.  Sutra 35.  Centre between the eyebrows.

The mind can be trained to steadiness through those forms of concentration which have relation to the sense perceptions.

Method IV.  Sutra 36.  Head centre.

By meditation upon Light and upon Radiance, knowledge of the Spirit can be reached and thus peace can be achieved.

[ 81 ]

Method V.   Sutra 37.   Sacral centre.

The chitta is stabilized and rendered free from illusion as the lower nature is purified and no longer indulged.

Method VI.   Sutra 38.   Throat centre.

Peace (steadiness of the chitta) can be reached through meditation on the knowledge which dreams give.

Method VII.   Sutra 39.   Heart centre.

Peace can also be reached through concentration upon that which is dearest to the heart.

These should be carefully considered, even if no details of procedure can here be given.   Only the principle and the law involved can be considered by the student.   It should be remembered also that all these centres have their correspondences in the etheric matter found in the region of the head and that it is when these seven head centres are awakened that their counterparts are also safely awakened.   These seven head centres correspond in the microcosm to the seven Rishis of the Great Bear, the prototypes of the seven Heavenly Men, and the centres above enumerated relate to the energy of the seven Heavenly Men Themselves.

It is not necessary to enlarge here upon these centres beyond indicating the following:

1.   The aspirant may regard each centre symbolically as a lotus.

2.   This lotus is formed of energy units moving or vibrating in a specific manner and these vibration-waves assume the forms we call the petals of the lotus.

3. Each lotus consists of:

   a. A certain number of petals,
   b. A pericarp or supporting calyx,
   c. A centre of pure white light called the "jewel."

4. Each centre corresponds to a sacred planet, the body of manifestation of one of the seven Heavenly Men.

5. Every centre has to be developed through the use of the Word. This word is AUM and it must appear in the vibrant centre eventually. When it shines forth perfectly within the wheel then that centre has perfectly awakened.

6. Certain of the qualities of the sun are the qualities of the centres.

a. Quality of the solar plexus............warmth.
b. Quality of centre at base of spine..kundalini fire.
c. Quality of the ajna centre between
   the eyebrows .........................................illuminating light.
d. Quality of the head centre............cold light.
e. Quality of the sacral centre...........moisture.
f. Quality of the throat centre...........red light.
g. Quality of the heart centre..............radiant or magnetic
                                           light.

In this sutra meditation upon light and radiance is enjoined and we learn that through this light and the ability to use it, knowledge of the spirit can be arrived at. At the centre of the "heart chakra" dwells Brahma, says the old Scripture and He reveals Himself in the light. The aspirant has therefore to become aware cf the "point of light within the wheel with twelve spokes" and as that point of light is dwelt upon, it reveals a road which must be travelled should the aspirant seek to arrive at his goal. The first thing which is revealed is darkness. This should be remembered. In terms of occidental mysticism this brings about the "dark night of the soul." We will not, however, dwell upon the mystical aspect as it is necessary for us to keep our conclusions as much as possible along the occult line. The truth, as expressed in terms of Christian mysticism, has been frequently and adequately covered.

**37. The chitta is stabilised and rendered free from illusion as the lower nature is purified and no longer indulged.**

This translation is a particularly free one, as the words used in the Sanskrit are somewhat difficult of exact interpretation. The thought conveyed is that as the organs of perception and as the sense contacts are continually negated by the real man (who no longer seeks to identify himself with them), then he becomes "free from passion." Heat, or desire for all objects, is overcome. He stands then free from his lower sense nature. This results in a corresponding mental stability and in an ability to concentrate, for the mind stuff is no longer subject to the modifications produced by sense reactions of any kind, either those we call good or those we call bad.

This has been strongly advocated in many of the systems and one of the methods suggested is constant meditation upon such great identities as Krishna, the Buddha and the Christ, who have freed Themselves from all sense reactions. This thought is brought out in some of the translations, but though indicated from one point of view, does not seem to be the main idea intended. Freedom from attachment is brought about as the fires of desire are overcome, and though the sacral centre is depicted as having specific relation to the sex nature, yet that sex nature (as it expresses itself on the physical plane) is symbolic of any attachment between the soul and any object of desire other than the spirit.

**38. Peace (steadiness of the chitta) can be reached through meditation on the knowledge which dreams give.**

The significant words in Sutra 38 are the phrase "the knowledge which dreams give" and in this connection the commentary on Sutra 10 is of interest. The oriental occultist uses the word "dream" in a much more technical sense than does the westerner and this must be fully grasped by the aspirant. To the oriental, the deepest dream condition is that in which the real man is sunk when in physical incarnation. This corresponds to that dream state which we recognize as caused by the vibration of the cells of the physical brain. Chaos, lack of continuity and ill regulated eventualities are present, coupled with an inability to recollect truly and accurately when awake. This condition is physical plane dreaming. Then there is the dream condition in which the man participates when immersed in sensuous perception of one kind or another, either of pleasure or of pain. This is experienced in the astral or emotional body. The knowledge given by the physical plane condition is largely instinctual; that achieved through the astral dream condition is largely sensuous. One is racial and group realisation, the other is relative to the notself and to man's relation to the not-self.

There comes in again a higher state of dream consciousness in which a faculty of another kind comes into play, and this might be called the imagination, bringing its own form of knowledge. Imagination involves certain mental states such as:

a.   Memory of things as they have been known, as states of consciousness,

b.   Anticipation of things as they may be known or of states of consciousness,

c.   Visualisation of the imaginary conditions and then the utilisation of the invoked image as a form, through which a new realm of realisation may be contacted, once the dreamer can identify himself with that which he has imagined.

In these three dream states we have the condition of the thinker in the three planes in the three worlds, from the state of ignorant savagery to that of the average enlightened man. It leads on then to a much higher state of dream consciousness.

The true use of the imagination necessitates a high degree of control and of mental power and

[ 86 ]

where this is present leads eventually to what is called the "state of samadhi." This is that condition wherein the adept can put the entire lower man to sleep, and himself pass into that realm wherein the "dreams of God" Himself are known, and in which knowledge of the "images" which the Deity has created can be contacted and seen. Thus the adept can intelligently participate in the great plan of evolution.

Beyond this state of samadhi lies the dream state of the Nirmanakayas and of the Buddhas, and so on up the scale of hierarchical life till that great Dreamer is known, who is the One, the only Narayana, the Lord of the World Himself, the Ancient of Days, our Planetary Logos. The student can only arrive at a very dim understanding of the nature of these dream states as he studies the idea conveyed in the earlier statement to the effect that, to the occultist, life on the physical plane is but a dream condition.

**39. Peace can also be reached through concentration upon that which is dearest to the heart.**

Sutra 39 in its very simplicity carries with it, its own powerful appeal. In it can be traced the various stages of acquirement—desire, longing, concentrated determination to possess, the negation of all that does not meet that requirement, the emptying of the hands so as to be free for new possession, then possession itself, satisfaction, peace. But with all things pertaining to the lower desires, the peace is but temporary, a new desire awakes and that which has been held so joyously is relinquished. Only that which is the fruition of the ages, only that which is the regaining of an old possession fully satisfies. Let the student therefore study and ascertain whether that which is dearest to his heart is temporal, transitory and ephemeral, or whether it is, as the great Lord has said, "treasure laid up in heaven."

We now come to the most comprehensive sutra in the book: (40). It might be pointed out here that these "seven ways to psychic peace," as they have been called, cover the seven methods of the seven rays in connection with the control of the psychic nature. It is important to emphasise this. These seven ways have a direct relation to the four initiations of the threshhold, for there is no major initiation for any son of God who has not achieved a measure of psychic peace. Students will find it of interest to work out these seven ways to peace in relation to one or other of the seven rays, assigning the way to the ray wherever it seems to them appropriate.

**40. Thus his realisation extends from the infinitely small to the infinitely great, and from annu (the atom or speck) to atma (or spirit) his knowledge is perfected.**

This translation does not adhere to the exact Sanskrit terms. It conveys nevertheless the exact meaning of the original which is the one thing of vital importance. An old verse from one of the hidden scriptures runs as follows and serves to elucidate the idea of this sutra:

"Within the speck God can be seen. Within the man God can reign. Within Brahma both are found; yet all is one. The atom is as God, God as the atom."

It is an occult truism that as a man arrives at a knowledge of himself, under the great law of analogy he arrives at the knowledge of God. This knowledge covers five great aspects:

1. Forms,
2. The constituents of form,
3. Forces,
4. Groups,
5. Energy.

Man must understand the nature of his body and of all his sheaths. This concerns his knowledge of form. He discovers that forms are made of atoms or "points of energy" and that all forms are alike in this respect. This knowledge concerns the constituents of form. He arrives next at an understanding of the aggregate of the energy of the atoms which constitute his forms, or, in other words, at a knowledge of the varying forces; the nature of these forces is determined by the rhythm, the activity and the quality of the atoms which form the sheath or sheaths. This knowledge concerns forces. Later he discovers analogous forms with analogous vibration and force demonstration, and this knowledge concerns groups. Consequently he finds his place and knows his work. Finally he arrives at a knowledge of that which concerns all forms, controls all forces and is the motive power of all groups. This knowledge concerns energy; it has to do with the nature of spirit. Through the medium of these five realisations man arrives at mastery, for realisation entails certain factors which might be enumerated as follows:

1. Aspiration,
2. Study and investigation,
3. Experiment,
4. Discovery,
5. Identification,
6. Realisation.

The adept can identify himself with or enter into the consciousness of the infinitesimally small. He can identify himself with the atom of substance and he knows what is as yet unknown to modern scientists. He realizes also that as the human kingdom (composed of human atoms) is the midway point or station on the ladder of evolution, therefore the infinitely small is as far away from him relatively as the infinitely great. It is as far a road to travel to embrace the consciousness of the minutest of all God's manifestations as it is to embrace the greatest, a solar system. Nevertheless, in all these ranges of consciousness, the method of mastery is the same—perfectly concentrated meditation, leading to perfected power over the mind. The mind is so constituted that it serves the purpose of both a telescope, bringing the seer into touch with the macrocosm, and a microscope bringing him into touch also with the minutest atom.

**41. To him whose vrittis (modifications of the substance of the mind) are entirely controlled there eventuates a state of identity with, and similarity to, that which is realised. The knower, knowledge and the field of knowledge become one, just as the crystal takes to itself the colours of that which is reflected in it.**

This sutra grows naturally out of the previous one. The perfected seer in his consciousness embraces the entire field of knowledge, from the standpoint of onlooker or perceiver and from the standpoint of identification. He is one with the atom of substance, he is able to cognize the minutest universe; he is one with the solar system, the vastest universe he is permitted to cognize in this greater cycle. His soul and their soul are seen to be identical—potentiality is seen in one, and (from the human standpoint) incomprehensible order leading to ultimate perfection is seen in the other. The activity which holds the electrons gathered around their centre is recognized as identical in nature with that which holds the planets in their orbits around the sun, and between these two divine manifestations the whole range of form is found.

The occult student has to realise that forms are diverse and many, but that all souls are identical with the Oversoul. The complete knowledge of the nature, quality, key and note of one soul (whether of a chemical atom, a rose, a pearl, a man or an angel) would reveal all souls upon the ladder of evolution. And the process is the same for all: *Recognition,* the use of the sense organs, including the sixth sense, the mind, in appreciation of the form and its constituents; *Concentration,* an act of the will whereby the form is negated by the senses and the knower passes behind it to that which vibrates in tune with his own soul. Thus knowledge is arrived at,—knowledge of that which the form (or field of knowledge) is seeking to express,—its soul, key or quality.

Then follows *Contemplation,* the identification of the knower with that within himself which is identical with the soul within the form. The two are then one and complete realisation is the case. This can be cultivated in a most practical way between human beings. There must be recognition of the contact that comes between two men who can see, hear and touch each other. A superficial form-recognition is the result. But another stage is possible wherein a man can pass behind the form and arrive at that which is the quality of his brother; he can touch that aspect of the consciousness which is analogous to his own. He becomes aware of the quality of his brother's life, of the nature of his plans, aspirations, hopes and purposes. He knows his brother, and the better he knows himself and his own soul, the deeper will be his knowledge of his brother. Finally, he can identify himself with his brother and become as he is, knowing and feeling as his brother's soul knows and feels. This is the meaning behind the occult words of St. John's Epistle "We shall be like Him for we shall see Him as He is."

# BOOK 1

It may be of value here if certain synonyms are again enumerated, which will, if borne in mind, clarify much of the teaching of the sutras, and enable the student to apply these thoughts in practical fashion to his own life.

Spirit ................Soul ..................Body.
Monad ................Ego ..................Personality.
Divine Self ......Higher Self .....Lower Self.
Perceiver ..........Perception .......That which is perceived.
Knower ..............Knowledge .......The field of knowledge.
Thinker ..............Thought ...........The mind (this is the crystal, reflecting the thought of the thinker).

It aids also to remember:

1. That on the physical plane the perceiver uses the five senses in order to arrive at the field of knowledge.

2. That all our three planes in the three worlds constitute the dense physical body of that One in Whom "we live and move and have our being."

3. That on the astral or emotional plane, the lower powers of clairvoyance and clairaudience are used by the perceiver and when misused reveal the serpent in the garden.

4. That on the mental plane psychometry and symbology (including numerology and geometry) are used by the perceiver to arrive at an understanding of the lower mental levels.

5. That only when these three are seen as lower and as constituting the form aspect does the perceiver arrive at a condition where he can begin to understand the nature of the soul and

[ 93 ]

comprehend the true significance of Sutras 40 and 41.

6. That, having reached that point, he begins to discriminate and to *use the mind* as the sixth sense, arriving thereby at that subjective quality or life which lies back of the field of knowledge (or form). This constitutes the nature of the soul within the form, and is, potentially and in fact, omniscient and omnipresent.

7. Having reached the soul in any form and contacted it through the medium of his own soul, he finds that all souls are one and can put himself with ease in the soul of an atom or of a humming bird, or he can expand his realisation in another direction and know himself one with God and with all superhuman existences.

**42. When the perceiver blends the words, the idea (or meaning) and the object, this is called the mental condition of judicial reasoning.**

In this sutra and the following one, Patanjali is enlarging upon an earlier formulation of the truth. (See Sutra 7.) He teaches that meditation is of two kinds:

1. *With an object or seed,* and therefore employing the rationalising judicial mind, the mental body with its concretising faculty, and its ability to create thought forms,

2. *Without an object or seedless,* and therefore employing a different faculty, and one which is only possible when the concrete mind is understood, and utilised with correctness. This correct

use involves the ability to "still the modifications of the mind," reduce the "chitta" or mind stuff to quietude so that it can take on the colouring of the higher knowledge and reflect the higher realities.

The perceiver has to arrive at a knowledge of subliminal things by the process, first of all, of awareness of the external form, then a passing beyond the external form to the internal state of that form, to that which produces externality (being force of some kind), until he arrives at that which is the cause of both. These three are called in this sutra:

The idea...........The cause back of the objective form.
The word...........The sound which produces form.
The object........The form produced by the sound to express the idea.

Students should realise that this covers the earlier meditative state and, because the lower mind is utilised in the process, is the *separative* method. Things become separated into their component parts and are found to be—as all else in nature—triple. Once this is grasped the occult significance and importance of all meditation becomes apparent and the method whereby occultists are made becomes clear. Always in the process of arriving at an understanding of nature, the occultist works inwards from the external form in order to discover the sound which created it, or the aggregate of forces which produced the external shape; every aggregate of forces has its own sound, produced by their interplay. Having discovered that, he penetrates still further inwards till he touches the cause, idea or divine thought (emanating from the Logos, planetary or solar), which gave rise to the sound, thus producing the form.

In creative work, the adept starts on the inside and—knowing the idea which he seeks to embody in form—he utters certain words or sounds and thus calls in certain forces which produce (through their interplay) a form of some kind. The higher the level on which the adept works the more elevated the ideas touched and the simpler cr more synthetic the sounds uttered.

Students of Raja Yoga have, however, to grasp the elementary facts concerning all forms and to familiarize themselves in their meditation with the work of separating the triplicities, so as to be able eventually to contact any of the component aspects *as they will*. In this way the nature of consciousness is understood, for the perceiver (who is trained in these differentiations) can enter into the consciousness of the atoms composing any tangible form, and can advance further and enter into the consciousness of the energies who produce the objective body. These are literally what has been called the "Army of the Voice." He can also contact eventually the consciousness of that Great Life who is responsible for the initial word. These are the great landmarks, but in between are many grades of lives responsible for the intermediate sounds and these can therefore be contacted and known.

**43. Perception without judicial reasoning is arrived at when the memory no longer holds control, the word and the object are transcended and only the idea is present.**

This condition is the state of "meditation without seed," free from the rational use of the mind, and its faculty to concretise. The object (which is brought into the mind consciousness through recollection or memory) is no longer considered, and the word which designates it and expresses its power is no longer heard. Only the idea of which the other two are expressions is realized, and the perceiver enters into the realm of ideas and of causes. This is pure contemplation, free from forms and thought. In it the perceiver looks out upon the world of causes; he sees with clear vision the divine impulses; then having thus contemplated the inner workings of the kingdom of God, he reflects back into the quiescent mental body or mind that which he has seen, and that mental body throws down the knowledge gained into the physical brain.

**44. The same two processes of concentration, with and without judicial action of the mind can be applied also to things subtle.**

This sutra is clear without much explanation. The word "subtle" has a wide meaning, but (from the standpoint of Patanjali) is most frequently applied to the essential something which we become aware of after we have employed the five senses; *i.e.*, the rose is the objective tangible form; its scent is the "thing subtle" back of the form. This expresses its quality to the occultist and is the result of the subtler elements producing its manifestation. The grosser elements produce the form; but within that gross form is a subtler one which we can only contact through acute perception or clarified sense. In the commentary found in Woods' translation the following words may serve to elucidate, and, if meditated upon by the more advanced students, will be found to be of profound occult significance:

". . . the atom of earth is produced by the five fire elements, among which the fire element of odour predominates. Likewise the atom of water is produced from the four fire elements among which the fire element of taste predominates. Likewise the atom of fire is produced from the three fire elements, excluding the fire element of odour and of taste, and among which the fire element of colour predominates. Likewise the atom of wind is produced from the two fire elements beginning with odour and of which two the fire element of touch predominates. Likewise the atom of air from the fire element sound alone."

If this idea is extended to the macrocosm, we will find that we can meditate upon the external form of God in Nature both with and without judicial action of the mind. Then, experience in meditation having been gained, and by an act of the will, the student can meditate on the subtle subjective nature of God as manifested under the great Law of Attraction, to which the Christian refers when he says "God is Love." The nature of God, the great "love" or attractive force, is responsible for the "things subtle" which are veiled by the things external.

**45. The gross leads into the subtle and the subtle leads in progressive stages to that state of pure spiritual being called Pradhana.**

Let the student remember here the following degrees or stages through which he must pass as he penetrates into the heart of the innermost:

1. The gross .........form, bhutas, rational tangible sheaths.
2. The subtle ........the nature or qualities, the tanmatras, the indryas, or the senses, the sense organs and that which is sensed.

These can be applied to all the planes of the three worlds with which man is concerned, and have a close relation to the pairs of opposites which he has to balance on the emotional plane. Behind all these is found that balanced state, called Pradhana, which is the cause of what is contacted physically and sensed subtly. This balanced state can well be called unresolvable primary substance, matter united with spirit, undifferentiated yet without form or distinguishing mark. Behind these three again is found the Absolute Principle but these three are all that man can know whilst in manifestation. Vivekananda in his commentary says as follows:

"The grosser objects are only the elements and everything manufactured out of them. The five objects begin with Tanmatras or five particles. The organs, the mind (the aggregate of all senses) egoism, the mind stuff (the cause of all manifestation) the equilibrium state of sattva, rajas and tamas (the three qualities of matter. A. B.),— called Pradhana (Chief) Prakriti (nature) or Avyakta (unmanifest) are all included in the category of five objects. The Purusa (the soul) alone is excepted from this definition.)."

Vivekananda apparently here translates purusa as soul, but it is usually translated spirit and refers to the first aspect.

### 46. All this constitutes meditation with seed.

The last four sutras have dealt with those forms of concentration which have been built up around an object. That object may concern that which is subtle and intangible from the physical plane standpoint, nevertheless (from the standpoint of the real or spiritual man) the fact of the not-self is involved. He is concerned with that which (in any of its aspects) may lead him into realms which are not primarily those of pure spirit. We need, however, to remember here that all these four stages are necessary and *must* precede any more spiritual realization. The mind of man is not in itself so constituted that it can apprehend the things of spirit. As he passes from one stage of "seeded" meditation to another, he ever approaches nearer to the seat of all knowledge, and will eventually contact that upon which he is meditating. Then the nature of the thinker himself, as pure spirit, will be apprehended, and the steps, stages, objects, seeds, organs, forms (subtle or gross) will all be lost sight of and only spirit be known. Both feeling and mind will then be transcended and only God Himself be seen; the lower vibrations will no longer be sensed; colour will no longer be seen; only light will be known; vision will be lost sight of, and the sound or word will alone be heard. The "eye of Shiva" will be left and with that the seer will identify himself.

In the above fourfold elimination, the stages of realization are hinted at—those stages which lead a man out of the world of form into the realm of the formless. Students will find it interesting to compare the four stages whereby "seeded meditation" progresses, with the four above. It might be pointed out also that in any meditation wherein *consciousness* is recognized, then an object is present; in any meditation wherein the perceiver is aware of that which is to be seen, then there is as yet a condition of form perception. Only when all forms and the field of knowledge itself are lost sight of, and the knower recognizes himself for what he essentially is (being lost in contemplation of his own pure spiritual nature), can ideal, formless, seedless, objectless meditation be arrived at. It is here that the language of the occultist and mystic both fail, for language deals with objectivity and its relation to spirit. Therefore this higher condition of meditation is likened to a sleep or trance condition, but is the antithesis of physical sleep or the trance of the medium, for in it the spiritual man is fully awake on those planes which transcend definition. He is aware, in a full sense, of his direct Spiritual Identity.

**47. When this super-contemplative state is reached, the Yogi acquires pure spiritual realisation through the balanced quiet of the Chitta (or mind stuff).**

The Sanskrit words employed in this sutra can only be adequately translated into clear terms by the use of certain phrases which make the English version clearer. Literally, the sutra might be stated to run as follows "Clear perspicuity follows through the quiet chitta." It should be remembered here that the idea involved is that of purity in its true sense, meaning "freedom from limitation," and therefore signifying the attainment of pure spiritual realization. Contact by the soul with the monad or spirit is the result, and knowledge of this contact is transmitted to the physical brain.

This is only possible at a very advanced stage of yoga practice, and when the mind stuff is utterly still. The Father in Heaven is known, as revealed by the Son to the Mother. Sattva (or rhythm) alone becomes manifest, rajas (activity) and tamas (inertia) being dominated and controlled. We should remember here that sattva has reference to the rhythm of the forms in which the yogi is functioning, and only as they express the highest of the three gunas (or qualities of matter) is the highest or spiritual aspect known. Only as rajas controls is the second aspect known; only as tamas holds sway is the lowest aspect known. There is an interesting analogy between the inertia (or tamas) aspect of matter and the condition of the bodies of the yogi when in the highest samadhi. Then the sattvic or rhythmic motion is so complete that to the eye of the average man a condition of quiescence is achieved which is the sublimation of the tamasic or inert condition of the densest substance.

The following words from the commentary dealt with in Woods' translation of the sutras will be found helpful:

"When freed from obscuration by impurity, the sattva of the thinking-substance, the essence of which is light, has pellucid steady flow not overwhelmed by the rajas and the tamas. This is the clearness. When this clearness arises in the super reflective balanced-state then the yogin gains the internal undisturbed calm (that is to say), the vision of the flash (sputa) of insight which does not pass successively through the serial order (of the usual processes of experience) and which has as its intended object the thing as it really is. . . . Impurity is an accretion of rajas and tamas. And it is the defilement which has the distinguishing characteristic of obscuration. Clearness is freed from this." (P. 93.)

The man has succeeded (through discipline, through following the means of yoga, and through perseverance in meditation) in dissociating himself from all forms, and in identifying himself with the formless.

He has arrived at the point at the heart of his being. From that point of pure spiritual realisation, he can increasingly work in the future. Through practice, he strengthens that realisation, and all life, work and circumstances are viewed as a passing pageant with which he is not concerned. Upon them, however, he can turn the searchlight of pure spirit; he himself is light and knows himself as part of the "Light of the World," and "in that light shall he see light." He knows things as they are and realizes that all which he has hitherto regarded as reality is but illusion. He has pierced the great Maya and passed behind it into the light which produces it and for him mistake is in the future impossible; his sense of values is correct; his sense of proportion is exact. He no longer is subject to deception but stands freed from delusion. When this point is realized, pain and pleasure no longer affect him; he is lost in the bliss of Self-Realization.

**48. His perception is now unfailingly exact, (or, his mind reveals only the Truth).**

Both translations are here given, as they seem to give together a truer idea than either does alone. The word "exact" is used in its occult sense and deals with the outlook of the Perceiver upon all phenomena. The world of illusion, or the world of form must be "exactly known." This means, literally, that the relation of every form to its *name* or originating word must be appreciated as it is. At the summation of the evolutionary process every form of divine manifestation must respond exactly to its name, or to the word which set up the original impulse and so brought a life into being. Therefore the first translation emphasises this idea and the three factors are hinted at.

1.  The idea,
2.  The word,
3.  The resultant form.

They also inevitably bring with them another triplicity,

1.  Time which connects the three,
2.  Space which produces the three,
3.  Evolution, the process of production.

One result of this is the demonstration of the law and the exact fulfilling of the purpose of God. This is realized by the yogi who has succeeded in eliminating all forms from his consciousness and has become aware of that which lies back of all forms. How he does this is revealed by the second translation. The mind stuff, being now perfectly still and the man being polarized in that factor which is not the mind nor any of the sheaths, can transmit to the physical brain unerringly, accurately and without mistake, that which is perceived in the Light of the Shekinah which streams from the Holy of Holies into which the man has succeeded in entering. The truth is known and the cause of every form in all the kingdoms of nature stands revealed. This is the revelation of

the true magic and the key to the great magical
work in which all true yogis and adepts participate.

**49.   This particular perception is unique and
reveals that which the rational mind (using
testimony, inference and deduction) cannot reveal.**

The meaning here might be stated to be that
the mind of man in its various aspects and uses
can reveal those things which concern objectivity,
but only identification with the spirit can reveal
the nature and world of the spirit.   "No man hath
seen God at any time, the only begotten Son, who
is in the bosom of the Father, he hath revealed
him."   Until a man knows himself as a Son of
God, until the Christ in each man is manifesting
and the Christ-life has full expression, and until
the man is one with that internal spiritual reality
which is his true self, the particular knowledge
dealt with here (knowledge of God and of spirit,
independent of matter or form) is impossible.
The testimony of the ages points to a spiritual
force or life in the world; the inference to be gar-
nered from the life experience of millions is that
spirit exists; the deduction to be gathered from
the consideration of the world or of the great
maya is that a Cause, self-persisting and self-ex-
isting, must be back of that maya.   Only the man,
however, who can pass behind all forms and can
transcend all the limitations in the three worlds
(mind, emotion and the things of sense, or the

"world, the flesh and the devil") can *know*, past all controversy and argument, that God *is*, and that he himself *is* God. Then he knows the truth, and that truth makes him free.

The field of knowledge, the instruments of knowledge and knowledge itself are transcended and the yogi comes to the great recognition that there is nothing except God; that His life is one and is to be found pulsating in the microscopic atom and in the macrocosmic atom also. With that life he identifies himself. He finds it at the heart of his own being and can there merge himself with the life of God as it is found in the ultimate primordial atom, or expand his realization until he knows himself as the life of the solar system.

### 50. It is hostile to, or supersedes all other impressions.

Previous to attaining this true perception, the onlooker has been dependent upon three other methods of ascertaining truth, all of them limited and imperfect. They are:

1. *Sense perceptions.* In this method the dweller in the body ascertains the nature of the objective world through the medium of his five senses. Objectivity or tangibility becomes known to him and he hears, sees, touches, tastes and smells the things of the physical world. He deals, however, with the *effects* produced by the subjective life, but has no clue to the causes or to the subjective energies of which they are the product. His interpretation of them is consequently false,

leading to wrong identification and an erroneous set of values.

2. *Mental perception.* Through the use of the mind the onlooker becomes aware of another grade of phenomena and is put en rapport with the thought world, or with that condition of substance in which is registered the thought impulses of our planet and its inhabitants, and with forms created by those vibratory impulses which express certain ideas and desires,—primarily at present the latter. Owing to the erroneous perception brought about through the use of the senses and the wrong interpretation of the things sensed, these thought forms are in themselves distortions of the reality, and express only those lower impulses and reactions which emanate from the lower kingdoms in nature. Students should remember that it is only when man is really beginning to use his mental body (and is not used by it) that he contacts the thought forms created by the guides of the race and justly perceives them.

3. *The super contemplative state.* In this condition perception is unfailingly accurate and the other modes of vision are seen in their right proportions. The senses are no longer required by the onlooker except in so far as he utilizes them for purposes of constructive work on their respective planes. He is now in possession of a faculty which safeguards him from error and of a sense which only reveals to him things as they are. The conditions governing this stage might be enumerated as follows:

[ 108 ]

## BOOK I

**1.** The man is polarized in his spiritual nature,

**2.** He recognizes himself and functions as the soul, the Christ,

**3.** He has the chitta or mind stuff in a state of quiescence,

**4.** The sutratma or thread is functioning adequately and the lower bodies are aligned upon it, producing a direct channel of communication with the physical brain,

**5.** The brain is trained to serve only as a delicate receiver of truth impressions,

**6.** The third eye is in process of unfoldment. Later, as the centres are awakened and brought into conscious control, they place the man en rapport with the various energy septenates in the seven planes of the system, and because the truth-perceiving faculty is developed, the man is thereby safeguarded from error and from danger.

This has been very clearly and ably stated by Charles Johnston in his commentary on this sutra as follows:

"Each state or field of the mind, each field of knowledge, so to speak, which is reached by mental and emotional energies, is a psychical state, just as the mind picture of a stage with the actors on it, is a psychical state or field. When the pure vision, as of the poet, the philosopher, the saint, fills the whole field, all lesser views and visions are crowded out. This high consciousness displaces all lesser consciousness. Yet, in a certain sense, that which is viewed as part, even by the vision of a sage, has still an element of illusion, a thin psychical veil, however pure and luminous that

[ 109 ]

veil may be. It is the last and highest psychic state."

**51. When this state of perception is itself also restrained (or superseded), then is pure samadhi achieved.**

The great teacher Patanjali, having led us through the various stages of the expanding consciousness, from "seeded" meditation to that in which the senses and the mind are superseded, carries us into a state for which we have no adequate terminology. The yogi of the East applies the word *Samadhi* to that state of consciousness wherein the world in which the spiritual man functions and the formless levels or planes of our solar system are contacted, seen and known. The field of knowledge of the three worlds, the realm of maya and of illusion, can be contacted at will by the seer using the instrument provided for him, but a new world opens up in which he sees his consciousness as one with all other energies, or conscious expressions of divine life. The last veil of illusion is withdrawn, the great heresy of separateness is seen in its true nature, and the seer can say with Christ:

"Neither pray I for these alone, but for them also which shall believe on me through their word; That they all may be one; as thou, Father, art in me, and I in thee, that they also may be one in us; that the world may believe that thou hast sent me. And the glory which thou gavest me I have given them; that they may be one, even as we are one: I in them, and thou in me, that they may be made perfect in one; and that the world may know that thou hast sent me, and hast loved them, as thou hast loved me." (John XVII. 20-23.)

## BOOK II

### THE STEPS TO UNION

a.  The five hindrances and their removal.
b.  The eight means defined.
Topic: The means of attainment.

# THE YOGA SUTRAS OF PATANJALI

## BOOK II

### The Steps to Union

1. The Yoga of action, leading to union with the soul is fiery aspiration, spiritual reading and devotion to Ishvara.

2. The aim of these three is to bring about soul vision and to eliminate obstructions.

3. These are the difficulty producing hindrances: avidya (ignorance) the sense of personality, desire, hate and the sense of attachment.

4. Avidya (ignorance) is the cause of all the other obstructions whether they be latent, in process of elimination, overcome, or in full operation.

5. Avidya is the condition of confusing the permanent, pure, blissful and the Self with that which is impermanent, impure, painful and the not-self.

6. The sense of personality is due to the identification of the knower with the instruments of knowledge.

7. Desire is attachment to objects of pleasure.

8. Hate is aversion for any object of the senses.

9. Intense desire for sentient existence is attachment. This is inherent in every form, is self-perpetuating, and known even to the very wise.

10. These five hindrances, when subtly known, can be overcome by an opposing mental attitude.

11. Their activities are to be done away with, through the meditation process.

12. Karma itself has its root in these five hindrances and must come to fruition in this life or in some later life.

[ 115 ]

# BOOK II

13. So long as the roots (or samskaras) exist, their fruition will be birth, life, and experiences resulting in pleasure or pain.

14. These seeds (or samskaras) produce pleasure or pain according as their originating cause was good or evil.

15. To the illuminated man all existence (in the three worlds) is considered pain owing to the activities of the gunas. These activities are threefold, producing consequences, anxieties and subliminal impressions.

16. Pain which is yet to come may be warded off.

17. The illusion that the Perceiver and that which is perceived are one and the same is the cause (of the pain-producing effects) which must be warded off.

18. That which is perceived has three qualities, sattva, rajas and tamas (rhythm, mobility and inertia); it consists of the elements and the sense organs. The use of these produces experience and eventual liberation.

19. The divisions of the gunas (or qualities of matter) are fourfold; the specific, the non-specific, the indicated and the untouchable.

20. The seer is pure knowledge (gnosis). Though pure, he looks upon the presented idea through the medium of the mind.

21. All that is exists for the sake of the soul.

22. In the case of the man who has achieved yoga (or union) the objective universe has ceased to be. Yet it existeth still for those who are not yet free.

23. The association of the soul with the mind and thus with that which the mind perceives, produces an understanding of the nature of that which is perceived and likewise of the Perceiver.

24. The cause of this association is ignorance or avidya. This has to be overcome.

25. When ignorance is brought to an end through non-association with the things perceived, this is the great liberation.

26. The state of bondage is overcome through perfectly maintained discrimination.

27. The knowledge (or illumination) achieved is seven-fold and is attained progressively.

28. When the means to yoga have been steadily practised, and when impurity has been overcome, enlightenment takes place, leading up to full illumination.

29. The eight means of yoga are, the Commandments or Yama, the Rules or Nijama, posture or Asana, right control of life-force or Pranayama, abstraction or Pratyahara, attention or Dharana, Meditation or Dhyana, Contemplation or Samadhi.

30. Harmlessness, truth to all beings, abstention from theft, from incontinence and from avarice, constitute yama or the five commandments.

31. Yama (or the five commandments) constitutes the universal duty and is irrespective of race, place, time or emergency.

32. Internal and external purification, contentment, fiery aspiration, spiritual reading and devotion to Ishvara constitutes nijama (or the five rules).

33. When thoughts which are contrary to yoga are present there should be the cultivation of their opposite.

34. Thoughts contrary to yoga are harmfulness, falsehood, theft, incontinence, and avarice, whether committed personally, caused to be committed or approved of, whether arising from avarice, anger or delusion (ignorance); whether slight in the doing, middling or great. These result always in excessive pain and ignorance. For this reason, the contrary thoughts must be cultivated.

35. In the presence of him who has perfected harmlessness, all enmity ceases.

36. When truth to all beings is perfected, the effectiveness of his words and acts is immediately to be seen.

37. When abstention from theft is perfected, the yogi can have whatever he desires.

38. By abstention from incontinence, energy is acquired.

39. When abstention from avarice is perfected, there comes an understanding of the law of rebirth.

40. Internal and external purification produces aversion for form, both one's own and all forms.
41. Through purification comes also a quiet spirit, concentration, conquest of the organs, and ability to see the Self.
42. As a result of contentment bliss is achieved.
43. Through fiery aspiration and through the removal of all impurity, comes the perfecting of the bodily powers and of the senses.
44. Spiritual reading results in a contact with the soul (or divine One).
45. Through devotion to Ishvara the goal of meditation (or samadhi) is reached.
46. The posture assumed must be steady and easy.
47. Steadiness and ease of posture is to be achieved through persistent slight effort and through the concentration of the mind upon the infinite.
48. When this is attained, the pairs of opposites no longer limit.
49. When right posture (asana) has been attained there follows right control of prana and proper inspiration and expiration of the breath.
50. Right control of prana (or the life currents) is external, internal or motionless; it is subject to place, time and number and is also protracted or brief.
51. There is a fourth stage which transcends those dealing with the internal and external phases.
52. Through this, that which obscures the light is gradually removed.
53. And the mind is prepared for concentrated meditation.
54. Abstraction (or Pratyahara) is the subjugation of the senses by the thinking principle and their withdrawal from that which has hitherto been their object.
55. As a result of these means there follows the complete subjugation of the sense organs.

# THE YOGA SUTRAS OF PATANJALI

*BOOK II*

**1. The yoga of action, leading to union with the soul is fiery aspiration, spiritual reading and devotion to Ishvara.**

We must here bear in mind that we are beginning the book which outlines the practical part of the work, which gives the rules which must be followed if the aspirant hopes to achieve, and which indicates those methods which will bring about the realization of spiritual consciousness. The objective has been dealt with in Book I. The aspirant naturally says on concluding Book I, "how desirable and how right, but *how* shall this be? What must I do? Where shall I begin?"

Patanjali starts at the very beginning and in this second book he indicates:

1. The basic personality requirements,
2. The hindrances which can then be noted by the earnest disciple,
3. The eight "means of yoga" or the eight kinds of activity which will bring about the needed results.

[ 119 ]

## BOOK II

The very simplicity of this outline makes its value exceedingly great; there is no confusion, no complex dissertations, but just a clear simple statement of the requirements.

It might be of value here if we dealt with the various "yogas" so as to give to the student a clear concept as to their distinctions and thus cultivate his discrimination. The principal yogas are three in number, the various other so-called "yogas" finding their place in one of these three groups:

1. Raja Yoga . . . the yoga of the mind or will,
2. Bhakti Yoga . . . the yoga of the heart or the devotee,
3. Karma Yoga . . . the yoga of action.

*Raja Yoga* stands by itself and is the king science of them all; it is the summation of all the others, it is the climax and that which completes the work of development in the human kingdom. It is the science of the mind and of the purposeful will, and brings the higher of man's sheaths in the three worlds under the subjection of the Inner Ruler. This science coordinates the entire lower threefold man, forcing him into a position where he is nothing but the vehicle for the soul, or God within. It includes the other yogas and profits by their achievements. It synthesises the work of evolution and crowns man as king.

*Bhakti Yoga* is the yoga of the heart; it is the bringing into submission of all the feelings, desires and emotions, to the one beloved, seen and known in the heart. It is the sublimation of all the lower loves and the bringing captive of all longings and desire, to the one longing to know the God of love and the love of God.

It was the "kingly" or crowning science of the last rootrace, the Atlantean, just as the science of Raja Yoga is the great science of our Aryan civilization. Bhakti Yoga made its exponent an arhat or led him to the fourth initiation. Raja Yoga makes him an adept and leads him to the portal of the fifth initiation. Both lead to liberation, for the arhat is released from the cycle of rebirth but Raja Yoga liberates him to complete service and freedom to work as a White Magician. Bhakti Yoga is the yoga of the heart, of the astral body.

*Karma Yoga* has a specific relation to physical plane activity, and to the working out into objective manifestation of all the inner impulses. In its ancient and simplest form it was the yoga of the third or Lemurian root race and its two best known expressions are:

a. Hatha Yoga,
b. Laya Yoga.

The former has specifically to do with the physical body, its conscious (not subconscious and automatic) functioning and all the various practices which give man control over the different organs and the entire mechanical apparatus of the physical body. The latter has to do with the etheric body, with the force centers or chakras found in that body and with the distribution of force currents and the awakening of the serpent fire.

It might be pointed out that if we divide the human torso into three departments it might be stated that:

1. Karma Yoga resulted in the awakening of the four centres below the diaphragm,

2. Bhakti Yoga resulted in their transmutation and transference into the two centres above the diaphragm, yet in the torso, the heart and the throat.

3. Raja Yoga synthesises all the forces of the body in the head and from there distributes and controls them.

Raja Yoga, which Patanjali primarily deals with, includes the effects of all the others. It is only possible when the others have been worked with, but not in the sense of working with them in this life. Evolution has brought all the sons of men (who are ready to be chelas or disciples), through the various races, and whilst in the Lemurian race (or else on the preceding chain or greater cycle) they were all hatha and laya yogins. This resulted in the development and control of the dual physical body, dense and etheric.

Whilst in the Atlantean race the desire or astral body was developed, and the flower of that race were true sons of bhakti yoga and true devotees. Now the highest of the three bodies must be brought to its fullest development and this Raja Yoga is intended to do and this is the object of Patanjali's work. The Aryan race will contribute this fuller development to the general economy, and the entire human family (with the exception of a percentage which entered the race too late to permit of the full flowering of the soul) will manifest as Sons of God with all the powers of the God unfolded and consciously used on the physical plane and in the physical body. Patanjali says that three things will bring this about, coupled with the following of certain methods and rules, and these three are:

1. Fiery aspiration, the domination of the *physical man* so that every atom of his body is afire with zeal and endeavor,

2. Spiritual reading, which has reference to the capacity of the *mental body* to see back of a symbol or to touch the subject lying back of the object,

3. Devotion to Ishvara, which relates to the *astral* or *emotional* body, the whole heart poured out in love to God—God in his own heart, God in the heart of his brother, and God as seen in every form.

Fiery aspiration is the sublimation of karma yoga. Devotion to Ishvara is the sublimation of bhakti yoga, whilst spiritual reading is the first step to Raja Yoga.

"Devotion to Ishvara" is a large and general term covering the relation of the personal self to the higher self, the Ishvara or Christ principle in the heart. It covers also the relation of the individual Ishvara to the universal or cosmic Ishvara; it deals with the realization of the soul in man that it is an integral part of the Oversoul. This

results in group consciousness which is the objective of the kingly science.

Devotion involves certain factors which it is
valuable for the devotee to realize.

1. A capacity to decentralize oneself, to change
one's attitude from self-centredness and selfishness to one of outgoing to the loved one. All
things are counted as loss provided the object of
one's devotion is attained.

2. Obedience to the beloved object once that
beloved is known. This has been called in some
translations "complete obedience to the Master"
and this is the true and accurate translation but
in view of the fact that the word *Master* connotes
(to the occult student) one of the adepts, we have
chosen to translate the word as "Ishvara," the one
God in the heart of man, the divine Jiva or "point
of divine life" at the centre of man's being. This
is the same in all men, whether savage or adept;
the difference only lies in degree of manifestation
and of control. Complete obedience to any guru
or mahatma in the sense of complete subjugation
of the will is never taught in the true science of
yoga. Subjugation of the lower man to the will
of the inner God is taught and all the methods
and rules of yoga are to this specific end. This
should be carefully borne in mind. "Spiritual
reading" is the most significant and occult preliminary thereto.

Every form is the result of thought and of
sound. Every form veils or conceals an idea or
concept. Every form, therefore, is but the symbol or attempted representation of an idea and

this is true without exception on all the planes of our solar system, wherein forms are found whether created by God, man or deva.

One object of a disciple's training is to enable him to ascertain that which lies back of any form in any kingdom of nature and thus ascertain the nature of the spiritual energy which brought it into being. The vastness of this cosmic symbolism will be apparent to even the most superficial thinker and the beginner upon the path of chelaship has to learn to separate the many forms into certain specific groups standing for certain basic ideas. He has to interpret the ideas lying back of specific symbols, and he has to look for the specific impulse latent in every form. He can begin practically to do this in the environment and in the place where he is. He can look for the idea which his brother's form veils; he can search for God behind the body of any and every man.

Thus the sutra under consideration takes the aspirant into the most practical part of life; it brings him face to face with three basic enquiries and as he seeks to answer them aright, he will inevitably equip himself to tread the path. These three enquiries are:

1. Towards what objective do all the longings and aspirations of my soul trend, towards God, or to things material?

2. Am I bringing my entire lower nature under the control of Ishvara or the true spiritual man?

3. Do I see God back of every form and circumstance in my daily contacts?

# BOOK II

## 2. The aim of these three is to bring about soul vision and to eliminate obstructions.

It is interesting to note here that the words "soul vision" precede the thought of the eliminated hindrances or obstructions, showing that the vision is possible even to those who have not yet perfected themselves. The vision comes in those moments of exaltation and high aspiration to which most of the sons of men are susceptible and provides the incentive needed to produce that determination and perseverance which the elimination of the obstruction necessitates. The words "elimination of the obstructions" or the "alteration of the hindrances" (as it is sometimes translated), is a large and generic expression and Hindu commentators point out that it involves even the eradication of the seeds of those hindrances, and their total destruction as by fire; that just as a burnt, dried up seed is no longer capable of propagation and becomes unfertile, producing no growth, so the seeds of the obstructions to the life of the Spirit are similarly rendered unfertile. These seeds are found in three groups, each producing a large crop of hindrances or obstructions on the three planes of man's evolution—the seeds latent in the physical body, those producing the obstructions of the astral body, and the seeds latent in the mental body. They are of three kinds in each case, making literally nine types or kinds of seeds:

1. Seeds brought over from previous lives,
2. Seeds sown in this life,

3. Seeds brought into the field of one's life from the family or race with which one is allied.

It is these seeds which produce the obstructions or hindrances to soul vision and the free play of spiritual energy and Patanjali says they are of five kinds and proceeds to deal with them specifically. By some commentators the word is translated distractions, and all three terms are equally correct and any of them can be used. It may perhaps be pointed out that:

1. The word *"obstruction"* is more technically correct when applied to the physical plane,

2. The word *"hindrance"* is more illuminating when applied to those things which, through the medium of the astral body, prevent soul vision,

3. The word *"distraction"* has more specific reference to the difficulties which assail the man who seeks to quiet the mind and so achieve soul vision.

3. **These are the difficulty producing hindrances: avidya (ignorance), and the sense of personality, desire, hate and the sense of attachment.**

These are the five wrong ideas or concepts which for aeons of time and throughout many lives, prevent the sons of men from realizing that they are sons of God. It is these concepts which lead men to identify themselves with that which is lower and material, and to forget the divine realities. It is these misconceptions which make a prodigal son of the divine Monad, and which send him forth into the far country to eat of the husks of mortal existence. It is these which must be overcome and eliminated before a man can "lift up his eyes" and see again the vision of the Father and the Father's Home and so be enabled to tread consciously the Path of return.

It might be pointed out that two of the hindrances, avidya and sense of personality, relate to man, the synthesis upon the physical plane, that desire has relation to his astral body or vehicle of feeling, and that hate and a sense of attachment are products of the sense of egoism (the ahamkara principle) which animate the mental body. Thus the threefold personality is the field for the seeds and in the soil of the personal life in the three worlds do these seeds propagate and flourish and grow up to obstruct and hinder the real man. These seeds must be destroyed, and in their destruction three things eventuate:

1. Karma is worked off,
2. Liberation is achieved,
3. The vision of the soul is perfected.

**4. Avidya (ignorance) is the cause of all the other obstructions, whether they be latent, in process of elimination, overcome, or in full operation.**

The comprehensiveness of this sutra is the first thing which attracts one's attention. It carries one in thought to the root cause of all evil and in its reference to the obstructions covers all possible conditions of their being. This verse sums up the condition of every man from the savage stage up through all intervening conditions to the state of arhatship, in which the final fetters of ignorance are cast off. It states that the reason evil exists, the reason selfishness and personal desires of any kind are evident, is found in the great basic condition which is the limitation of form itself, avidya or ignorance.

The aspirant is reminded right at the beginning of his investigations into the laws of spiritual unfoldment, that two factors must be taken into account which are based on the fact of manifestation itself:

1. The fact of the not-self towards which the divine points of spiritual life are attracted, and which in the period of evolution absorbs them,

2. The fact of the limitations which form-taking necessitates.

The above two factors must be recognized as true of the solar Logos, the planetary Logos, a man or an atom. Every form of divine life (the infinitesimally small and the infinitely great) veils or hides a fraction of spiritual energy. The result to the point of spiritual existence is necessarily a shutting in, a cutting off, and a circumscribing of itself, and only the contacts of existence itself and the struggle of the spiritual unit within the form can bring about eventual release.

For the time being and during the process of incarnation, the veiled point of life remains in ignorance of that which lies outside of itself and progressively has to fight its way out to ever increasing freedom and liberty.

## BOOK II

First the sphere of its own form is the sole thing it is aware of and it remains in ignorance of all outside of itself. The contacts, brought about by desire, are the factors whereby ignorance works out into knowledge, and the man (for we will only consider the human unit in this connection, though the basic laws hold good for all forms of divine life) gradually becomes aware of himself as he is and conscious of his environment. As this environment is triple (physical, astral and mental) and as he has three vehicles whereby he can contact the three worlds, the period covered in this awakening is immense. The old commentary says in this connection:

"In the Hall of Ignorance the triple sheaths are known. The solar life at its densest point is contacted and man emerges fully human."

Then the man becomes aware of something else, the *group* to which he belongs, and he does this through a finding of his own inner reality as latent in his personality. He learns that he, the human atom is a part of a group or centre in the body of a heavenly Man, a planetary Logos and that he must develop awareness of:

   a.   His group vibration,
   b.   His group purpose,
   c.   His group centre.

This is the stage of the probationary path or the Path of Discipleship up to the third initiation, and the old commentary proceeds:

"Within the Hall of Learning, the central mystery is contacted. The method of release is seen, the law is well fulfilled, and man emerges well-nigh adept."

[ 130 ]

## BOOK II

Finally, the man enters the Hall of Wisdom to which he was admitted occasionally (and with increasing frequency) after the first great initiation, and learns of the place his group holds in the planetary plan, catching a glimpse also of the cosmic scheme. Ignorance (as we understand the term) is, of course, negated, but it cannot be too frequently emphasized that there remains much unknown even to the adept, and that the Christ Himself, the great World Teacher, knows not all that is the content of the awareness of the King of the World. The Yoga Sutras of Patanjali only deal, however, with the overcoming of the ignorance which holds a man upon the wheel of rebirth and which prevents him unfolding the true powers of the soul. The old commentary says in connection with this final stage:

"Within the Hall of Wisdom, light fully shines upon the adept's ways. He knows and sees the seventh part and visions all the rest. He is himself a septenate and from this Hall emerges God."

**5. Avidya is the condition of confusing the permanent, pure, blissful and the Self, with that which is impermanent, impure, painful and the not-self.**

This condition of ignorance, or the "state of avidya" is characteristic of all those who as yet do not discriminate between the real and unreal, between death and immortality, and between light and darkness. It governs, therefore, life in the three worlds, for the correspondence between avidya on the physical plane as experienced by man in incarnation is to be found on all planes. It is a limitation of Spirit itself and a necessary corollary of form-taking. The spiritual unit is born blind and senseless. It comes into form at the beginning of the ages and cycles of rebirth in a state of total unawareness. It has to become aware of that which is around it; to do this it has first to develop the senses whereby contact and awareness become possible. The method and process through which the human being has evolved five senses or avenues of approach to the not-self are well known and any standard physiological text book can supply the needed information. Three factors must be borne in mind in connection with the spiritual unit:

1. The senses have to be evolved,
2. Their recognition and use must follow,
3. A period succeeds wherein the spiritual man utilizes the senses in the fulfillment of his desire, and in so doing identifies himself with his apparatus of manifestation.

He is doubly blind, for he is not only born blind and senseless but he is mentally blinded also, and does not see himself or things as they are but makes the mistake of regarding himself as the material form, and this he does for many cycles. He has no sense of values or of proportion but looks upon the transient, suffering, unclean, material, lower man (his three sheaths in their totality) as himself, the reality. He cannot dissociate himself from his forms. The senses are part of the forms; they are not the spiritual man, the dweller in the form. They are part of the not-self and the medium of its contact with the planetary not-self.

Through discrimination and dispassion the self, who is permanent, pure, and blissful, can eventually dissociate itself from the not-self which is impermanent, impure, and full of pain. When this is not realized, the man is in a condition of avidya. When it is in process of accomplishment, the man is a follower of vidya or knowledge, a fourfold path. When the soul is known as it is and the not-self is relegated to its rightful place as a sheath, vehicle or implement, then knowledge itself is transcended and the knower stands alone. This is liberation and the goal.

**6. The sense of personality is due to the identification of the knower with the instruments of knowledge.**

This verse is the commentary upon the previous one. The student should remember that the knower, the spiritual man, has various instruments for contacting his environment and thus becoming increasingly aware:

1. His three sheaths or bodies which are his medium of contact on three planes:

    a. The physical body,
    b. The emotional or astral body,
    c. The mental body.

2. On the physical plane he has his five senses, hearing, touch, sight, taste and smell.

[ 133 ]

# BOOK II

3. The mind, the great sixth sense which has a triple use. As yet for the majority of men it has but one use:

Its first and commonest use is a gathering of the realized contacts together and their transmission as information to the ego or knower, much in the same way as the nervous system telegraphs to the brain the external contacts it makes. It is this use of the mind which produces primarily the sense of personality which begins to fade out as the other uses become possible.

A second use of the mind is the one which the first five means of yoga bring about—the power to transmit to the brain the thoughts, wishes and will of the ego or soul. This brings into the personal self on the physical plane a recognition of the reality and the sense of identification with the not-self becomes steadily less.

The third use of the mind is its use by the soul as an organ of vision whereby the realm of the soul itself is contacted and known. The final three means of yoga bring this about.

It should be emphasized that this is a most important fact to note. If the aspirant will regard the development and full use of the sixth sense as his immediate objective, and will bear in mind the three purposes for which it is intended, he will make rapid progress, the sense of personality will fade away and identification with the soul will ensue. This is one of the greatest of the fetters which hold the sons of men captive. It is here that the axe must be laid to the root of the tree.

## BOOK II

**7. Desire is attachment to objects of pleasure.**

This is not a literal translation by any means but gives the basic idea so clearly that it is best to translate the sutra as above.

These objects of pleasure cover all the attachments which a man forms from the savage state of infant humanity up to advanced degrees of discipleship; they cover desire for gross objects on the physical plane as well as attachment to those things, occupations and reactions which the emotions or intellectual pursuits will offer; they cover the whole gamut or range of sensuous experience from the response of the savage to warmth and a good meal to the rapture of the mystic. Desire is a generic term covering the outgoing tendency of spirit towards form life. It may mean the delight of a cannibal for that which he eats, the love of a man for his family, the appreciation of the artist for a beautiful painting, or the adoration of the devotee for Christ or his guru. It is all attachment in some degree or another, and the progress of the soul seems to be in this dispensation from one object of sense to another until that time comes when he is thrown back *alone* upon himself. He has exhausted all objects of attachment, and even his guru seems to have left him alone. Only one reality is left, that spiritual reality which is himself, and his desire then turns inward. It is no longer outgoing but he finds the kingdom of God within. All desire then leaves him. He makes contacts, and continues to manifest and work upon the planes of illusion but he works from the centre where dwells his divine self, the sum total of all desire, and there is nothing to lure him forth into the byways of pleasure or of pain.

### 8. Hate is aversion for any object of the senses.

This sutra is the reverse of the preceding one. The true yogi neither feels aversion or desire. He is balanced between these pairs of opposites. Hate causes separation, whereas love reveals the unity underlying all forms. Hate is the result of concentration upon form and of a forgetfulness of that which every form (in more or less degree) reveals; hate is the feeling of repulsion and leads to a withdrawal of the man from the object hated; hate is the reverse of brotherhood and therefore is the breaking of one of the basic laws of the solar system. Hate negates unity, causes barriers to be built and produces those causes which lead to crystallization, destruction and death. It is energy used to repudiate instead of to synthesize and therefore runs counter to the law of evolution.

Hate is really the result of the sense of personality and of ignorance plus misapplied desire. It is almost the culmination of the other three. It was the sense of personality and of extreme ignorance coupled with desire for personal gain which produced hatred of Abel in the heart of Cain and caused the first murder, or the destruction of a brother's form. This should be carefully considered, for hate in some degree, aversion to some extent, is present in every human heart. Only, however, when it is entirely overcome by love or the sense of unity will death, danger and fear pass out of the ken of the human family.

**9. Intense desire for sentient existence is attachment. This is inherent in every form, is self-perpetuating, and known even to the very wise.**

This form of attachment is the basic cause of all manifestation. It is inherent in the relationship of the two great opposites, spirit and matter; it is the governing factor in logoic manifestation and this is the reason why even "the very wise" are subject to it. This form of attachment is an automatic self-reproducing, self-perpetuating faculty, and it should be remembered that the overcoming of this tendency, even when carried to its highest stage by the adept, is but a relative overcoming. As long as the Logos of our solar system, or the Absolute Spirit, incarnates through the medium of a solar system, this tendency will be present in the highest planetary Spirit and the most elevated spiritual existence. All that is possible in overcoming attachment, or killing out desire, is to develop the power to balance the pairs of opposites on any particular plane so that one is no longer held by the forms of that plane and withdrawal becomes possible. Very secondary meanings are given by the ordinary student to the words attachment, desire, and their killing out. They are interpreted in terms of the student's small advancement. They are but English words which most inadequately and only symbolically seek to express an occult work. They can only be truly understood in terms of the law of Attraction and Repulsion and through an understanding of the system of occult vibrations.

The will to live or to manifest is part of the divine Life impulse, and therefore is right. The will to be or to manifest upon any specific plane or through any specific group of forms is not right when that sphere of manifestation is outgrown, and when any peculiar set of forms have served their purpose of providing media for experience-contacts and can teach no further lessons, evil enters in, for a tendency to evil is but a tendency to revert to the use of forms and practices which the Indweller has outgrown. For this reason, the gross animal sins are universally regarded as evil because it is generally recognized that the dweller in the form of man has outgrown the third or animal kingdom.

An adept, therefore, has transcended attachment to forms on three planes (physical, astral and mental) and has killed out all longing for the forms of those planes. When the life or Spirit withdraws itself, the form dies, occultly. When the thought of the ego or higher self is occupied with its own plane, there is no energy outgoing towards the matter of the three worlds and so no form-building and form-attachment is there possible. This is in line with the occult truism that "energy follows thought," and in line too with the teaching that the body of the Christ principle, (the buddhic vehicle) only begins to coordinate as the lower impulses fade out. It is consistent also with the fact that the causal vehicle, the body of the higher self on the abstract levels of the mental plane gains in beauty, size and activity with greater rapidity during the stages of discipleship than was previously possible in the entire cycle of previous incarnations. Egoic energy is not strictly outgoing, but is directed more literally to its own self-development. Attachment to form or the attraction of form for Spirit is the great involutionary impulse. Repulsion of form and consequent form disintegration is the great evolutionary urge.

**10. These five hindrances, when subtly known, can be overcome by an opposing mental attitude.**

The words "subtly known" could be paraphrased as "when realized by the inner man," and the thought back of the words has been well explained by Dvivedi in his Comment as follows:

"Having described the nature of 'distractions,' the author points out the way to suppress them. They are divided into two kinds, subtle and gross. The first are those which exist in a dormant condition in the form of impressions, whereas the second are those that are concretely affecting the mind. The first can be completely suppressed only by gaining mastery over the whole of their support, viz. the thinking principle."

# BOOK II

This is the first work of the aspirant to yoga. He must realize the nature of the obstacles and then set in to overcome them, doing the work from the mental plane. He has to gain control of the apparatus of thought; then he has to learn how to use that apparatus, and when this has been accomplished, he begins to offset the hindrances by counter currents. The hindrances themselves are the result of wrong habits of thought and the misuse of the thinking principle. When they are subtly known as the *seeds* which produce the "obstacle-producing forms," then they can be exterminated in the latent stages by right habits of thought resulting in the setting up of the liberty-producing means.

Ignorance (avidya) must be supplanted by the true vidya or knowledge, and as is well-known, in this fourth race on this fourth globe and in the fourth round, the four vidyas and the four noble truths and the four basic elements form the sum total of this knowledge.

The four vidyas of the Hindu philosophy might be enumerated as follows:

1.  Yajna Vidya.—The performance of religious rites in order to produce certain results. Ceremonial magic. Is concerned with sound, therefore with the Akasa or the ether of space. The "Yajna" is the invisible deity who pervades space.

2.  Mahavidya.—The great magic knowledge. It has degenerated into Tantrika worship. Deals with the feminine aspect, or the matter (mother) aspect. The basis of black magic. True maha-

[ 140 ]

yoga has to do with the form (2nd aspect) and its adaptation to Spirit and its needs.

3. Guhya vidya.—The science of mantrams. The secret knowledge of mystic mantrams. The occult potency of sound, of the Word.

4. Atman vidya.—True spiritual wisdom.

The four noble truths have been stated for us in the words of the Buddha in the following terms:

"Now the Exalted One thus addressed the brethren:
'Through not understanding, through not penetrating the Four Aryan Truths, brethren, we have run on and wandered round this long, long journey (or rebirth), both you and I. What are those four?

The Aryan Truth of Ill: the Aryan Truth of the Arising of Ill: the Aryan Truth of the Ceasing of Ill: the Aryan Truth of the Way leading to the Ceasing of Ill.

But, brethren, when these Four Aryan Truths are understood and penetrated, then is uprooted the craving for existence, cut off is the thread that leadeth to rebirth, then is there no more coming to be.'

Thus spake the Exalted One. When the Happy One had thus spoken, the Master added this further:
    Blind to the Fourfold Aryan Truths of things,
    And blind to see things as they really are,
    Long was our journeying thro' divers births.
    Gone is the cord of life when these are seen.
    No more becoming when Ill's root is cut."

The four elements have been stated for us in the following extract from the *Secret Doctrine* (I. 95):

"The Golden Egg was surrounded by seven natural Elements, four ready (ether, fire, air, water), three secret."

## BOOK II

**11. Their activities are to be done away with through the meditation process.**

The "opposing mental attitude" referred to in the previous sutra has distinct reference to the seeds or the latent tendencies as they subsist in the mental body and in the body of desire. This mental attitude has to become one of active mental meditation and one-pointed thought if the activities of the physical body are to be subjected to a like control. Much that we do is automatic and the result of long continued emotional and mental habits. Instinctively, from ancient practice and through subjection to a world of tangible forms, our physical plane activities are governed by the five hindrances. These have to be suppressed and the work of dealing with the latent seeds and with suppressing the external activities must proceed simultaneously. The steady opposition of the mental attitude deals with one; meditation which brings in the three factors of the thinker, the mind and the physical brain will take care of the other, and this must not be forgotten, otherwise theory will not become intelligent practice. This meditation process is dealt with in Book III and need not be enlarged upon here.

**12. Karma itself has its root in these five hindrances and must come to fruition in this life or in some later life.**

Just as long as man on the physical plane is subject to, or governed by these hindrances, just so long will he initiate those activities which will produce inevitable effects, and just so long will he be tied to the wheel of rebirth and be condemned to form-taking. The student should carefully note that these five hindrances are the cause of all the activities of the lower personality or the lower man. Everything he does is based on one or other of them and there is no action of the average man in the three worlds which is not the outcome of ignorance and its accompanying erroneous identifications and reactions.

As the hindrances are overcome and ignorance, the field of them all, is superseded by divine wisdom, there are fewer and fewer effects to work out on the physical plane, and the chains which link a man to the great wheel of physical manifestation are severed one by one. These chains are triple just as the field of ignorance is triple, being the three great planes of consciousness which are the field of human evolution. When the field of ignorance becomes the field of conscious experience and when the chains are felt to be fetters and limitations, the would be chela has made a tremendous step forward in the liberating process. When he can carry the struggle inward into what Ganganatha Jha calls "the unmanifested life" and which we frequently call "the subtler planes" he is entering the Hall of Learning and is severing those fetters which kama (or desire) and the wrong use of the mind have so subtly forged. Later he will enter the Hall of Wisdom and be taught certain esoteric and occult methods of hastening the liberating process.

## BOOK II

**13.** So long as the roots (or samkaras) exist, their fruition will be birth, life, and experiences resulting in pleasure or pain.

The predominant work of the occult student is the manipulation of force, and the entering of that world wherein forces are actively set in motion which result in phenomenal effects. He has to study and comprehend practically and intelligently the working of the law of Cause and Effect, and he leaves off dealing with effects and centres his attention on their producing causes. In relation to himself, he comes to realise that the primary cause of the phenomenon of his objective existence in the three worlds is the ego itself, and that the secondary causes are the aggregate of those fundamental egoic impulses which have led to the development of response to sense contacts on the three planes. These impulses have produced effects which (being under the law) must work out into objectivity on the physical plane. Therefore there is much importance attached to the necessity for establishing direct egoic contact, via the thread or sutratma, for only in this way can the aspirant ascertain the causes lying back of the present manifestations of his life, or begin to deal with the samkaras or seeds of his future activities. These seeds are kama-manasic (or partially emotional and partially mental) in nature, for desire is potent in its effects and produces the physical vehicle in its two aspects.

a. Lower manas, or concrete mind is the basic factor in the production of the etheric body.

b. Kama, or desire is the prime factor in calling the dense physical vehicle into being.

The two together are responsible for manifested existence.

It is well known that the tree of life is depicted with the roots above and the flowering leaves downwards. In the tiny tree of life of the ego the same symbolic presentation holds true. The roots are found on the mental plane. The flowering forth into objectivity and fruition is to be seen on the physical plane. Therefore it is necessary for the aspirant to lay the axe to the root of the tree, or to deal with the thoughts and desires which produce the physical body. He must enter the subjective realm if he wants to deal with that which will continue to keep him on the wheel of rebirth. When the seeds are eradicated, fruition is not possible. When the root is separated from its externalities on any of the three planes, then the life-energy no longer flows downwards. The three words birth, life and experience sum up human existence, its object, method and goal and with them we need not deal. The whole subject of karma (or the law of Cause and Effect) is dealt with in this sutra, and is of too vast a subject to be enlarged upon here. Suffice it to say that, from the standpoint of the Yoga Sutras, karma is of three kinds:

1. *Latent Karma.* Those seeds and causes which are yet undeveloped and inactive and must work out to fruition in some part of the present or subsequent lives.

2. *Active Karma.* Those seeds or causes

which are in process of fruition and for which the present life is intended to provide the needed soil for the flowering forth.

3. *New Karma.* Those seeds or causes which are being produced in this life, and which must inevitably govern the circumstances of some future life.

The beginner in this science of yoga can begin dealing with his active karma, interpreting each life-event and every circumstance as providing conditions wherein he can work off a certain specified series of effects. He can endeavor so to watch his thoughts that new seeds are not sown so that no future karma can be brought to fruition in some later life.

The seeds of latent karma are more difficult for the neophyte to work with and it is here that his Master can help him—manipulating his circumstances and dealing with his surroundings in the three worlds in order that this type of karma may more quickly work out and be done with.

**14. These seeds (or samskaras) produce pleasure or pain according as their originating cause was good or evil.**

It might be noted that good is that which relates to the one principle, to the reality indwelling all forms, to the Spirit of man as it reveals itself through the soul, and to the Father as He manifests through the Son. Evil relates to the form, to the vehicle, and to matter and really concerns the relation of the Son to his body of manifestation. If the Son of God (cosmic or human) is limited, and imprisoned and blinded by his form, that is the power of evil over him. If he is aware of his own self, unfettered by forms, and free from the thralldom of matter that is the power of good. Complete freedom from matter causes bliss or pleasure—the joy of realisation. Evil causes pain, for just in so far as the Inner Ruler is limited by his body of manifestation just so far does he suffer.

**15. To the illuminated man all existence (in the three worlds) is considered pain owing to the activities of the gunas. These activities are threefold, producing consequences, anxieties and subliminal impressions.**

The three "gunas" are the three qualities of matter itself, sattva, rajas and tamas, or rhythm, activity and inertia, and are inherent in all forms. The student needs to remember that every form on every plane is thus characterised, and this is true of the highest form as of the lowest, the manifestation of these qualities only differing in degree.

To the man who is achieving perfection it becomes increasingly apparent how every form through which he, the divine spiritual man is manifesting, causes limitation and difficulty. The physical vehicle of the adept, though constructed of substance predominatingly sattvic in nature, equilibrised and rhythmic, yet serves to confine him to the world of physical endeavor and limits the powers of the true man. Speaking generally it might be said that:

1.  The attribute of inertia (or tamas) characterises the lower personal self, the sheaths of the
threefold lower man.

2.  The attribute of activity is the prime characteristic of the soul, and it is this quality which
causes the intense activity and constant labor of
the man as he seeks experience and later, as he
seeks to serve.

3.  The attribute of rhythm, or balance, is the
quality of the spirit or monad and it is this tendency to perfection which is the cause of man's
evolution in time and space and the factor which
carries all life through all forms to the consummation.  Let us bear in mind here, however, that
these three qualities are the qualities of the substance through which the triple spirit is manifesting in this solar system.  The nature of spirit
itself we know not as yet, for we cannot think
except in terms of form, however, transcendental
those forms may be.  Only those souls who have
attained the highest initiation and can pass beyond our solar ring-pass-not know somewhat of
the essential nature of that which we call spirit.

Coming to the practical manifestation of the
gunas in the three worlds (in relation to man) it
can be noted that:

1.  The attribute of balance or rhythm distinguishes the mental vehicle.  When the mental
body is organized and man is being directed by
his mind, his life becomes stabilised and organized
also and the direction of his affairs proceeds in a
balanced manner.

2.  The quality of activity or mobility is the

characteristic of the emotional or astral nature
and, when this is dominant the life is chaotic, violent, emotional and subjected to every mood and
feeling. It is primarily the quality of the desire
life.

3. Inertia is the quality dominating the physical body and the whole objective of the ego is to
break down that inertia and drive its lowest vehicle into an activity which will bring about the
desired ends. Hence the use and necessity for the
guna of mobility and the full play of the emotional or desire nature in the earlier stages of
endeavor.

Pain is the product of these form activities, for
pain is the result of the inherent difference between the pairs of opposites, spirit and matter.
Both the factors are "at peace" essentially until
brought into conjunction and both resist each
other and produce friction and suffering when
united in time and space.

Patanjali points out that this pain is comprehensive, covering past, present and future.

1. *Consequences.* Pain is brought about
through the activity of the past and the working
out of karma as it is expressed in the adjusting of
mistakes, the paying of the price of error. The
settling of past obligations and debts is ever a
sorrowful process. Certain past eventualities ne-
cesitate present conditions both of heredity, environment and type of body, and the form, both
of vehicle and group relations, is painful to the
soul, who is confined thereby.

2. *Anxieties.* This concerns the present and

is sometimes translated—apprehensions. If the student will study this term he will note that it covers not only the fear of evil in suffering, but also the fear of failure in the spiritual body in service. These equally cause pain and distress and parallel the awakening of the real man to a realisation of his heritage.

3. *Subliminal impressions*, has relation to the future and concerns those forebodings as to death, suffering and need which dominate so many of the sons of men. It is the unknown and its possibilities that we fear both for ourselves and others, and this in its turn produces pain.

**16. Pain which is yet to come may be warded off.**

The Sanskrit words here give a twofold idea. They infer first of all that certain types of coming "misery" (as some translations give it) may be avoided by a right adjustment of a man's energies so that through his changed attitude of mind, painful reactions are no longer possible, and through the transmutation of his desires old "pains" are impossible. It infers secondly that life will be so lived in the present that no causes will be set in motion along the line of pain-producing effects. This dual inference will cause in the life of the yogi a dual discipline involving a set determination to practise non-attachment, and a steady discipline of the lower nature. This will bring about a mental activity of such a nature that old tendencies, longings and desires no longer attract, and no activities are indulged in which can produce later karma, or results.

That which is past can only now be worked out, and that type of karma, bringing pain, sorrow and misery in its train must be allowed to follow out its course. Present karma, or that precipitation of effects which the ego plans to disperse in the present life-cycle must equally play its part in the emancipation of the soul. It is, however, possible for the spiritual man so to govern the lower man that the happenings of karma (or the effects as they work out into the physical objective world) may cause no pain or distress, as they will be seen and met by the non-attached yogi. Nor will further pain-producing causes be allowed to be set in motion.

**17. The illusion that the Perceiver and that which is perceived are one and the same, is the cause (of the pain-producing effects) which must be warded off.**

This sutra brings us right back to the great basic duality of manifestation, the union of spirit and matter. It is their interplay which produces all the form-producing modifications or activities on the various planes and which is the cause of the limitations which pure consciousness has imposed upcn itself. In a small commentary such as this it is impossible to enter with any fullness into this subject. All that it is possible to do is to touch upon the subject as it affects man himself. It might be summed up as follows:—All pain and sorrow is caused by the spiritual man identifying himself with his objective forms in the three worlds and with the realm of phenomena in which those forms have their activities. When he can detach himself from the kingdom of the senses and know himself as the "one who is not that which is seen and touched and heard" then he can free himself from all form-limitations and stand apart as the divine perceiver and actor. He will use forms as he desires in order to attain certain specific ends but is not deluded into regarding them as himself. Students would do well to learn to hold the consciousness that in the three worlds (which is all that concerns the aspirant at this stage) he is the highest factor in the well-known triplicities:

| | | |
|---|---|---|
| The Perceiver | Perception | That which is perceived, |
| The Thinker | Thought | Thought forms, |
| The Knower | Knowledge | The field of knowledge, |
| The Seer | Sight | That which is seen, |
| The Observer | Observation | That which is observed, |
| The Spectator | Vision | The Spectacle, |

and many others equally well known.

The great objective of Raja Yoga is to free the thinker from the modifications of the thinking principle so that he no longer merges himself in the great world of thought illusions nor identifies himself with that which is purely phenomenal. He stands free and detached and uses the world of the senses as the field of his intelligent activities and no longer as the field of his experiments and experience-gaining endeavours.

It must be remembered that the means of perception are the six senses; *i.e.* hearing, touch, sight, taste, smell and the mind, and that these six must be transcended and known for what they are. The means of perception reveal the great maya or world of illusion which is composed of forms of every kind, built of substance which must be studied as to its atomic and molecular construction and as to the basic elements which give to that substance its specific differentiations and qualities. For purposes of study the student will do well to remember that he must investigate the nature of the following factors in the polar opposite to spirit which we call matter:

1. Atoms,
2. Molecular matter,
3. The elements,
4. The three gunas or qualities,
5. The tattvas or force differentiations in their seven forms.

Through an understanding of the nature and distinctions of matter he will come to a comprehension of the world of form which has held his spirit a prisoner for so long. This Patanjali points out in the next sutra.

**18. That which is perceived has three qualities, sattva, rajas and tamas (rhythm, mobility and inertia); it consists of the elements and the sense organs. The use of these produces experience and eventual liberation.**

This is one of the most important sutras in the book for in a few concise words we have summed up for us the nature of substance, its constitution, its purpose and reason. Much time might be given to a consideration of each sentence, and the words, "the qualities," "the elements," "the senses," "evolution" and "liberation" express the sum total of the factors concerned in the growth of man. These five are that with which the human unit is the most concerned and cover his career from the moment when he first took incarnation and throughout the long cycle of lives until he passes through the various gates of initiation out into the larger life of the cosmos.

First *inertia* distinguishes him, and his forms are of so heavy and gross a nature that many and violent contacts are needed before he becomes aware of his surroundings and later intelligently appreciates them. The great elements of earth, water, fire and air play their part in the building of his forms and are incorporated into his very being. His various sense organs slowly become active; first, the five senses and then when the second quality of rajas or activity is firmly established, the sixth sense or the mind begins to develop also. Later he begins to perceive in all around him in the phenomenal world, the same qualities and elements as in himself, and his knowledge rapidly grows. From that he passes to a distinction between himself as the Perceiver and that which he perceives as his forms and their world of being. The sixth sense becomes increasingly dominant and is eventually controlled by the true man who passes then into the sattvic state where he is harmonised in himself and con-

sequently with all around him. His manifestation
is rhythmic and in tune with the great whole. He
looks on at the spectacle and sees to it that those
forms through which he is active in the world of
phenomena are duly controlled and that all his
activities are in harmony with the great plan.

When this is so, he is part of the whole yet freed
and liberated from the control of the world of
form, of the elements and of the senses. He uses
them; they no longer use him.

**19.  The divisions of the gunas (or qualities
of matter) are fourfold; the specific, the non-
specific, the indicated and the untouchable.**

It is interesting to note here that the gunas or
qualities (the sum total of the attributes or aspects of the substance of our solar system) are
fourfold. In this septenary division we have an
analogy to the septenates found throughout our
manifested universe. First we have the major
three aspects of thought-substance:

1. Sattvic substance ........rhythm, equilibrium,
                              harmony,
2. Rajasic substance........mobility, activity,
3. Tamasic substance......inertia, stability.

These three are divided into:

1. The  specific..............manifested  elements,
                             form,
2. The unspecific..........the senses, force reac-
                           tions, the tanmatras,
3. The indicated...........primary substance....the
                          tattvas, atomic matter,

[ 155 ]

4. The untouchable....the great Existence who is the sum total of all these.

This sutra is intended to cover the technicalities of the form aspect of manifestation whether referring to the manifestation of a human atom or of a solar deity, and simply indicates the natural triplicity of substance. its septenary nature, and its various mutations. It expresses the nature of that aspect of divine life which is called Brahma by the Hindu, and the Holy Spirit by the Christian. This is the third aspect of the Trimurti or Trinity, the aspect of active intelligent matter, out of which the body of Vishnu or of the cosmic Christ is to be built in order that Shiva, the Father or the spirit may have a medium of revelation. It might therefore be of use if the nature of the four divisions of the three gunas were indicated, after giving the synonyms for these gunas.

*The three gunas:*

1. The qualities of matter,
2. The aspects of thinking substance, or of the universal mind,
3. The attributes of force-matter,
4. The three potencies.

These triplicities should be carefully studied as it is through them that consciousness in its various degrees becomes possible. We are here dealing with the great illusion of forms with which the Real Man identifies himself to his sorrow and pain throughout the long cycle of manifestation and from which he must eventually be liberated.

A still vaster thought is also involved: the imprisoning of the life of a solar Logos in the form of a solar system, its evolutionary development through the medium of that form and the eventual perfection and release of that life from the form at the conclusion of a great solar cycle. The lesser cycle of man is involved in the greater and his attainment and the nature of his liberation is only relative to the greater whole.

1. *The specific division of the gunas.*

This specific or particularised division of the gunas is divided into sixteen parts which deal primarily with man's reaction to the tangible objective world.

a. *The five elements:* ether, air, fire, water and earth. These are the directly involved effects of the unspecific or subjective sound or word.

b. *The five sense organs:* the ear, the skin, the eye, the tongue and the nostrils, those physical organs or channels through which identification with the tangible world becomes possible.

c. *The five organs of action:* voice, hands, feet, the excretory organs and the organs of generation.

d. *The mind.* This is the sixth sense, the organ which synthesises all the other sense organs and eventually will make their use a thing of the past.

These sixteen means of perception and activity in the phenomenal world are channels for the real thinking man; they demonstrate his active reality and are the sum total of the physical facts relating to every incarnated son of God. Similarly in their cosmic connotation, they are the sum total of the facts demonstrating the reality of a cosmic incarnation. "The Word is made flesh" both individually and in a cosmic sense.

2. *The unspecific division of the gunas.*

These are six in number and concern that which lies back of the specific; they deal with that which is subjective and intangible, and with the *force* display which produces the specific forms.

Technically these are called in the Hindu books the tanmatras. They have to do with consciousness more than form and are the "special modifications of buddhi or consciousness" (Ganganatha Jha). They are:

1. The element of hearing, or that which produces the ear,—the rudiment of hearing,

2. The element of touch or that which produces the mechanism of touch, the skin, etc.,—the rudiment of touch,

3. The element of sight, or that which produces the eye,

4. The element of taste, or that which produces the mechanism of taste.

5. The element of smell, or that which produces the mechanism of smell.

Back of these five lies the sixth tanmatra or modification of the consciousness principle, the "feeling of personality" as it has been called, the "I am I" consciousnes, the ahamkara principle. It is this which produces the sense of personal reality and of one's being a separated unit of consciousness. It is the basis of the great "heresy of separateness" and the cause of the real or spiritual man being lured into the great illusion. It is this which forces man for long aeons to identify himself with the things of the senses and it is this too which eventually brings him to the position where he seeks liberation.

3. *The indicated.*

Back of the sixteen specialized divisions and back of the six unspecialized, lies that which is the cause of them all, which is called in the Hindu books Buddhi, or pure reason, the intellect apart from the lower mind, sometimes called the intuition, whose nature is love-wisdom. This is the Christ-life or principle, which in the process of taking incarnation or form, as we know it, manifests forth as the specific and the unspecific. It is as yet for the majority only *"indicated."* We surmise it is there. The work of Raja Yoga is to bring forth into full knowledge this vague surmise so that theory becomes fact and that which is latent and believed to exist may be recognized and known for what it is.

4. *The untouchable.*

Finally we come to the fourth division of the gunas or aspects, that "in which we live and move and have our being," the untouchable or unknown God. This is the great form of existence in which our little forms are found. This is the sum total of the thinking substance of which our little minds are part; this is the whole manifestation of God through the medium of the cosmic Christ of which each little Son of God is a part. Of this untouchable and unknown the mind of man cannot as yet conceive.

**20. The seer is pure knowledge (gnosis). Though pure, he looks upon the presented idea through the medium of the mind.**

Reference has already been made to the excellent translation of this sutra as given by Johnston which runs as follows: "The seer is pure vision. Though pure, he looks out through the vesture of the mind." Ganganatha Jha throws still further light upon it in the words "The spectator is absolute sentience, and though pure, still beholds intellected ideas." The thought conveyed is that the true man, the spectator, perceiver or thinker is the sum total of all perception, be it through the avenues of the senses or of the lower mind; he is in himself knowledge, clear vision or true perception. All that exists in the three worlds exists because of and for him; he is the cause of its being and when he no longer seeks it or endeavours to vision it, for him it exists not. This sutra is one of the key verses in the book, and gives the clue to the entire science of yoga. Certain thoughts lie hid in its formulation which cover the whole ground of this science and students would do well to give much attention to this. It has a mantric effect and if stated as an affirmation and used constantly by the aspirant will eventually demonstrate to him the truth of the statement that "as a man thinketh, so is he."

"I am pure knowledge. Though pure, I look

upon presented ideas through the medium of the mind."

We have here:

1.   *The seer* or the one who looks on and considers (from his divine standpoint) this world of effects, this great maya of illusion,

2.   *The presented idea.* The thought conveyed here is that every form which passes before the spectator in the great panorama of life in the three worlds is a "presented-idea," and that these presented ideas are therefore embodied thoughts of some kind and must be regarded as such. The task of the occultist is to work with the force which lies back of every form and not so much with the form which is but the effect of some cause. This method of endeavour can only be developed gradually. The spectator passes gradually from the forms and their true significance in his own immediate environment and in his own tiny world, through the various forms of the world process until the world of causes stands revealed to him, and the world of effects assumes a secondary position.

He perceives first the forms in the three worlds. Gradually then he becomes aware of that which caused them and of the type of force which brought them into being. Later he discovers the idea which they embody and, tracing them progressively onward or back to their originating source, he comes into touch with the great lives which are the cause of manifestation. He thus passes out of the realm of objectivity, out of the mental, emotional and physical worlds into the realm of the soul or of the subjective cause of this triple manifestation. This is the world of ideas and therefore of pure knowledge, pure reason and divine mind. Later, at a very advanced stage he touches the one Life which synthesises the many lives, the one Purpose which blends the many ideas into one homogeneous plan.

3. *The mind.* This is the instrument which the seer employs in order to perceive presented ideas or thought forms. For purposes of clarification it might be noted that the presented ideas fall into five groups of thought forms:

a. The tangible objective forms in the physical world of every day. With these the seer has for long identified himself in the earlier and more savage stages of human existence.

b. The moods, feelings and desires, which all have form in the astral world, the world of the emotions.

c. The thought forms in their myriad distinctions which crowd the mental world.

Through these "presented ideas," the seer achieves knowledge of the not-self.

d. The thought forms which he can create himself after he has learned to control his instrument the mind and can discriminate between the illusory world of present ideas and those realities which constitute the world of spirit.

Through this process he arrives at a knowledge of himself. Throughout the great experience of knowing the not-self and knowing himself, he uses the mind as his medium of search, of explanation and of interpretation, for the senses and all his channels of contact, telegraph constant information and reactions to the mind via the lower instrument of the brain. Having reached this stage the seer is then able to use the mind in a reverse manner. Instead of turning his attention to the not-self or the illusory world of effects and instead of studying his own lower nature, he can now, owing to the mental control achieved, arrive at the fifth stage:

e. The ideas presented by the world of spiritual life, the realm of spiritual knowledge, and the kingdom of God in the truest sense.

Through this, the seer arrives at a knowledge of God as He is and comes to an understanding of the nature of spirit. The mind then serves a triple purpose:

a. Through it, the seer looks out upon the realm of causes, the spiritual realm.

b. By its means, the world of causes can be interpreted in terms of the intellect.

c. By using it correctly, the seer can transmit to the physical brain of the lower personal self (the reflection in the world of effects of the true man) that which the soul sees and knows. This triangle is then formed and comes into working activity: The seer or spiritual man, the mind, his medium of investigation, or the window through which he looks out (whether upon the world of effects, upon himself, or upon the world of cause) and the brain, which is the receiving plate upon which the seer can impress his "pure knowledge" using the mind as an interpreter and transmitting agency.

## BOOK II

**21.   All that is exists for the sake of the soul.**

Man in his arrogance should not take this
sutra to mean that all that is created exists for
him.   The sense is much wider than this.   The
soul referred to is that of the Supreme Being
of which the soul of man is but an infinitesimal
part.   Man's tiny world, his small environment
and contacts, exist for the sake of the experience
they bring him and the final liberation they bring
about; he is the cause of their manifestation and
they are the result of his own thought power.
But around him and through him is to be found
that greater whole of which he is a part, and the
entire vast universe, planetary and solar, exists
for the sake of the vaster Life in whose body he
is but an atom.   The whole world of forms is
the result of the thought activity of some life;
the whole universe of matter is the field for the
experience of some existence.

**22.   In the case of the man who has achieved
yoga (or union) the objective universe has
ceased to be.   Yet it existeth still for those who
are not yet free.**

This sutra holds the germ of the entire science
of thought.   Its premise is based upon the realisation that all that we behold are modifications of
thought substance, that the thinker creates his
own world, whether he be God or man.   When a
man through the science of yoga (that science
which deals with the "suppression of the activities

of the thinking principle" or with mind control),
has achieved full power over the mind and over
mental substance or thought matter, he is freed
from the control of those forms which hold the
majority of men captive in the three worlds.

He stands then apart from the great illusion;
the bodies which have hitherto held him no longer
do so; the great currents of ideas and thoughts
and desires which have their origin through the
"modifications of the thinking principle" of men
imprisoned in the three worlds no longer sway
or affect him; and the myriad thought forms
which are the result of these currents in the mental, astral and physical worlds no longer shut him
away from the realities or from the true subjective world of causes, and of force emanations.
He is no longer deceived and can discriminate between the real and the unreal, between the true
and the false, and between the life of the spirit
and the world of phenomena. He becomes subject then to the currents of thought, and the
world of ideas emanating from great spiritual
entities, from spiritual lives, and the great plan
of the Architect of the Universe can unroll itself
before him. He is liberated and free and subject
only to the new conditions of the life of the man
who has made the great at-one-ment. The laws
of the three worlds are not superseded but are
transcended, for the greater always includes the
lesser and though—for purposes of service—he
may choose to limit himself to a seemingly three
dimensional life, yet he goes forth into the
world of higher dimensions at his pleasure, and

when needed for the extension of the kingdom
of God.

The object of this science of yoga is to reveal
to man the mode of this liberation and how he can
free himself. Hence the trend of Patanjali's
teaching up to this point has been to indicate
man's place in the scheme, to put his finger upon
the basic cause of man's restlessness and urge
towards activity of one kind or another; to show
the reason for the existence of the great world of
effects and to tempt the aspirant to an investigation of the world of causes; and so to demonstrate the need for further unfoldment and the
nature of the hindrances to that unfoldment that
the man will be ready to say: If this is all so,
what are the means whereby this union with the
real and this dispersal of the great illusion may
be brought about? This second book presents the
eight great means of yoga, giving thus a clear and
concise outline of the exact steps to be followed
for the needed regulation of the physical, psychic
and mental life.

> **23. The association of the soul with the
> mind and thus with that which the mind per-
> ceives, produces an understanding of the nature
> of that which is perceived and likewise of the
> Perceiver.**

In this sutra the attention of the student is
drawn to the primary quality which he must develop, that of discrimination. Its meaning is
therefore very clear. The pairs of opposites,
spirit and matter, purusha and prakriti, are

brought into close association and that union must come to be recognised by the soul, the perceiving consciousness. Through the process of this blending of the dualities, the soul, the thinker, comes to a comprehension of the nature which is his very own, the spiritual nature, and the nature of the phenomenal world which he perceives, contacts and uses. The organ of perception is the mind and the five senses, and from the standpoint of the soul, they form one instrument. For a long period and through many incarnations the soul or thinker identifies himself with this organ of perception and in the earlier stages with that also which he perceives through its use. He regards the phenomenal body he uses, the physical body, as himself, as witness the expression: "I am tired" or "I am hungry." He identifies himself with his body of feeling or desire, and says "I am cross," or "I want money." He identifies himself with the mental vehicle and regards himself as thinking thus and so. It is this identification which results in the theological differences, and the doctrinal and sectarian diversities everywhere to be found, and in this fifth root race and particularly in this fifth subrace this identification reaches its apotheosis. It is the era of the personal self, not of the spiritual Self. This realisation of the lower nature is part of the great evolutionary process but must be followed by a realization of the other polar opposite, the spiritual Self. This is brought about by the soul beginning to practise discrimination, at first theoretically and intellectually (hence the great value of the present era of criticism and polemical discussion, as it forms part of the planetary discriminative process) and later experimentally. This discrimination leads eventually to three things:

1. An understanding of the distinction between spirit and matter,

2. A comprehension of the nature therefore of the soul which is the product of this union, and is the son, produced by the union of the father-spirit and of the mother-matter,

3. A development whereby the soul begins to identify itself with the spiritual aspect and not with the phenomenal world of forms. This later stage is greatly aided and hastened through the practice of Raja Yoga and hence the determination of the Hierarchy to give this science to the critical discriminating West. It should be borne in mind that the soul passes through great stages in the unifying process and that the word *yoga* covers the evolutionary development of the human Monad.

1. The union of the soul with the form and its identification with the matter aspect,

2. The union of thinking man or the self-conscious reflection in the three worlds with the spiritual man on its own plane,

3. The union of the spiritual man or divine thinker with its Father in Heaven, the Monad or spirit aspect. Stage I covers the period from the first incarnation up to the treading of the Probationary Path. Stage II covers the period of the Probationary Path up to the third initiation

upon the Path of Discipleship. Stage III covers
the final stages of the Path of Initiation.

**24. The cause of this association is igno-
rance or avidya. This has to be overcome.**

Ignorance of the real nature of the soul and an
urge to find out its own nature and its powers is
the cause of the soul's identifying itself with the
organs of perception, and with that which they
perceive or bring within the consciousness of the
soul. When through this ignorance and its consequences, the soul fails to find what it is seeking,
there comes the stage when the search takes on a
different form and the soul itself searches for
reality. It might be expressed thus.

Identification with the phenomenal world and
the use of the outgoing organs of perception covers the period which the real man spends in what
is called the Hall of Ignorance. Satiety, restlessness and a search for the knowledge of the self or
soul characterises the period spent in the Hall of
Learning. Realization, expansion of consciousness and identification with the spiritual man
cover the period spent in the Hall of Wisdom.
The terms human life, mystic life and occult life
apply to these three stages.

**25. When ignorance is brought to an end
through non-association with the things perceived, this is the great liberation.**

During the process of incarnation, the seer, the
soul, is submerged in the great maya or illusion.
He is imprisoned by his own thought forms and

thought creations and in those of the three worlds also. He regards himself as part of the phenomenal world. When, through experience and discrimination, he can distinguish between himself and those forms, then the process of liberation can proceed and eventually culminate in the great renunciation which once and for all sets a man free from the three worlds.

This process is a progressive one and cannot be effected all at once. It covers two stages:

1. The stage of probation, or, as the Christian expresses it, the Path of Purification,

2. The stage of discipleship in two parts:

a. Discipleship itself or the steadfast training and discipline administered to the personal lower self by the soul, directed by his guru or master,

b. Initiation, or the progressive expansions of consciousness through which the disciple passes under the guidance of the master.

Certain words describe this dual process:

a. Aspiration,
b. Discipline,
c. Purification,
d. The practice of the means of yoga or union,
e. Initiation,
f. Realisation,
g. Union.

**26. The state of bondage is overcome through perfectly maintained discrimination.**

A word here on discrimination will be of value as it is the first great method of attaining liberation or freedom from the three worlds. Based as it is on a realisation of the essential duality of nature, and regarding nature as a result of the union of the two polarities of the Absolute All, spirit and matter, discrimination is at first an attitude of mind and must be sedulously cultivated. The premise of the duality is admitted as a logical basis for further work and the theory is tested out in an effort to prove the truth. The aspirant then definitely assumes the attitude of higher polarity (that of spirit, manifesting as the soul or inner ruler) and seeks in the affairs of every day to discriminate between the form and the life, between the soul and the body, between the sum total of the lower manifestation (physical, astral and mental man) and the real self, the cause of the lower manifestation.

He seeks in the affairs of every day to cultivate a consciousness of the real and a negation of the unreal and this he carries into all his relationships and into all his affairs. He accustoms himself, through persistent unbroken practise, to distinguish between the self and the not-self, and to occupy himself with the affairs of spirit and not with those of the great maya or world of forms. This distinction is at first theoretical, then intellectual but later assumes more reality and enters into the happenings of the emotional and physical world. Finally the following of this method eventuates in the entrance of the aspirant into an entirely new dimension and his identification with a life and a world of being dissociated from the three worlds of human endeavour.

## BOOK II

When this is so the new environment becomes familiar to him so that he knows not only the form but the subjective Reality which produces or causes the existence of the forms.

Then he passes on to the cultivation of the next great quality which is dispassion or desirelessness. A man may be able to distinguish between the real and the true, between the substance and the Life which animates it and yet desire or "go out" towards the form existence. This too must be overcome before perfect liberation, emancipation or freedom is attained. In one of the old commentaries in the archives of the Lodge of Masters, the following words are found:

> "It suffices not to know the way nor to feel the force which serveth to extract the life from out of the forms of maya. A moment of great portent must take place wherein the chela breaketh by one act and through a word of Power the illusory sutratma which bindeth him to form. Like the spider which gathereth up the thread again within himself whereby he ventured forth into unknown realms, so the chela withdraweth himself from all the forms in the three realms of being which have hitherto enticed."

The above merits close consideration and can be linked to the thought embodied in the occult phrase: "Before a man can tread the Path, he must become that Path himself."

**27. The k n o w l e d g e (or illumination) achieved is sevenfold, and is attained progressively.**

The Hindu teaching holds that the states of mind-consciousness are seven in number. The sixth sense and its use bring about seven modes of thought, or—to put it more technically—there are seven major modifications of the thinking principle. These are:

1. *Desire for knowledge.* It is this which drives forth the Prodigal Son, the soul into the three worlds of illusion, or (to carry the metaphor further back still) it is this which sends forth the Monad or Spirit into incarnation. This basic desire is what causes all experience.

2. *Desire for freedom.* The result of experience and of the investigations which the soul carries on in its manifold life-cycles is to cause a great longing for a different condition and a great desire for liberation and for freedom from the wheel of rebirth.

3. *Desire for happiness.* This is a basic quality of all human beings, though it shows itself in many different ways. It is based upon an inherent faculty of discrimination and upon a deep seated capacity to contrast the "Father's" home and the Prodigal's present condition. It is this inherent capacity for "bliss" or happiness which produces that restlessness and urge to change which lies back of the evolutionary urge itself. It is the cause of activity and progress. Dissatisfaction with the present condition is based upon a dim memory of a time of satisfaction and of bliss. This has to be regained before peace can be known.

4. *Desire to do one's duty.* The first three modifications of the thinking principle eventually bring evolving humanity to the state where the

motive for life comes to be simply the fulfillment
of one's dharma. The longing for knowledge, for
freedom, and for happiness has brought the man
to a state of utter dissatisfaction. Nothing brings
him any true joy or peace. He has exhausted
himself in the search for joy for himself. Now
he begins to widen his horizon and to search
where (in the group and in his environment),
what he seeks may lie. He awakens to a sense of
responsibility to others and begins to seek for
happiness in the fulfillment of his obligations to
his dependents, his family, friends and all whom
he contacts. This new tendency is the beginning
of the life of service which leads eventually to
a full realization of the significance of group
consciousness. H.P.B. has said that a sense of
responsibility is the first indication of the awakening of the ego or the Christ principle.

5. *Sorrow.* The greater the refinement of
the human vehicle, the greater the response of
the nervous system to the pairs of opposites, pain
and pleasure. As a man progresses and rises
on the ladder of evolution in the human family
it becomes apparent that his capacity to appreciate sorrow or joy is greatly increased. This
becomes terribly true in the case of an aspirant
and of a disciple. His sense of values becomes
so acute and his physical vehicle so sensitized that
he suffers more than the average man. This
serves to drive him forward with increasing activity in his search. His response to outer contacts is ever more rapid and his capacity for pain,
physical and emotional, becomes greatly in-

creased. This is apparent in the fifth race and particularly in the fifth subrace in the increasing frequency of suicide. The capacity of the race to suffer is due to the development and refinement of the physical vehicle and to the evolution of the body of feeling, the astral.

6. *Fear.* As the mental body develops and the modifications of the thinking principle become more rapid, fear and that which it produces begin to demonstrate. This is not the instinctual fear of animals and of the savage races, which is based upon the response of the physical body to physical plane conditions, but the fears of the mind, based upon memory, imagination and anticipation, and the power to visualize. These are difficult to overcome and can only be dominated by the ego or soul itself.

7. *Doubt.* This is one of the most interesting of the modifications for it concerns causes more than effects. The man who doubts can be described perhaps as doubting himself as an arbiter of his fate, his fellowmen as to their nature and reactions, God, or the first cause as witnessed by the controversies built up around religion and its exponents, nature itself, which doubt urges him on to constant scientific investigation and finally, the mind itself. When he begins to question the capacity of the mind to explain, interpret and comprehend, he has practically exhausted the sum total of his resources in the three worlds.

The tendency of these seven states of mind, produced through the experience of the man upon the Wheel of Life is to bring him to the point where he feels that physical plane living, sentiency and mental processes have nothing to give and utterly fail to satisfy him. He reaches the stage which Paul refers to when he says "I count all things but loss that I may win Christ."

The seven stages of illumination have been described by a Hindu teacher as follows:

1. The stage wherein the chela realizes that he has run the whole gamut of life experience in the three worlds and can say "I have known all that was to be known. Nothing further remains to know." His place on the ladder is revealed to him. He knows what he has to do. This relates to the first modification of the thinking principle, desire for knowledge.

2. The stage wherein he frees himself from every known limitation, and can say "I have freed myself from my fetters." This stage is long but results in the attainment of freedom and relates to the second of the modifications dealt with above.

3. The stage wherein the consciousness shifts completely out of the lower personality and becomes the true spiritual consciousness, centered in the real man, the ego or soul. This brings in the consciousness of the Christ nature which is love, peace and truth. He can say now "I have reached my goal. Nothing remains to attract me in the three worlds." Desire for happiness is satisfied. The third modification is transcended.

4. The stage wherein he can say with truth "I have fulfilled my dharma, and accomplished my whole duty." He has worked off karma, and

fulfilled the law. Thus he becomes a Master and a wielder of the law. This stage has relation to the fourth modification.

5. The stage wherein complete control of the mind is achieved and the seer can say "My mind is at rest." Then and only then, when complete rest is known can the true contemplation and samadhi of the highest kind be known. Sorrow, the fifth modification, is dispelled by the glory of the illumination received. The pairs of opposites are no longer at war.

6. The stage wherein the chela realises that matter or form have no longer any power over him. He can then say "The gunas or qualities of matter in the three worlds no longer attract me; they call forth no response from me." Fear therefore is eliminated for there is nothing in the disciple which can attract to him evil, death or pain. Thus equally the sixth modification is overcome and realisation of the true nature of divinity and utter bliss takes its place.

7. Full self-realisation is the next and final stage. The initiate can now say, with full conscious knowledge, "I am that I am" and he *knows* himself as one with the All-Self. Doubt no longer controls. The full light of day or completed illumination takes place and floods the whole being of the seer.

These are the seven stages upon the Path, the seven stations of the cross as the Christian puts it, the seven great initiations and the seven ways to bliss. Now the "Path of the just shineth ever more and more until the perfect day."

## BOOK II

## THE EIGHT MEANS

**28. When the means to Yoga have been steadily practised and when impurity has been overcome, enlightenment takes place leading up to full illumination.**

We now come to the practical part of the book, wherein instruction is given as to the method to pursue if full yoga, union, or at-one-ment is to be achieved. The work might be described as twofold:

1. The practice of the right means whereby union is brought about,

2. The discipline of the lower threefold man so that impurity in any of the three bodies is eradicated.

This steadfast application to the twofold work produces two corresponding results, each dependent upon its cause:

1. *Discrimination* becomes possible. The practice of the means, leads the aspirant to a scientific understanding of the distinction existing between the self and the not-self, between spirit and matter. This knowledge is no longer theoretical and that to which the man aspires, but is a fact in the experience of the disciple and one upon which he bases all his subsequent activities.

2. *Discernment* takes place. As the purificatory process is carried on, the sheaths or bodies which veil the reality become attenuated and no longer act as thick veils, hiding the soul, and the world wherein the soul normally moves. The aspirant becomes aware of a part of himself,

hitherto hidden and unknown. He approaches the heart of the mystery of himself and draws closer to the "Angel of the Presence" which can only be truly seen at initiation. He discerns a new factor and a new world and seeks to make them his own in conscious experience upon the physical plane.

It should be noted here that the two causes of revelation, the practice of the eight means to yoga and the purification of the life in the three worlds, deal with the man from the standpoint of the three worlds and bring about (in the man's physical brain) the power to discriminate between the real and the unreal and to discern the things of the spirit. They cause also certain changes of conditions within the head, reorganize the vital airs and act directly upon the pineal gland and the pituitary body. When these four:

1. Practise,
2. Purification,
3. Discrimination,
4. Discernment,

are part of the life of the physical plane man, then the spiritual man, the ego or thinker on his own plane attends to his part of the liberating process and the final two stages are brought about from above downwards. This sixfold process is the correspondence upon the Path of Discipleship, of the individualizing process, wherein animal man, the lower quaternary (physical, etheric, astral and lower mental) received that twofold expression of spirit, atma-buddhi, spiritual will and spiritual love, which completed him and made him

[ 179 ]

truly man. The two stages of development which are brought about by the ego within the purified and earnest aspirant, are:

1. *Enlightenment.* The light in the head, which is at first but a spark, is fanned to a flame which illumines all things and is fed constantly from above. This is progressive (see previous sutra), and is dependent upon steadfast practise, meditation and earnest service.

2. *Illumination.* The gradually increasing downpour of fiery energy increases steadily the "light in the head," or the effulgence found in the brain in the neighborhood of the pineal gland. This is to the little system of the threefold man in physical manifestation what the physical sun is to the solar system. This light becomes eventually a blaze of glory and the man becomes a "son of light" or a "sun of righteousness." Such were the Buddha, the Christ, and all the great Ones who have attained.

**29. The eight means of yoga are: the Commandments or Yama, the Rules or Nijama, posture or Asana, right control of life-force or Pranayama, abstraction or Pratyahara, attention or Dharana, meditation or Dhyana, and contemplation or Samadhi.**

It will be noted that these means or practices are apparently simple, but it must be carefully remembered that they do not refer to anything accomplished on one or other plane in some one body, but to the simultaneous activity and practice of these methods in all three bodies at once, so that the entire threefold lower man practices the means as they refer to the physical, the astral, and the mental vehicles. This is often forgotten. Therefore, in the study of these various means to yoga or union, we must consider them as they apply to the physical man, then to the emotional man and then to the mental man. The yogi, for instance, has to understand the significance of right breathing or of posture as they relate to the triple aligned and coordinated lower man, remembering that it is only as the lower man forms a coherent rhythmic instrument that it becomes possible for the ego to enlighten and illuminate him. The practise of breathing exercises, for instance, has led the aspirant frequently to concentrate upon the physical apparatus of breath to the exclusion of the analogous practice of rhythmic control of the emotional life.

It may be of use here if (before we take up the consideration of the means, one by one) we tabulated them carefully, giving their synonyms where possible:

### Means I.

*The Commandments*. Yama. Self-control or forbearance. Restraint. Abstention from wrong acts. These are five in number and relate to the relation of the disciple (or chela) to others and to the outside world.

### Means II

*The Rules*. Nijama. Right observances. These are likewise five in number and are frequently

called the "religious observances" because they
relate to the interior life of the disciple and to
that tie, the sutratma or link which relates him
to God, or to his Father in Heaven. These two,
the five Commandments and the five Rules are
the Hindu correspondence to the ten Commandments of the Bible and cover the daily life of the
aspirant, as it affects those around him, and
his own internal reactions.

### Means III.

*Posture*. Asana. Right Poise. Correct attitude. Position. This third means concerns the
physical attitude of the disciple when in meditation, his emotional attitude towards his environment or his group, and his mental attitude towards ideas, thought currents and abstract concepts. Finally, the practice of this means coordinates and perfects the lower threefold man so
that the three sheaths can form a perfect channel for the expression or manifestation of the life
of the spirit.

### Means IV.

*Right control of the life-force*. Pranayama.
Suppression of the breath. Regulation of the
breath. This refers to the control, regulation and
suppression of the vital airs, the breath and the
forces or shaktis of the body. It leads in reality
to the organization of the vital body or the etheric
body so that the life current or forces, emanating
from the ego or spiritual man on his own plane,

can be correctly transmitted to the physical man in objective manifestation.

### Means V.

*Abstraction.* Pratyahara. Right withdrawal. Restraint. Withdrawal of the senses. Here we get back of the physical and the etheric bodies, to the emotional body, the seat of the desires, of sensory perception and of feeling. Here can be noted the orderly method which is followed in the pursuit of yoga or union. The physical plane life, external and internal is attended to; the correct attitude to life in its triple manifestation is cultivated. The etheric body is organized and controlled and the astral body is re-oriented, for the desire nature is subdued and the real man withdraws himself gradually from all sense contacts. The next two means relate to the mental body and the final one to the real man or thinker.

### Means VI.

*Attention.* Dharana. Concentration. Fixation of the mind. Here the instrument of the Thinker, the Real Man, is brought under this control. The sixth sense is coordinated, understood, focussed and used.

### Means VII.

*Meditation.* Dhyana. The capacity of the thinker to use the mind as desired and to transmit to the brain, higher thoughts, abstract ideas, and idealistic concepts. This means concerns higher and lower mind.

## BOOK II

### Means VIII.

*Contemplation.* Samadhi. This relates to the ego or real man and concerns the realm of the soul. The spiritual man contemplates, studies or meditates upon the world of causes, upon the "things of God." He then, utilizing his controlled instrument, the mind (controlled through the practise of concentration and meditation) transmits to the physical brain, via the sutratma or thread which passes down through the three sheaths to the brain, that which the soul knows, sees and understands. This produces full illumination.

### MEANS I. THE COMMANDMENTS

**30. Harmlessness, truth to all beings, abstention from theft, from incontinence and from avarice, constitute yama or the five commandments.**

These five commandments are simple and clear and yet, if practised, would make a man perfect in his relationships to other men, to supermen and to the subhuman realms. The very first command to be harmless is in reality a summation of the others. These commandments are curiously complete and cover the triple nature; in studying all these means we shall note their relation to one or other part of the lower threefold manifestation of the ego.

### I. Physical Nature.

1. *Harmlessness.* This covers a man's physical acts as they relate to all forms of divine mani-

festation and concerns specifically his *force* nature or the energy which he expresses through his physical plane activities. He hurts no one, and injures nobody.

2. *Truth.* This concerns primarily his use of speech and of the organs of sound, and relates to "truth in the inmost part" so that truth in externality becomes possible. This is a large subject, and deals with the formulation of a man's belief regarding God, people, things and forms through the medium of the tongue and voice. This is covered in the aphorism in *Light on the Path.* "Before the voice can speak in the presence of the Master it must have lost the power to wound."

3. *Abstention from theft.* The disciple is precise and accurate in all his affairs and appropriates nothing which is not rightly his. This is a large concept covering more than the fact of actual physical appropriation of others' possessions.

## II. Astral Nature.

4. *Abstention from incontinence.* This is literally desirelessness and governs the out-going tendencies to that which is not the self, which finds physical plane expression in the relation between the sexes. It must be remembered here, however, that this expression is regarded by the occult student as only one form which the out-going impulses take, and a form which allies a man closely with the animal kingdom. Any impulse which concerns the forms and the real man

and which tends to link him to a form and to the
physical plane is regarded as a form of incontinence. There is physical plane incontinence and
this should have been left behind by the disciple
long ago. But there are also many tendencies
towards pleasure seeking with consequent satisfaction of the desire nature and this, to the true
aspirant, is likewise regarded as incontinence.

### III. Mental Nature.

5. *Abstention from avarice.* This deals with
the sin of covetousness which is literally theft
upon the mental plane. The sin of avarice may
lead to any number of physical plane sins and is
very powerful. It concerns mental force and is
a generic term covering those potent longings
which have their seat not only in the emotional
or kamic (desire) body, but in the mental body
also. This commandment to abstain from avarice is covered by St. Paul when he says "I have
learned in whatsoever state I am, therewith to be
content." That state has to be attained before
the mind can be so quieted that the things of the
soul can find entrance.

**31. Yama (or the five commandments) con-
stitutes the universal duty and is irrespective
of race, place, time or emergency.**

This sutra makes clear the universality of certain requirements, and by a study of these five
commandments which form the basis of what the
Buddhist calls "right conduct," it will be seen

that they form the basis of all true law and that
their infringement constitutes lawlessness. The
word translated duty or obligation, could well be
expressed by that comprehensive term *dharma*
in respect to others. Dharma means literally the
proper working out of one's obligations (or
karma) in the place, surroundings and environment where fate has put one. Certain governing factors in conduct must be observed and no
latitude is permitted in these respects no matter
what one's nationality, no matter what the locality
in which one finds oneself, and no matter what
age one may be or what emergency may arise.
These are the five immutable laws governing
human conduct and when they are followed by
all the sons of men, the full significance of the
term "peace to all beings" will be comprehended.

## MEANS II. THE RULES

**32. Internal and external purification, con-
tentment, fiery aspiration, spiritual reading and
devotion to Ishvara constitutes nijama (or the
five rules).**

As said above, these five rules govern the life
of the lower personal self and form the basis of
character. The yoga practices which so much
interest the western thinker and aspirant, and
which lure him on with their apparent ease of accomplishment and richness of reward (such as
psychic unfoldment) are not permitted by the
true guru or teacher until yama or nijama have

been established as controlling factors in the daily life of the disciple. The commandments and the rules must first be kept, and when his outer conduct to his fellowmen and his inner discipline of life is brought into line with these requirements, then he can safely proceed with the forms and rituals of practical yoga, but not till then.

It is the failure to recognize this that leads to so much of the trouble among students of yoga in the west. There is no better basis for the work of Eastern occultism than strict adherence to the requirements laid down by the Master of all the Masters in the *Sermon on the Mount*, and the self-disciplined Christian, pledged to purity of life and unselfish service, can take up the practise of yoga much more safely than his more worldly and selfish yet intellectual brother. He will not run the risks that his unprepared brother takes.

The words "*internal and external purity*" relate to the three sheaths in which the self is veiled and must be interpreted in a dual sense. Every sheath has its densest and most tangible form and this must be kept clean, for there is a sense in which the astral and mental bodies can be kept cleansed from impurities coming to them from their environment, just as the physical body must be kept cleansed from similar impurities. The subtler matters of those bodies must be kept equally cleansed and this is the basis of that study of magnetic purity which is the cause of so many observances in the East which seem inexplicable to the Westerner. A shadow cast upon food by a foreigner produces impure conditions; this is based upon the belief that certain types of force emanations produce impure conditions and though the method of counteracting these conditions may savour of dead letter ritual yet the thought back of the observance remains still the truth. So little is as yet known about force emanations from the human being, or acting upon the human mechanism, that what may be called "scientific purification" is as yet in its infancy.

*Contentment* is productive of conditions wherein the mind is at rest; it is based upon the recognition of the laws governing life and primarily the law of karma. It produces a state of mind wherein all conditions are regarded as correct and just, and as those in which the aspirant can best work out his problem and achieve the goal for any specific life. This does not entail a settling down and an acquiescence producing inertia, but a recognition of present assets, an availing oneself of one's opportunities and letting them form a background and a basis for all future progress. When this is done rightly the three remaining rules can be more easily kept.

*Fiery aspiration* will be dealt with more fully in the next book, but it is well to point out here that this quality of "going forth" towards the ideal or of straining towards the objective must be so profound in the aspirant to yoga that no difficulties can turn him back. Only when this quality has been developed and proved and when it is found that no problem, no darkness and no

[ 189 ]

time element can hinder, is a man permitted to become the disciple of some Master. Fiery effort, steady persistent longing and enduring faithfulness to the ideal visioned are the *sine qua non* of discipleship. These characteristics must be found in all three bodies, leading to the constant disciplining of the physical vehicle, the steady orientation of the emotional nature and the mental attitude which enables a man to "count all things but loss" if he can only arrive at his goal.

*Spiritual reading* will be found to concern the development of the sense of subjective realities. It is fostered by study as understood in the physical sense, and by the endeavour to arrive at the thoughts which words convey. It is developed by a close scrutiny of the causes which lie back of all desires, aspirations and feelings, and thus is related to the desire or astral plane. It deals with the reading of symbols or geometrical forms ensouling an idea or thought and this concerns the mental plane. This will be dealt with later in Book III.

*Devotion to Ishvara* may be briefly stated to constitute the attitude of the lower threefold self to the service of the ego, the inner ruler, the God or Christ within. This will be triple in its manifestation, bringing that lower personal self into a life of obedience to the Master within the heart; eventually bringing the aspirant into the group of some adept or spiritual teacher, and leading him also into devoted service to Ishvara or the divine Self as found in the hearts of all men and back of all forms of divine manifestation.

**33. When thoughts which are contrary to yoga are present there should be the cultivation of their opposite.**

The translation by Johnston gives the same idea in very beautiful words and the method is adequately brought out. He says:

"When transgressions hinder, the weight of the imagination should be thrown upon the opposite side."

The entire science of the balancing of the pairs of opposites is given in these two translations, neither one being fully complete without the other. It is often difficult to translate the ancient Sanskrit terms by one word or phrase, for in that language a term will stand for an entire idea and will require several phrases in order to convey the true meaning in the more limited English tongue.

Certain basic concepts are embodied in this sutra and for the sake of clarity might be tabulated as follows:

1. As a man thinketh so is he. That which works out into physical objectivity is always a thought, and according to that thought or idea so will be the form and life-purpose.

2. Thoughts are of two kinds; those tending to form-building, to limitation, to physical plane expression; those tending away from the lower three planes and therefore from the form aspect as we know it in the three worlds, and leading to union (yoga or at-one-ment) with the soul, the Christ aspect.

[ 191 ]

3.   When it is found that the thoughts habitually cultivated are productive of astral and physical reactions and results it must be realized that they are inimical to yoga; they hinder the at-one-ing process.

4.   Contrary thoughts to these must then be cultivated; these can be easily ascertained for they will be the direct opposite of the inhibiting thoughts.

5.   The cultivation of the thoughts which will tend to yoga and lead a man to a knowledge of his real self and consequent union with that self involves a triple process:

a.   The new thought concept, definitely formulated and found to be contrary to the old thought current, must be ascertained and considered.

b.   The use of the imagination comes next in order to bring the thought into manifestation. This brings in the realm of desire and consequently the astral or emotional body is affected.

c.   Then follows definite visualization of the effect of that which has been thought and imagined, as it will manifest in the physical plane life.

This will be found to generate energy.   This means consequently that the etheric body becomes vitalized or energized by the new thought current and certain transformations and re-organizations take place which eventually cause a complete change in the activities of the physical plane man.   The constant cultivation of this effects an entire transformation in the threefold lower man, and eventually the truth of the Christian phraseology becomes apparent, "only Christ is seen and heard," only the real or spiritual man can be seen expressing himself through a physical medium, as Christ did through His instrument and disciple, Jesus.

**34. Thoughts contrary to yoga are harmfulness, falsehood, theft, incontinence, and avarice, whether committed personally, caused to be committed or approved of, whether arising from avarice, anger or delusion (ignorance); whether slight in the doing, middling or great. These result always in excessive pain and ignorance. For this reason, the contrary thoughts must be cultivated.**

It wll be noted that the five Commandments deal specifically with those "thoughts contrary to yoga" or union, and that the keeping of the Commandments will bring about:

a. Harmlessness instead of harmfulness,
b. Truth instead of falsehood,
c. Abstention from theft instead of stealing,
d. Self-control instead of incontinence,
e. Contentment instead of avarice or covetousness.

No excuse is left to the aspirant, and the truth is borne in on him that transgression of the Commandments is equally productive of results whether the violation is trifling or very great. A "contrary thought" *must* produce its effect and the effect is dual; pain, and ignorance or delusion. There are three words which the occult student associates ever with the three worlds:

1. *Maya or illusion,* having reference to the world of forms in which the true self finds itself when in incarnation, and with which it ignorantly identifies itself for long aeons;

2. *Delusion,* the process of wrong identification, in which the self deludes itself, and says "I am the form;"

3. *Ignorance* or avidya, the result of this wrong identification and at the same time the cause of it.

The self is clothed in form; it is deluded in the world of illusion. Every time, however, that "thoughts contrary to yoga" are knowingly entertained, the self submerges itself still more in the illusory world and adds to the veil of ignorance. Every time that the "weight of the imagination" is thrown on the side of the real nature of the self and turned away from the world of the not-self, the illusion is lessened, the delusion becomes weakened, and ignorance is gradually superseded by knowledge.

**35. In the presence of him who has perfected harmlessness, all enmity ceases.**

This sutra demonstrates to us the working out of a great law. In Book IV. Sutra 17, Patanjali tells us that the perception of a characteristic, of a quality and of an objective form is dependent upon the fact that in the perceiver similar characteristics, qualities and objective capacity are to be found. This similarity is the basis of perception. The same truth is hinted at in the first

*Epistle of St. John* where the words are found "We shall be like Him for we shall see Him as He is." Only that can be contacted which is already present or partially present in the perceiver's consciousness. If enmity and hatred are therefore to be found by the perceiver, it is because in him the seeds of enmity and hatred are present. When they are absent naught but unity and harmony exists. This is the first stage of universal love, the practical endeavour on the part of the aspirant to be at one with all beings. He begins with himself and sees to it that the seeds of harmfulness in his own nature are eradicated. He deals, therefore, with the cause which produces enmity towards him and others. The natural result is that he is at peace and others are at peace with him. In his presence even wild beasts are rendered impotent and this by the condition of the mind-state of the aspirant or yogin.

**36. When truth to all beings is perfected, the effectiveness of his words and acts is immediately to be seen.**

This question of truth is one of the great problems which the aspirant has to solve, and he who attempts to speak only that which is entirely accurate will find himself confronted by very definite difficulties. Truth is entirely relative whilst evolution proceeds, and is progressive in its manifestation. It might be defined as the demonstration on the physical plane of as much of the divine reality as the stage in evolution and the medium employed permit. Truth, therefore, involves the ability of the perceiver or aspirant to see correctly the amount of the divine which a form (tangible, objective, or of words) clothes. It involves, therefore, the capacity to penetrate to the subject and to contact that which every form veils. It involves also the ability of the aspirant to construct a form (tangible, objective, or of words) which will convey the truth as it is. This is in reality the first two stages of the great creative process:

1. Correct perception,
2. Accurate construction,

and it leads on to the consummation dealt with in the sutra under consideration—the effectiveness of all words and acts to convey reality or truth as it is. This sutra gives the clue to the work of the magician and is the basis for the great science of mantras or of words of power which are the equipment of every adept.

Through an understanding of,

a. The law of vibration,
b. The science of sound,
c. The purpose of evolution,
d. The present cyclic stage,
e. The nature of form,
f. The manipulation of atomic substance,

the adept not only sees truth in all things but comprehends how to make truth visible, thus aiding the evolutionary process and "casting images upon the screen of time." This he does through certain words and acts. For the aspirant, the development of this capacity comes through a constant effort to fulfill the following requirements:

1. Strict attention to every formulation of words used,

2. The wise use of silence as a factor of service,

3. The constant study of the causes lying back of every act so that the reason for the effectiveness or non-effectiveness of action is understood.

4. A steady endeavour to see the reality in every form. This literally involves a study of the law of cause and effect, or karma, the object of the karmic law being to bring the opposite pole of Spirit, matter, into strict conformity with the requirements of spirit so that matter and form can perfectly express the nature of spirit.

**37. When abstention from theft is perfected, the yogi can have whatever he desires.**

In this is to be found the clue to the great law of supply and demand. When the aspirant has learned to "desire nothing for the separated self" he can then be trusted with the riches of the universe; when he makes no demand for the lower nature and claims nothing for the three-fold physical man, then all that he desires comes to him unasked and unclaimed. In some translations the words are found "all jewels are his."

It must be remembered with care that the theft referred to has reference not only to the taking of things tangible and physical, but has reference also to abstention from theft on the emotional or mental planes. The aspirant takes nothing;

emotional benefits, such as love and favor, dislike or hatred are not claimed by him and absorbed when they do not belong to him; intellectual benefits, the claiming of a reputation not warranted, the assumption of some one else's duty, favour or popularity are all equally repudiated by him and he adheres with strictness to that which is his own. "Let every man attend to his own dharma" and fulfill his own role, is the Eastern injunction. "Mind your own business" is the Western attempt to teach the same truth and convey the injunction that we each of us must not steal from another the opportunity to do right, to measure up to responsibility and to do his duty. This is the true abstention from theft. It will lead a man perfectly to meet his own obligations, to shoulder his own responsibility and to fulfill his own duty. It will lead him to refrain from appropriating anything that belongs to his brother in the three worlds of human endeavour.

### 38. By abstention from incontinence, energy is acquired.

Incontinence is usually regarded as the dissipation of the vitality or the virility of the animal nature. The power to create upon the physical plane and to perpetuate the race is the highest physical act of which man is capable. The dissipation of the vital powers through loose living and incontinence is the great sin against the physical body. It involves the failure to recognize the importance of the procreative act, the inability to resist the lower desires and pleasures, and a loss of self control. The results of this failure are apparent throughout the human family at this time in the low health average, in the full hospitals, and the diseased, enfeebled and anemic men, women and children everywhere to be found. There is little conservation of energy, and the very words "dissipation" and dissipated men" carry a lesson.

The first thing a disciple has to do is to learn the true nature of creation and to conserve his energy. Celibacy is not enjoined. Self-control is. In the relatively short cycle of lives, however, in which the aspirant fits himself to tread the path, he may have to pass a life or maybe several in a definite abstention from the act of procreation in order to learn complete control and to demonstrate the fact that he has completely subdued the lower sex nature. The right use of the sex principle along with entire conformity to the law of the land is characteristic of every true aspirant.

Apart from a consideration of this subject along the lines of the conservation of energy, there is another angle from which the aspirant approaches the problem and that is the transmutation of the vital principle (as manifested through the physical organism) into the dynamic demonstration of it as manifested through the organ of sound, or creation, through the word, the work of the true magician. There is as all students of occultism know, a close connection between the organs of generation and the third major centre, the throat centre. This is apparent physiologically in the change of voice seen during the adolescent period. Through the true conservation of energy and abstention from incontinence, the yogi becomes a creator on the mental plane through the use of the word and of sounds, and the energy which can be dissipated through the activity of the lower centre is concentrated and transmuted into the great creative work of the magician. This is done through continence, pure living and clean thinking, and not through any perversions of occult truth such as sex magic and the enormities of the sex perversions of various so-called occult schools. The latter are on the black path and do not lead to the portal of initiation.

**39. When abstention from avarice is perfected, there comes an understanding of the law of rebirth.**

This sutra gives in unequivocal terms the great teaching that it is desire for form of some kind which brings the spirit into incarnation. When desirelessness is present, then the three worlds can no longer hold the yogi. We forge our own chains in the furnace of desire and of a various longing for things, for experience and for form life.

When contentment is cultivated and present, gradually these chains drop off and no others are forged. As we disentangle ourselves from the world of illusion, our vision becomes cleared, and the laws of being and of existence become apparent to us and are little by little understood. The how and the why of life are answered. The reason for and the method of physical plane existence is no longer a problem, and the yogi understands why the past has been and what its characteristics are; he understands the reason for the present life cycle and experience and can make practical application of the law each day, and he knows well what he has to do for the future. Thus he frees himself, desires nothing in the three worlds and re-orients himself to the conditions in the world of spiritual being.

In these qualities we have the carrying out of the five Commandments.

**40. Internal and external purification produces aversion for form, both one's own and all forms.**

This paraphrase of Sutra 40 does not adhere to the technical translation of the Sankrit words on account of the misunderstanding of the words used. Literally the translation runs "internal and external purification produces hatred for one's own body and non-intercourse with all bodies." The tendency of students in the West to interpret literally necessitates a somewhat freer translation. The Eastern student, more versed in the symbolic presentation of truth is not so liable to make mistakes along this line. In considering this sutra it should be remembered that purity is a quality of spirit.

# BOOK II

Purification is necessarily of various kinds and relates to the four vehicles (the physical body, the etheric body, the emotional body and the mental body) through which man contacts the three worlds of his endeavor. We might, therefore, distinguish between them as follows:

a. External purity ....physical vehicle ...dense body,
b. Magnetic purity ....etheric vehicle .......internal purity,
c. Psychic purity ........astral vehicle .......emotional purity,
d. Mental purity ........mental vehicle .......purity of the concrete mind.

It should be most carefully borne in mind that this purity concerns the substance out of which each of these vehicles is composed. It is attained in three ways:

1. Elimination of impure substance or of those atoms and molecules which limit the free expression of spirit, and which confine it to the form so that it can have neither free ingress nor egress;

2. Assimilation of those atoms and molecules which will tend to provide a form through which spirit can adequately function;

3. The protection of the purified form from contamination and deterioration.

On the Path of Purification or of Probation, this eliminative process is commenced; on the Path of Discipleship, the rules for the constructive or assimilative process are learnt and on the Path of Initiation (after the second initiation,) the protective work is begun.

In the occident the rules of external purification, of sanitation and of hygiene are well known and largely practised. In the orient, the rules

of magnetic purification are better known and
when the two systems are synthesized and mu-
tually recognized, the physical sheath in its dual
nature will eventually be brought to a high degree of refinement.

In this cycle, however, the interest of the Hierarchy is being largely centred on the question
of psychic purity and this is the reason for the
trend of the occult teaching at present developing. It is away from what is commonly understood by psychic development, lays no emphasis
on the lower psychic powers and seeks to train
the aspirant in the laws of the spiritual life.
This produces a realization of the nature of the
psyche or soul, and a control of the lower psychic
nature. The great "push" of the hierarchical endeavour for this century, 1926-2026, will be along
these lines, combined with a dissemination of the
laws of thought. Hence the necessity for the
promulgation of the teaching given in the Yoga
Sutras. They give the rules for mind control but
the nature of the psychic powers and the development of the psychic consciousness are also largely
dealt with.

The entire third book deals with these powers
and the theme of the sutras as a whole might be
briefly stated to be the development of mind control with a view to soul-contact and the consequent control of the lower psychic powers, their
unfoldment parallelling that of the higher powers.
This should be emphasized. Aversion for form or
"desirelessness," which is the generic term covering this condition of mind, is the great impulse

which eventually leads to complete liberation from form.

It is not that form or form taking is in itself evil. Both forms and the process of incarnation are right and proper in their place but for the man who has no further use for experience in the three worlds, having learnt the needed lessons in the school of life, form and rebirth become evil and must be relegated to a position outside the life of the ego. That the liberated man may choose to limit himself by a form for specific purposes of service is true, but this he does through an act of the will and self-abnegation; he is not impelled thereto by desire but by love of humanity and a longing to stay with his brothers till the last of the sons of God has reached the portal of liberation.

**41. Through purification comes also a quiet spirit, concentration, conquest of the organs, and ability to see the Self.**

It should be remembered that both the Commandments and the Rules (Yama and Nyama) have to do with the lower fourfold self, functioning in the three worlds, and frequently called the lower quaternary. We have seen in the preceding sutra that the purification required is fourfold and concerns four vehicles. The results of this purity are also fourfold and have reference equally to the four sheaths. These results are, in the order of the vehicles:

## BOOK II

1. Conquest of the organs..............The physical body,
2. A quiet spirit................................The emotional vehicle,
3. Concentration ...............................The lower mind or the mental body,
4. Ability to see the self...................The synthetic result of the triple condition of the above sheaths.

The "*conquest of the organs*" has reference specially to the senses and is the result of magnetic purity or the refinement of the etheric body. In this connection students should bear in mind that the physical body is not a principle, but is built in exact conformity with the etheric body. This etheric body is the magnetic vehicle on the physical plane and attracts (according to its own nature and constituents) those atoms and particles of substance out of which the dense physical is constructed. When the sense perceptions are refined and when the vibratory condition of the vital body is justly attuned, the organs of the senses are entirely dominated and controlled by the real man and put him in contact eventually with the two highest subplanes of the physical plane and not with the lower astral as is now the case. The correct order of this control of the organs of physical perception or of the five senses is as follows:

1. Correct intellectual perception of the ideal on the mental plane.

2. Pure desire, freed from love of form on the emotional or astral plane,

3. Correct use and development of the five cen-

tres up the spine (base of spine, sacral centre, solar plexus, heart and throat centres), each of which is found in the etheric body and is allied with one or other of the five senses,

4. Consequent correct reaction of the sense organs to the requirements of the true or spiritual man.

In connection with the astral body, the result of purification is a quiet spirit, or the "gentle stillness" of the vehicle so that it can adequately reflect the Christ principle, or the buddhic nature. The relation of the astral or kamic principle (using the middle vehicle of the threefold lower man) to the buddhic principle using the middle vehicle of the spiritual triad (or atma-buddhi-manas), should be carefully considered. Quieted emotions, and the control of the desire nature ever precede the re-orientation of the lower. Before the desire of a man can be towards things spiritual he has to cease to desire the things of the world, and of the flesh. This produces an interlude of great difficulty in the life of neophyte, and the process is symbolized for us in the use of the word "conversion" in orthodox Christian circles; it involves "a turning round" with its consequent temporary turmoil, but eventual quietness.

In the mental body, the effect of purification is the development of the capacity to concentrate or to be one-pointed. The mind no longer flits hither and thither but becomes controlled and quiescent and receptive to the higher impress.

As this is discussed fully in book three we need not deal further with it here.

When these three results of purification are making themselves felt in the life of the aspirant, he nears a certain climax which is a sudden perception of the nature of the soul. He gets a vision of the reality which is himself, and finds out the truth of the words of the Christ that "the pure in heart shall see God." He beholds the soul and henceforth his desire is for ever towards reality and away from the unreal and the world of illusion.

**42. As a result of contentment bliss is achieved.**

There is little to say in connection with this sutra except to point out that all pain, displeasure and unhappiness are based upon rebellion, and that, from the point of view of the occultist, rebellion but stirs up increased trouble, and resistance only serves to feed the evil, whatever it may be. The man who has learnt to accept his lot, wastes no time in vain regrets, and his entire energy can then be given to the perfect fulfillment of his dharma, or obligatory work. Instead of repining, and clouding the issues of life with worry, doubt and despair, he clarifies his path by the quiet realization of life as it is and a direct appreciation of what he may make of it. Thus no strength, time or opportunity is lost, and steady progress towards the goal is made.

**43. Through fiery aspiration and through the removal of all impurity, comes the perfecting of the bodily powers and of the senses.**

Though the two causes of the perfecting process are aspiration and purification, yet these two form really only one and are the two aspects of the discipline of the Probationary Path. The old commentary which forms the esoteric basis of the inner teaching on Raja Yoga has some sentences which will be found of value here in conveying the correct concept:

> "As the breath of fire streams upward through the system, as the fiery element makes its presence felt, that which is hindering is seen to disappear, and that which was obscure becomes illuminated.
>
> The fire ascends and barriers are burned; the breath expands, and limitations disappear. The seven, hitherto quiescent, stir to life. The ten portals, sealed and closed or partially ajar, swing wide.
>
> The five great means of contact rush into activity. Obstacles are overcome, and barriers no longer hinder. The purified one becomes the great receiver and the One is known."

In these words the purification by fire and by air is dealt with and this is the purification undergone on the path of yoga. Purification by water has been submitted to in the later stages of the life of the highly evolved man, prior to treading the Path of Discipleship, and is hinted at in the words "waters of sorrow" so often used. Now the fiery ordeal is undergone and the entire lower nature is passed through the fire. This is the first meaning and the one with which the aspirant is most concerned. It is called forth when he can, from his heart, send forth the call for fire, embodied in the words:

"I seek the Way; I yearn to know. Visions I see, and fleeting deep impressions. Behind the Portal, on the other side, lies that which I call home, for the circle hath been well-nigh trod, and the end approacheth the beginning.

I seek the Way. All ways my feet have trod. The Way of Fire calls me with fierce appeal. Naught in me seeks the way of peace; naught in me yearns for earth.

Let the fire rage, the flames devour; let all the dross be burnt; and let me enter through that Gate, and tread the Way of Fire."

The breath of God is felt as the cleansing breeze also and is the response of the soul to the aspiration of the disciple. The soul then "inspires" the lower man.

The secondary meaning has of course direct reference to the work of the kundalini or serpent fire at the base of the spine as it responds to the soul vibration (felt in the head, in the region of the pineal gland, and called "the light in the head"). Mounting upward, it burns out all obstructions in the spinal etheric channel and vitalizes or electrifies the five centres up the spine and the two in the head. The vital airs within the ventricles of the head are also swept into activity and produce a cleansing, or rather eliminating effect therein. With this the student has as yet nothing to do, beyond seeing to it that as far as in him lies, the aspiration of his heart is of the needed "fiery" character, and that the steady purification of his physical, emotional and mental nature, proceeds as desired. When this is the case, the response of the soul will be effective and the consequent reactions within the etheric centres will take place safely, under law, and normally.

The three verses quoted above deal with,

a. The seven centres, hitherto quiescent,

b. The ten closed portals, the ten orifices of the physical body,

c. The five senses, through which contact with the physical plane takes place,

and in these terms the entire outgoing and ingoing activities of the physical plane man are comprehended.

When these have all been brought under the direction of the soul, or inner ruler, then unity with the soul is effected, and consequently identification with that one in whom we live and move and have our being.

### 44. Spiritual reading results in a contact with the Soul (or divine One).

This might perhaps more literally be translated as "the reading of symbols produces contact with the soul." A symbol is a form of some kind which veils or hides a thought, an idea or a truth and it might be laid down therefore as a general axiom that every form of every kind is a symbol, or the objective veil of a thought. This when applied, will be found to refer equally to a human form, which is intended to be the symbol (or made in the image) of God; it is an objective form veiling a divine thought, idea or truth, the tangible manifestation of a divine concept. The goal of evolution is to bring to perfection, this objective symbolic form. When a man knows that, he ceases to identify himself with the symbol which is his lower nature. He begins to function consciously as the divine inner subjective self, using the lower man to veil and hide his form, and daily dealing with that form so that it is moulded and wrought into an adequate instrument of expression. The idea is also carried forward into the daily life, in the attitude of the man to every form (in the three kingdoms of nature) he contacts. He seeks to see below the surface and to touch the divine idea.

This is the fourth of the Rules and concerns the man's inner attitude to the objective universe. It might be said therefore that the rules concern a man's attitude towards:

1. His own lower nature...................internal and external purification,
2. His karma or lot in life...............contentment,
3. His soul or ego ...............................fiery aspiration,
4. Environment and physical plane contacts ...........................................spiritual reading,
5. The one Existence, God.................devotion to Ishvara.

Thus a "right attitude" to all things covers this set of rules.

**45. Through devotion to Ishvara the goal of meditation (or samadhi) is reached.**

The goal of meditation is ability to contact the divine inner self, and through the contact, to come to a realization of the unity of that self with all selves and the All-Self, and this, not just theoretically, but as a fact in nature. This comes about when a state called "samadhi" is achieved wherein the consciousness of the thinker is transferred out of the lower brain consciousness into that of the spiritual man or soul on its own plane. The stages of this transfer might be stated to be as follows:

1. Transfer of the consciousness of the body, the outgoing instinctual consciousness of the physical man, into the head. This necessitates a conscious withdrawal of the consciousness to a point within the brain in the neighborhood of the pineal gland, and its conscious definite centering there.

2. Transfer of the consciousness out of the head or brain into the mind or mental body. In this transfer, the brain remains keenly alert and the withdrawal is consciously undertaken via the etheric body, using the brahmarandra or opening at the top of the head. At no point is the man in trance, unconscious or asleep. He actively undertakes and carries forward this abstracting or withdrawing process.

3. Transfer of the consciousness from out of the mental body into that of the ego, the soul, lodged in the causal body or egoic lotus. There is then brought about a condition in which the brain, the mental body and the egoic body form a coherent quiescent unit, alive, alert, positive and steady.

4. The state of samadhi or spiritual contem-

plation can then be entered, when the soul looks out upon its own world, sees the vision of things as they are, contacts reality and "knows God."

Following upon this comes the stage in which the spiritual man transmits to the brain via the mind that which is visioned, seen, contacted and known; and in this way, the knowledge becomes part of the brain contents and is available for use upon the physical plane.

This is the goal of the meditation process, and the results in their many distinctions are the subject of Book III. and are produced by conformity to the eight means of yoga dealt with in Book II. Only devotion to Ishvara or true love of God, with its accompanying qualities of service, love of man, and patient endurance in well-doing, will carry a man along this arduous path of discipline, purification and hard work.

## MEANS III. POSTURE

**46. The posture assumed must be steady and easy.**

This sutra is one that has led our occidental students into a great deal of trouble for they have interpreted it in an entirely physical sense. That it has a physical meaning is true but taken in reference to the lower threefold nature it might be said that it refers to a steady immovable position of the physical body when in meditation, a firm steadfast unwavering condition of the astral or emotional body in the passage through worldly existence, and an unfluctuating steady mind, one that is absolutely under control. Of these three, it might be said that the physical posture is of the least importance, and that the position in which the aspirant can the soonest forget that he possesses a physical body is the best. It might be generally laid down that an upright position in a comfortable chair, with the spine erect, the feet crossed naturally, the hands folded in the lap, the eye closed, and the chin a little dropped is the best posture for the occidental aspirant. In the East there is a science of postures and about eighty-four different positions, some of them most intricate and painful, are listed. This science is a branch of hatha yoga and is not to be followed by the fifth root-race; it is a remnant of that yoga which was necessary and sufficient for the Lemurian root-race man, who needed to learn physical control. Bhakti yoga, or the yoga of the devotee was the yoga of the Atlantean or fourth root-race man, plus a little hatha yoga. In this fifth root-race, the Aryan, hatha yoga should fall into desuetude altogether where the disciple is concerned, and he should occupy himself with Raja Yoga plus bhakti yoga—he should be a mental devotee.

The *Lemurian* disciple learned to control the physical body and to devote it to the service of Ishvara through hatha yoga, with aspiration towards emotional control.

The *Atlantean* disciple learned to control the emotional body and to devote it to the service of Ishvara through bhakti yoga, with aspiration towards mental control.

## BOOK II

The *Aryan* disciple has to learn to control the mental body and devote it to the service of Ishvara through Raja Yoga, with aspiration towards knowledge of the indweller, the soul. Thus in this root-race, the entire lower man, the personality is subjugated and the "Transfiguration" of humanity takes place.

**47. Steadiness and ease of posture is to be achieved through persistent slight effort and through the concentration of the mind upon the infinite.**

This covers the two aspects which in meditation produce difficulty, the comfort of the body and the control of the mind. It is noteworthy that the effort to attain forgetfulness of the physical body through correct posture is brought about through steady gentle persistent practise, rather than through the violent forcing of the body into postures and attitudes unaccustomed and uncomfortable. When this can be done and when the mind can be so engrossed upon a consideration of the things of the soul, then steadiness and ease characterize the man on the physical plane. He is forgetful of the physical vehicle and hence can concentrate the mind, and his concentration of the mind is then so one-pointed that thought of the body becomes impossible.

**48. When this is attained, the pairs of opposites no longer limit.**

The pairs of opposites concern the desire body and it is significant that in the preceding sutra

[ 215 ]

only the mind and the physical body were dealt with. In this sutra the emotional nature, expressing itself through desire fails to be influenced by the pull of any attractive force. The astral body becomes quiescent and non-assertive, unresponsive to any lure from the world of illusion.

There is a great mystery concerned with the astral body of man and with the astral light, and the nature of the mystery is still only known to advanced initiates. The astral light is thrown into objectivity by two producing factors, and the astral body of a man is responsive to two types of energy. They seem essentially in themselves to lack character or form but to be dependent for manifestation upon "that which is above and that which is below." The desire nature of man, for instance, seems to respond to the lure of the great world of illusion, the maya of the senses, or to the voice of the ego, using the mental body. Vibrations reach the astral body from the physical plane and from the mental world, and according to the nature of the man and to the point in evolution which he has reached, so will be the response to the higher or the lower call.

The astral body is either attentive to the egoic impression or swayed by the million voices of earth. It apparently has no voice of its own, no character of its own. This has been pictured for us in the Gita where Arjuna stands midway between the two opposing forces of good and evil and searches for the right attitude to both. The astral plane is the battleground of the soul, the place of victory or the place of defeat; it is the

[ 216 ]

kurukshetra, upon which the great choice is made.

In these sutras concerning posture, the same idea lies latent. The physical plane and the mental plane are emphasized and it is brought out that when they are adjusted rightly, when poise on the physical plane and one pointedness on the mental plane are attained, then the pairs of opposites no longer limit. The point of balance is reached and the man is liberated. The scales of a man's life are absolutely adjusted and he stands free.

## MEANS IV. PRANAYAMA

**49. When right posture (asana) has been attained there follows right control of prana and proper inspiration and expiration of the breath.**

Here again we come to a sutra that has led to much misunderstanding and much mischief. Teaching on the control of prana is prevalent and has led to the following of breathing exercises and to the practices dependent for their success upon the suspension of the breathing process. Most of this has been caused by a belief in the occidental mind that prana and breath are synonymous terms. This is by no means the case. Vivekananda points this out in his commentary on the sutra in the following words:

"When the posture has been conquered, then this motion is to be broken and controlled, and thus we come to pranayama; the controlling of the vital forces of the body. Prana is not breath, though it is usually so translated. It is the sum total of the cosmic energy. It is the energy that is in each body, and its most apparent manifestation is the motion of the lungs. This motion is caused by prana drawing in the breath, and is what we seek to control in pranayama. We begin by controlling the breath, as the easiest way of getting control of the prana."

Prana is the sum total of the energy in the body (and this applies equally to the planetary and the solar body). It therefore concerns the inflow of energy into the etheric body and its outflow through the medium of the physical body. In the physical body this is symbolized for us in the necessary inspiration and exhalation of the breath. By stressing the physical act of breathing, much of the true sense of this sutra has been lost.

Certain things should be remembered as one studies pranayama. First, that one of the main purposes of the etheric body is that it acts as a stimulator and the energizer of the dense physical body. It is almost as if the dense physical body had no independent existence but simply acted as it was swayed and motivated by the etheric body. The etheric body is the force or vital body and it permeates every part of the dense vehicle. It is the background, the true substance of the physical body. According to the nature of the force animating the etheric body, according to the activity of that force in the etheric body, according to the aliveness or the sluggishness of the most important parts of the etheric body (the centres up the spine) so will be the corresponding activity of the physical body. Similarly and symbolically, according to the wholeness of the breathing apparatus, and according to the ability of that apparatus to oxygenate and render pure the blood, so will be the health or wholeness of the dense physical body.

It should also be remembered that the key to the just response of the lower to the higher, lies in rhythm, and in the ability of the physical body to respond or vibrate in rhythmic unison with the etheric body. Students have found out that this is much facilitated by steady even breathing, and the majority of the breathing exercises when emphasized to the exclusion of the previous three means to yoga (the Commandments, Rules and Posture) have a definite effect upon the etheric centres and may lead to disastrous results. It is most necessary that students should follow the means of yoga in the order in which they are given by Patanjali, and so see to it that the purificatory process, the discipline of the outer and inner life and one-pointedness of the mind should be aimed at, prior to attempting the regulation of the etheric vehicle through breathing, and the awakening of the centres.

The work done through pranayama might briefly be stated to be the following:

1. The oxygenation of the blood and hence the cleansing of the blood currents and consequent physical health.

2. The bringing of the physical body into a vibration synchronous with that of the etheric

body. This results in the complete subjugation of the dense physical body and its bringing into line with the etheric body. The two parts of the physical vehicle form a unit.

3. The transmission of energy via the etheric body to all parts of the dense physical body. This energy may come from various sources:

a. From the planetary aura. In this case it is planetary prana, and so concerns primarily the spleen and the health of the physical body.

b. From the astral world via the astral body. This will be purely kamic or desire force and will affect primarily the centres below the diaphragm.

c. From the universal mind or manasic force. This will be largely thought force and will go to the throat centre.

d. From the ego itself, stimulating primarily the head and heart centres.

Most people receive force only from the physical and astral planes, but disciples receive force also from the mental and egoic levels.

**50. Right control of prana (or the life currents) is external, internal or motionless; it is subject to place, time and number and is also protracted or brief.**

This is a most difficult sutra to understand and its meaning has been made purposely abstruse, owing to the dangers incident to the control of the bodily forces. The ideas and teaching conveyed fall into three parts:

I. The external, internal or motionless control

of the life currents of the body (dense and etheric). This concerns:

1. The breathing apparatus and the use of the breath.
2. The vital airs and their radiation.
3. The centres, and their awakening.
4. The kundalini fire and its right progression up the spine.

II. The astrological significance and the relation of the man to his group, planetary or otherwise. This is dealt with in the words "place, time and number."

III. The process of illumination and the production of response in the physical man via the brain to the higher impressions. This ability to respond to the voice of the ego and to become quiescent and receptive must precede the last four means of yoga which do not so immediately concern the dense physical plane or the etheric levels of consciousness.

It will be obvious that much of the teaching conveyed in this sutra can only safely be given directly by the teacher to the pupil, after a proper study of the bodily conditions of that pupil. It is not possible nor right to give in a book intended for the general public those rules, practices and methods which enable the trained disciple to bring his dense physical vehicle into instantaneous synchronization with his etheric body, to densify and irradiate his aura so as to produce certain magnetic results in his environment, and to awaken his centres so that certain psychic powers are displayed. The methods for arousing the kundalini fire and blending it with the downpouring egoic force must also be left for direct teaching by a master in this science to his pupil. There is extreme danger attendant upon the premature awakening of the fire, and the consequent destruction of certain protective structures in the etheric body and the breaking down of the barriers between this world and the astral world, before the pupil is properly "balanced between the pairs of opposites. There is a menace in the premature growth of the lower psychic powers before the higher nature is awakened, and the effect upon the brain can be seen as insanity in some form or other, mild or the reverse. A few explanatory words can, however, be given which will enable the true occult student to gain that information which, if correctly used, acts as a key to the possession of more. This is ever the occult method. Let us, therefore, deal briefly with our three points.

I. The *external* control of the prana or life currents concerns those breathing exercises and rhythmic practices which bring the physical organs, allied with the etheric centres, into proper condition. These physical organs are themselves never specifically dealt with by the white magician or occultist. They are dealt with in black magic, and consist of the brain, the lungs, the heart, the spleen and the generative organs.

The black magician definitely utilizes these physical parts of the body to generate a type of force which is a mixture of etheric force and dense physical energy, to enable him to do certain forms of magical work and also to produce effects on the physical bodies of animals and men. It is the knowledge of this which is the basis of voodooism and of all those practices which cause the depletion and death of men and women who obstruct the path of the black magician or are regarded by him as enemies. With these the aspirant to the mysteries of the Brotherhood of the great White Lodge has nothing to do. He brings about the merging of the two parts of the dense physical, and the synchronization of the rhythm of the two bodies and the consequent unity of the entire lower man through attention to the etheric breath and rhythm. This inevitably produces the "external control of the life currents."

The *internal* control of the life currents is brought about in three ways:

1.  By an intellectual understanding of the nature of the etheric body and the laws of its life.

2.  Through a consideration of the types of energy and of their apparatus, the system of centres, to be found in the etheric body.

3.  Through certain developments and knowledge which come to the aspirant when he is ready (having attended to the previous means of yoga) and which give him the ability to tap certain types of forces, energies, or shaktis, to utilize them correctly through the medium of his own centres and to produce effects which come under the descriptive terms, illuminative, purificatory, magnetic, dynamic, psychic, and magic.

The *motionless* control of the life currents is the effect of the proper development of the other two, external and internal control and must be present before the fifth means of yoga, withdrawal or abstraction becomes possible. It simply indicates perfectly balanced synchronization and the complete unification of the two parts of the physical body so that there is no impediment to the outgoing or incoming forces. When motionless control is reached, the yogi can withdraw from his physical body at will or can pull in that body and manipulate at will any of the seven great planetary forces.

It should be borne in mind that the ideal condition is here dealt with and that no aspirant can achieve this means of yoga without working simultaneously at the other means also. The study of the parallelism in nature is of value here.

II. The astrological significance is also hinted at here in the three words, "place, time, and number." In these words the universal triplicities must be recognized, and right control of the life currents must be seen to be related to karma, opportunity and form; there are certain words which when rightly understood give the key to all practical occultism and make the yogi a master of life. They are:

| Sound | Number | Colour | Form |
| Word | Life | Light | Body |

and these are recognized as subject to the space-idea and the time-element. It should be borne in mind, in this connection, that "space is the first entity" (*Secret Doctrine* I. 583) and that cyclic manifestation is the law of life.

[ 224 ]

## BOOK II

When this is recognized, the entity, expressing itself cyclically, will make its presence felt through differentiation, through the colour or quality of the veiling form and through the form itself. These factors make up the sum total of the expression of any identity, God or man, and the appearance of any man in exoteric expression on the physical plane is dependent upon the rhythmic or cyclic outgoing or indrawing energy of the great Life in whom he lives and moves and has his being. This is the basis of the science of astrology or the relationship of the planet, or planets to the human being and of their relation to the stars and the various signs of the zodiac.

Some knowledge of this is essential to the right control of the life currents, so that the disciple can avail himself of the "times and seasons" wherein progress can be expedited.

III. The process of illuminating the lower man becomes possible through the right control of the pranas and this "illuminating process" is an exact science for which these four means of yoga have prepared the way. The fires of the body are justly arranged, the "motionless" condition can be somewhat reached, the vital airs in the head are "at peace" and the entire lower man awaits one of two processes:

a. The withdrawal of the true or spiritual man in order to function on some higher plane,

b. Or the bringing down into the lower brain consciousness, of light, illumination and knowledge from the planes of the ego.

[ 225 ]

**51. There is a fourth stage which transcends those dealing with the internal and external phases.**

We have seen how the control of the life currents can be either externally active, internally active or balanced. This triple process brings the entire lower personal man into a condition, first of rhythmic response to the inner motivating factor (in this case, the ego or spiritual man on his own plane) and then of complete quiescence or stillness. This latter condition of receptive waiting, if one might so call it, is succeeded by one of a form of higher activity. This is literally the imposition of a new rate of vibration on the lower, the sounding forth of a new note, emanating from the inner spiritual man which produces certain definite effects in the three sheaths which constitute the lower self and which veil the divinity which is man. These changes are dealt with in the next two sutras.

The work of the average aspirant is most frequently given to preparing the sheaths so that this fourth stage can become possible. His attention is concentrated upon the attainment of:

1. The conscious coordination of the three bodies or sheaths,
2. Their due alignment,
3. The regulation of the rhythm of the sheaths so that they are synchronized with each other and with the rate of the egoic impression,
4. Their unification into one coherent whole

so that the man is literally the three in one and the one in three,

5. Quiescence, or the attitude of positive receptivity to the higher inspiration and downflow of egoic life and energy.

It may help the student if he realizes that the right control of prana involves the recognition that energy is the sum total of existence and of manifestation, and that the three lower bodies are energy bodies, each forming a vehicle for the higher type of energy and being themselves transmitters of energy. The energies of the lower man are energies of the third aspect, the Holy Ghost or Brahma aspect. The energy of the spiritual man is that of the second aspect, the Christ force, or buddhi. The object of evolution in the human family is to bring this Christ force, the principle of buddhi, into full manifestation upon the physical plane and this through the utilization of the lower triple sheath. This triple sheath is the Holy Grail, the cup which is the receiver and container of the life of God. When the lower man is brought into proper response through attention to the four means of yoga already considered, two results begin to manifest in him and he is ready to use the remaining four means which will reorient him and bring him eventually to liberation.

**52. Through this, that which obscures the light is gradually removed.**

The first result is the gradual wearing away, or attenuation of the material forms which hide the reality. This does not mean the wasting away of the forms but the steady refining and transmutation of the matter with which they are constructed so that they become so purified and clarified that the "Light of God" which they have hitherto hidden, can shine forth in all its beauty in the three worlds. This can be demonstrated as literally true upon the physical plane, for through the work of purification and the control of the life currents the light in the head becomes so apparent that it can be seen by those who have supernatural vision, as radiations extending all around the head, thus forming the halo so well known in pictures of the saints. The halo is a fact in nature and not just a symbol. It is the result of the work of Raja Yoga and is the physical demonstration of the life and light of the spiritual man. Vivekananda says, speaking technically (and it is good for Western occult students to master the technique and terminology of this science of the soul which the East has held in trust for so long) :

"The chitta has, by its own nature, all knowledge. It is made of sattva particles, but is covered by rajas and tamas particles, and by pranayama this covering is removed."

### 53. And the mind is prepared for concentrated meditation.

Johnston's edition gives a beautiful rendering of this sutra in the words: "Thence comes the mind's power to hold itself in the light—," the idea being that once the condition of quiescence has been reached, and the fourth stage of super-normal impression has been made possible, the remaining means of yoga, abstraction, attention, meditation and contemplation can be properly undertaken. The mind can be gripped and used and the process of transmitting the knowledge, light and wisdom from the ego or soul, to the brain via the mind can be safely undertaken.

## MEANS V.   ABSTRACTION

**54.   Abstraction (or Pratyahara) is the subjugation of the senses by the thinking principle and their withdrawal from that which has hitherto been their object.**

This sutra summarizes for us the work done in the control of the psychic nature, and gives us the result achieved when the thinker, through the medium of the mind, the thinking principle, so dominates the senses that they have no independent expression of their own.

Before attention, meditation and contemplation, (the last three means of yoga) can be properly undertaken, not only must the outer conduct be corrected, not only must inner purity be arrived at, not only must the right attitude towards all things be cultivated and the life currents consequently controlled, but the capacity to subjugate the outgoing tendencies of the five senses must be worked at. So the aspirant is taught the right withdrawal or abstraction of the consciousness which is outgoing towards the world of phenomena, and must learn to centre his consciousness in the great central station in the head from whence energy can be consciously distributed as he participates in the great work, from whence he can make a contact with the realm of the soul and in which he can receive the messages and impressions which emanate from that realm. This is a definite stage of achievement and is not simply a symbolic way of expressing one-pointed interest.

The various avenues of sense perception are brought into a quiescent condition. The consciousness of the real man no longer surges outwards along its five avenues of contact. The five senses are dominated by the sixth sense, the mind and all the consciousness and the perceptive faculty of the aspirant is synthesized in the head, and turns inward and upward. The psychic nature is thereby subjugated and the mental plane becomes the field of man's activity. This withdrawal or abstracting process proceeds in stages:

1.  The withdrawal of the physical consciousness, or perception through hearing, touch, sight, taste and smell. These modes of perception become temporarily dormant, and man's perception becomes simply mental and the brain consciousness is all that is active on the physical plane.

2.  The withdrawal of the consciousness into the region of the pineal gland, so that man's point of realization is centralized in the region between the middle of the forehead and the pineal gland.

3.  The next stage is that of abstracting the

consciousness into the head centre, the thousand petalled lotus or sahasara, by knowingly withdrawing the consciousness out of the head. This can be done in full waking consciousness when certain rules are learned and certain work accomplished. These can obviously not be given in such a work as this. The majority of people have to master the first two stages and learn to control the avenues of perception, the five senses.

4. The abstracting of the consciousness into the astral body and thus freeing it from the physical plane.

5. A still further withdrawal into the mental body or the mind so that neither the physical nor the astral any longer limit or confine the man.

When this can be done, true meditation and contemplation becomes possible.

Dvivedi says in his commentary on this sutra: "Abstraction consists in the senses becoming entirely assimilated to, or controlled by the mind. They must be drawn away from their objects and fixed upon the mind and assimilated to it, so that by preventing the transformation of the thinking principle, the sense also will follow it and be immediately controlled. Not only this but they will be ever ready to contribute collectively toward the absorbing meditation of any given thing at any moment."

The result, therefore, of correct abstraction or withdrawal is briefly:

1. The synthesis of the senses by the sixth sense, the mind.

2. The alignment of the threefold lower man so that the three bodies function as a coordinated unit.

3. The freeing of the man from the limitations of the bodies.

4. The consequent ability of the soul or ego to impress and illuminate the brain through the medium of the mind.

**55. As a result of these means there follows the complete subjugation of the sense organs.**

In Book I a general indication was given of the objective of Raja Yoga and of the hindrances to its practice coupled with an indication of the benefits. In Book II which we have just completed, the hindrances are specifically dealt with, the method of correcting them is indicated and then the means of yoga are taken up, five out of the eight being considered and explained. These five means, when duly followed, bring a man to the point where his lower psychic nature is being controlled, the senses are being mastered and he can begin to undertake the subjugation of the sixth sense, the mind.

The methods whereby the mind is controlled and the aspirant becomes complete master of the entire lower man are taken up in the next book. The remaining three means of yoga are explained and then the results of yoga are given in detail. Students will find it useful to note the graded and accurate method outlined in this marvellous treatise. It is valuable to note its brevity and yet its concise and complete nature. It is the text book of an exact science and within its few short pages are gathered all the rules, necessary in the Aryan rootrace, for the complete control of the mind, which should be the contribution of that race to the evolutionary process.

# BOOK III.

## Union Achieved and Its Results

a. Meditation, and its stages
b. Twenty-three results of meditation
   Topic: The powers of the soul

# THE YOGA SUTRAS OF PATANJALI

## BOOK III.

### Union Achieved and Its Results

1. Concentration is the fixing of the chitta (mind stuff) upon a particular object. This is dharana.
2. Sustained concentration (dharana) is meditation (dhyana).
3. When the chitta becomes absorbed in that which is the reality (or idea embodied in the form), and is unaware of separateness or the personal self, this is contemplation or samadhi.
4. When concentration, meditation and contemplation form one sequential act, then is sanyama achieved.
5. As a result of sanyama comes the shining forth of the light.
6. This illumination is gradual; it is developed stage by stage.
7. These last three means of yoga have a more intimate subjective effect than the previous means.
8. Even these three, however, are external to the true seedless meditation (or samadhi) which is not based on an object. It is free from the effects of the discriminative nature of the chitta (or mind stuff).
9. The sequence of mental states is as follows: the mind reacts to that which is seen; then follows the moment of mind control. Then ensues a moment wherein the chitta (mind stuff) responds to both these factors. Finally these pass away, and the perceiving consciousness has full sway.
10. Through the cultivation of this habit of mind there will eventuate a steadiness of spiritual perception.

# BOOK III

11. The establishing of this habit, and the restraining of the mind from its thought-form-making tendency, results eventually in the constant power to contemplate.

12. When mind control and the controlling factor are equally balanced, then comes the condition of one-pointedness.

13. Through this process the aspects of every object are known, their characteristics (or form), their symbolic nature, and their specific use in time-conditions (stage of development) are known and realised.

14. The characteristics of every object are acquired, manifesting or latent.

15. The stage of development is responsible for the various modifications of the versatile psychic nature and of the thinking principle.

16. Through concentrated meditation upon the triple nature of every form, comes the revelation of that which has been and of that which will be.

17. The Sound (or word), that which it denotes (the object) and the embodied spiritual essence (or idea) are usually confused in the mind of the perceiver. By concentrated meditation on these three aspects comes an (intuitive) comprehension of the sound uttered by all forms of life.

18. Knowledge of previous incarnations becomes available when the power to see thought-images is acquired.

19. Through concentrated meditation, the thought images in the minds of other people become apparent.

20. As, however, the object of those thoughts is not apparent to the perceiver, he sees only the thought and not the object. His meditation excludes the tangible.

21. By concentrated meditation upon the distinction between form and body, those properties of the body which make it visible to the human eye are negated (or withdrawn) and the yogi can render himself invisible.

22. Karma (or effects) are of two kinds: immediate karma or future karma. By perfectly concentrated

meditation on these, the yogi knows the term of his experience in the three worlds. This knowledge comes also from signs.

23. Union with others is to be gained through one-pointed meditation upon the three states of feeling—compassion, tenderness and dispassion.

24. Meditation, one-pointedly centered upon the power of the elephant, will awaken that force or light.

25. Perfectly concentrated meditation upon the awakened light will produce the consciousness of that which is subtle, hidden or remote.

26. Through meditation, one-pointedly fixed upon the sun, will come a consciousness (or knowledge) of the seven worlds.

27. A knowledge of all lunar forms arises through one-pointed meditation upon the moon.

28. Concentration upon the Pole-Star will give knowledge of the orbits of the planets and the stars.

29. By concentrated attention upon the centre called the solar plexus, comes perfected knowledge as to the condition of the body.

30. By fixing the attention upon the throat centre, the cessation of hunger and thirst will ensue.

31. By fixing the attention upon the tube or nerve below the throat centre, equilibrium is achieved.

32. Those who have attained self-mastery can be seen and contacted through focussing the light in the head. This power is developed in one-pointed meditation.

33. All things can be known in the vivid light of the intuition.

34. Understanding of the mind-consciousness comes from one-pointed meditation upon the heart centre.

35. Experience (of the pairs of opposites) comes from the inability of the soul to distinguish between the personal self and the purusa (or spirit). The objective forms exist for the use (and experience) of the spiritual man. By meditation upon this, arises the intuitive perception of the spiritual nature (the purusa).

36. As the result of this experience and meditation, the higher hearing, touch, sight, taste and smell are developed, producing intuitional knowledge.

37. These powers are obstacles to the highest spiritual realisation, but serve as magical powers in the objective worlds.

38. By liberation from the causes of bondage through their weakening and by an understanding of the mode of transference (withdrawal or entrance), the mind stuff (or chitta) can enter another body.

39. By subjugation of the upward life (the udana) there is liberation from water, the thorny path, and mire, and the power of ascension is gained.

40. Through subjugation of the samana, the spark becomes the flame.

41. By the means of one-pointed meditation upon the relationship between the akasha and sound, an organ for spiritual hearing will be developed.

42. By one-pointed meditation upon the relationship existing between the body and the akasha, ascension out of matter (the three worlds) and power to travel in space is gained.

43. When that which veils the light is done away with, then comes the state of being called discarnate (or disembodied), freed from the modification of the thinking principle. This is the state of illumination.

44. One-pointed meditation upon the five forms which every element takes, produces mastery over every element. These five forms are the gross nature, the elemental form, the quality, the pervasiveness and the basic purpose.

45. Through this mastery, minuteness and the other siddhis (or powers) are attained, likewise bodily perfection and freedom from all hindrances.

46. Symmetry of form, beauty of colour, strength and the compactness of the diamond, constitute bodily perfection.

47. Mastery over the senses is brought about through concentrated meditation upon their nature, peculiar attributes, egoism, pervasiveness and useful purpose.

# BOOK III

48. As a result of this perfection, there comes rapidity of action like that of mind, perception independent of the organs, and mastery over root substance.

49. The man who can discriminate between the soul and the spirit achieves supremacy over all conditions and becomes omniscient.

50. By a passionless attitude towards this attainment and towards all soul-powers, the one who is free from the seeds of bondage, attains the condition of isolated unity.

51. There should be entire rejection of all allurements from all forms of being, even the celestial, for the recurrence of evil contacts remains possible.

52. Intuitive knowledge is developed through the use of the discriminative faculty when there is one-pointed concentration upon moments and their continuous succession.

53. From this intuitive knowledge is born the capacity to distinguish (between all beings) and to cognize their genus, qualities and position in space.

54. This intuitive knowledge, which is the great Deliverer, is omnipresent and omniscient and includes the past, the present and the future in the Eternal Now.

55. When the objective forms and the soul have reached a condition of equal purity, then is At-one-ment achieved and liberation results.

# THE YOGA SUTRAS OF PATANJALI

*BOOK III.*

## Union Achieved and Its Results

**1. Concentration is the fixing of the chitta (mind stuff) upon a particular object. This is dharana.**

We have now reached the part of the Yoga Sutras which deals specifically with mind control and with the effect of that control. The first fifteen sutras are given to the control of the mind and how it is to be attained and the remaining forty sutras concern the results which take place after this control has been gained. Twenty-four results are enumerated, and these are all along the line of expansions of consciousness and the demonstration of psychic faculties, both lower and higher.

The first step towards this unfoldment is concentration, or the ability to hold the mind steadily and unwaveringly upon that which the aspirant chooses. This first step is one of the most difficult stages in the meditation process and involves constant unremitting ability to keep bringing the mind back to that "object" upon which the aspirant has chosen to concentrate. The stages in concentration are themselves well marked and can be stated as follows:

1.  The choice of some "object" upon which to concentrate,

2.  The withdrawing of the mind-consciousness from the periphery of the body, so that the avenues of outer perception and contact (the five senses) are stilled, and the consciousness is no longer outgoing,

3.  The centering of the consciousness and its steadying within the head at a point midway between the eyebrows,

4.  The application of the mind, or the paying of close attention to the object chosen for concentration,

5.  The visualization of that object, imaginative perception of it and logical reasoning about it,

6.  The extension of the mental concepts which have been formed from the specific and particular to the general and the universal or cosmic,

7.  An attempt to arrive at that which lies back of the form considered, or to reach the idea which is responsible for the form.

This process gradually steps up the consciousness and enables the aspirant to arrive at the life side of manifestation instead of the form side. He begins however with the form or "object." Objects upon which to concentrate are of four kinds:

## BOOK III

1.  *External objects*, such as images of the deity, pictures or forms in nature,

2.  *Internal objects*, such as the centres in the etheric body,

3.  *Qualities*, such as the various virtues, with the intent to awaken desire for these virtues and thus to build them into the content of the personal life,

4.  *Mental* concepts or those ideas which embody the ideals lying back of all animated forms. These may take the form of symbols or of words.

In one of the Puranas the idea embodied in concentration is expressed most beautifully. The aspirant is told, after he has made use of the first five means of yoga (dealt with in Book II), that he "should make a localization of the mind stuff upon some auspicious support" and this localization is illustrated by a description of the fixing of the attention upon a form of God.

"The incarnated form of the Exalted One leaves one without desire for any other support. This should be understood to be fixed attention, when the mind stuff is fixed upon this form. And what is this incarnate form of Hari on which one should ponder, let that be heard by thee, O Ruler of Men. Fixed attention is not possible without something on which to fix it." (Vishnu Purana VI. 7. 75-85.)

Then follows a description of the incarnated form of the Exalted One, concluding with these words:

". . . upon Him let the yogin ponder; and lost in Him, concentrate his own mind until, O, King, the fixed attention becomes firmly fixed upon Him only. While

[ 245 ]

performing this or while doing, as he wills, some other action wherein his mind does not wander, he should then deem this fixed attention to be perfected." (Naradiya Purana LXVII. 54-62.)

It is the realization of the necessity for "objects" in concentration that originated the demand for images, sacred sculptures and pictures. All these objects entail the use of the lower concrete mind and this is the necessary preliminary stage. Their use brings the mind into a controlled condition so that the aspirant can make it do just what he chooses. The four types of objects mentioned above carry the aspirant gradually inwards and enable him to transfer his consciousness from the physical plane into the etheric realm, from thence into the world of desire or of the emotions, and so into the world of mental ideas and concepts. This process, which is carried on within the brain, brings the entire lower man into a state of one-pointed coherent attention, all parts of his nature being directed to the attainment of fixed attention or a concentration of all the mental faculties. The mind then is no longer scattering, unsteady and outgoing, but is fully "fixed in attention." Vivekananda translates "dharana" as "holding the mind to one thought for twelve seconds."

This clear, one-pointed, still perception of an object, without any other object or thought entering into one's consciousness is most difficult of achievement, and when it can be done for the space of twelve seconds, true concentration is being achieved.

2. **Sustained Concentration (dharana) is meditation (dhyana).**

Meditation is but the extension of concentration and grows out of the facility a man achieves in "fixing the mind" at will on any particular object. It falls under the same rules and conditions as concentration and the only distinction between the two is in the *time* element.

Having achieved the capacity to focus the mind steadily upon an object, the next step is developing the power to hold the mind stuff or chitta unwaveringly occupied with that object or thought for a prolonged period. The Purana quoted above continues:

"An uninterrupted succession of presented ideas single in intent upon His form, without desire for anything else, that, O King, is contemplation. It is brought about by the first six aids of yoga."

The word contemplation here is synonymous with meditation. This meditation is still with seed or with an object.

Dvivedi says in his comment on this sutra:

". . . Dhyana is the entire fixing of the mind on the object thought of (to the extent of making it one with it). In fact, the mind should, at the time, be conscious only of itself and the object." The man's attitude becomes pure fixed attention; his physical body, his emotions, surroundings, and all sounds and sights are lost sight of and the brain is conscious only of the object which is the topic or seed of meditation, and the thoughts which the mind is formulating in connection with that object.

**3. When the chitta becomes absorbed in that which is the reality (or idea embodied in the form), and is unaware of separateness or of the personal self, this is contemplation or samadhi.**

The simplest way in which to comprehend this sutra is to realize that every form or object is a manifested life of some kind or another. In the early stages of the meditation process, the student becomes aware of the nature of the form and of his relation to it. The two states in which he is conscious of himself and of the object of his meditation are entirely mental conditions; they exist within his mind.

This condition is followed by one in which his realization travels inward on to the subjective plane and he becomes aware of the *nature* of the life which is expressing itself through the form. Quality and subjective relationships engross his attention and the form aspect is lost sight of, but still the sense of separateness or of duality persists. He is still aware of himself and of that which is the not-self. Similarity of quality and response to analogous vibration are his, however.

In the two stages of dharana and dhyana, of concentration and of meditation, the mind is the important factor and is the producer in the brain. A great Hindu teacher, *Kecidhvaja*, expresses this idea in the following words:

"The soul has the means. Thinking is the means. It is inanimate. When thinking has completed its task of release, it has done what it had to do and ceases." (From the Vishnu Parana. VI. 7:90.)

The truth of this makes any description or explanation of the high state of samadhi or contemplation exceedingly difficult, for words and phrases are but the effort of the mind to submit to the brain of the personal self that which will enable it to appreciate and comprehend the process.

In contemplation, the yogi loses sight of:

1. His brain consciousness or the physical plane apprehensions as to time and space.

2. His emotional reactions to the subject of his meditation process.

3. His mental activities, so that all the "modifications" of the thinking process, all the emotional reactions of the desire-mind (kama-manas) vehicle are subdued and the yogi is unaware of them. He is, however, intensely alive and alert, positive and awake, for the brain and the mind are held by him in a steady grip, and are used by him without any interference on their part.

This literally means that the independent life of these forms through which the real self is functioning is still, quieted and subdued, and the real or spiritual man, awake on his own plane, is able to function with full use of the brain, sheaths and mind of the lower self, his vehicle or instrument. He is, therefore, centred in himself or in the soul aspect. All sense of separateness or of the lower personal self are lost sight of, and he becomes identified with the *soul* of that form which has been the object of his meditation.

Unhindered by the mind stuff, or by the desire

nature he "enters into" that condition which has four outstanding characteristics:

1. *Absorption in the soul consciousness* and therefore awareness of the soul of all things. Form is no longer seen, and the vision of the reality, veiled by all forms, is revealed.

2. *Liberation from the three worlds* of sense perception, so only that is known and contacted which is free from form, from desire and from lower concrete mental substance.

3. *Realization of oneness* with all souls, subhuman, human, and superhuman. Group consciousness somewhat expresses the idea, just as separated consciousness, or realization of one's own individual identity, characterizes consciousness in the three worlds.

4. *Illumination* or perception of the light aspect of manifestation. Through meditation the yogi knows himself to be light, a point of fiery essence. Through facility in the meditation process he can focus that light on any object he chooses and come "en rapport" with the light which that object is hiding. That light is then known to be one in essence with his own light-centre, and comprehension, communication and identification then become possible.

**4. When concentration, meditation and contemplation form one sequential act, then is sanyama achieved.**

This is a most difficult idea to express for we have not in the English language the equivalent of the Sanskrit term "sanyama." It is the synthesis of the three stages of the meditation process and is only possible to that student who has learnt and mastered the three states of mind control. Through that mastery he has produced certain results, which are as follows:

1. He has freed himself from the three worlds of mind, emotion and physical plane existence. They no longer attract his attention. He is not concentrated upon, or engrossed by them.

2. He can focus his attention at will and can hold his mind steady indefinitely, whilst working intensively in the mental world, should he so choose.

3. He can polarize or centre himself in the consciousness of the ego, soul or spiritual man, and knows himself as separate from the mind, the emotions, desires, feelings and form which constitute the lower man.

4. He has learnt to recognize that lower man (the sum total of mental states, of emotions and physical atoms) as simply his instrument for communicating at will with the three lower planes.

5. He has acquired the faculty of contemplation or the attitude of the real Identity towards the realm of the soul and can look out on the soul-realm in a sense corresponding to the way a man can use his eyes to see on the physical plane.

6. He can transmit to the brain, via the controlled mind, that which he sees, and can thus impart knowledge of the self and of its kingdom to the man on the physical plane.

This is perfectly concentrated meditation and

the power so to meditate is called sanyama in this sutra. It is the attainment of the power of meditation which is the objective of the Raja Yoga system. Through this achievement, the yogi has learnt to differentiate between the object and that which the object veils or hides. He has learnt to pierce through all veils and contact the reality behind. He has achieved a working knowledge of duality.

There is yet a higher consciousness than this, that realization which is covered by the term unity, but as yet it is not his. This is, however, a very high stage and produces in the physical man astounding effects and introduces him to various forms of phenomena.

**5. As a result of sanyama comes the shining forth of the light.**

There are several terms used here by various commentators and translators and it might be of interest to consider some of them, for in the various interpretations will come a full understanding of the Sanskrit terms.

Briefly, the idea involves the conception that the nature of the soul is light, and that light is the great revealer. The yogi, through steady practise in meditation, has reached the point where he can at will, turn the light which radiates from his very being, in any direction, and can illumine any subject. Nothing can therefore be hid from him and all knowledge is at his disposal. This power is therefore described as:

## BOOK III

1.  *Illumination of perception.*   The light of the soul pours forth and the man on the physical plane, in his brain consciousness, is thereby enabled to perceive that which before was dark and hidden from him.   The process may technically be described in the following concise terms:

a.   Meditation,

b.   Polarization in the soul or egoic consciousness,

c.   Contemplation, or the turning of the soul-light upon that which is to be known or investigated,

d.   The subsequent pouring down of the knowledge ascertained, in a "stream of illumination" into the brain, via the sutratma, the thread-soul, silver cord, or magnetic link.   This thread passes through the mind and illumines it.   The thoughts engendered in the automatic response of the chitta (or mind stuff) to the knowledge conveyed, are then impressed upon the brain and the man, in his physical consciousness, becomes cognizant of what the soul knows.   He becomes illumined.

As this process becomes more frequent and steady, a change takes place in the physical man. He becomes more and more synchronized with the soul.   The time element in transmission recedes into the background and the illumination of the field of knowledge by the light of the soul and the illumining of the physical brain, becomes an instantaneous happening.

The light in the head increases in a corresponding degree and the third eye develops and functions.   On the astral and mental plane a corresponding "eye" develops, and thus the ego or soul can illumine all the three planes in the three worlds as well as the soul realm.

2. *Lucidity of consciousness.* A man becomes lucid and clear sighted. He is conscious of a growing power in himself which will enable him to explain and solve all problems, and not only this, but "lucidly to speak" and thus become one of the teaching forces of the world. All knowledge, consciously acquired by self illumination must be shared, and clearly imparted to others. It is the corollary of illumination.

3. *The shining forth of insight.* This gives a new angle on the subject and a most important one. It is the definition of the capacity to "see into" a form, to arrive at that subjective reality which has made the objective sheath what it is. This insight is more than understanding, sympathy or comprehension. They are but the effects of it. It is the capacity to pierce through all forms and arrive at that which they veil, because that reality is identical with the reality in oneself.

4. *The illumining of the intellect.* Unless the mind or intellect can grasp and transmit that which the soul knows, the mysteries remain unexplained to the physical brain and the knowledge possessed by the soul must remain nothing more than a beautiful and unattainable vision. But once the intellect is illumined, it can transmit to and impress upon the brain those hidden things which only the sons of God on their own plane know. Hence the need for Raja Yoga or the

science of union through mind control and development.

**6. This illumination is gradual; it is developed stage by stage.**

The evolutionary nature of all growth and unfoldment is dealt with here and the aspirant is reminded that nothing is accomplished at once but only as the result of long and steady effort.

One thing that every aspirant to the mysteries should remember is that growth that is gradual, and relatively slow, is the method of every natural process and this soul unfoldment is, after all, but one of the great processes of nature. All that the aspirant has to do is to provide the right conditions. The growth then will take care of itself normally. Steady perseverance, patient endurance, the achievement of a little every day, are of more value to the aspirant than the violent rushing forward and the enthusiastic endeavour of the emotional and temperamental person. The undue forcing of one's development carries with it certain most definite and specific dangers. These are avoided when the student realizes that the path is long and that an intelligent understanding of each stage of the path is of more value to him than the results achieved through the premature awakening of the psychic nature. The injunction to grow as the flower grows, carries with it a tremendous occult truth. There is an injunction in Ecc. VII. 16, which carries this thought, "Be not righteous over much, . . . why shouldest thou die?"

**7. These last three means of yoga have a more intimate subjective effect than the previous means.**

The first five means of yoga have for their primary objective the preparation of the would-be yogi. Through keeping the Commandments and the Rules, through the achievements of poise and rhythmic control of the energies of the body, and through the power to withdraw his consciousness and centre it in the head, the aspirant is enabled to take full advantage of, and safely to cultivate the powers of concentration, meditation and contemplation.

Having contacted the subjective in himself and become aware of that which is interior, he can begin to work with the interior, internal and intimate means.

The entire eight means of yoga themselves only prepare a man for that state of spiritual consciousness which transcends thought, which is apart from any of the seeds of thought, which is formless, and which can only be described (and then inadequately) by such terms as unification, realization, identification, nirvanic consciousness, etc.

It is useless for the neophyte to attempt to comprehend until he has developed the internal instrument for comprehension; it is fruitless for the man of the world to question and seek to be shown unless at the same time he is willing (as in the acquirement of any science) to learn the A.B.C. and graduate in the technique.

Johnston in his commentary says:

". . . The means of growth previously described were concerned with the extrication of the spiritual man from psychic bondages and veils; while this threefold power is to be exercised by the spiritual man thus extricated and standing on his feet, viewing life with his open eyes."

**8. Even these three, however, are external to the true seedless meditation (or samadhi) which is not based on an object. It is free from the effects of the discriminative nature of the chitta (or mind stuff).**

In all the previous stages the thinker has been aware of both himself, the knower, and of the field of knowledge. In the earliest stages he was aware of triplicity, for the instrument of knowledge was likewise recognised, later to be transcended and forgotten. Now comes the final stage, the object of all yoga practices, where *unity* is known and even duality is seen to be a limitation. Naught remains but awareness of the self, of that omniscient, omnipotent knower who is one with the All, and whose very nature is awareness and energy. As has been well said:

"There are therefore these two types of perception: That of living things and that of the Life; that of the soul's works and that of the soul itself."

The expounder of yoga is now desirous of describing the results of meditation (some along the line of the higher psychism and some along the line of the lower); the next seven sutras, therefore, deal with the nature of the objects seen and the control of the mind as the real man seeks to focus the illuminating ray of his mind upon them.

In studying these results of meditation in the psychic realm, it should be borne in mind that the eight means of yoga do produce definite effects in the lower nature and that this causes certain unfoldments and experiences to take place; these put the aspirant more consciously en rapport with the interior planes in the three worlds. This is a safe and necessary process provided it is the outcome of the awakening of the man on his own plane, and the turning of the eye of the soul, via the mind and the third eye, upon these planes. The presence of the lower psychic power may, however, mean that the soul is (from the physical plane standpoint) asleep and unable to use its instrument, and that these experiences are therefore only the result of the activity of the solar plexus producing awareness of the astral plane. This type of psychism is a *reversion* to the animal state and to the child stage of the human race. It is undesirable and dangerous.

**9. The sequence of mental states is as follows: the mind reacts to that which is seen; then follows the moment of mind control. Then ensues a moment wherein the chitta (mind stuff) responds to both these factors. Finally these pass away, and the perceiving consciousness has full sway.**

If the student will look at any of the translations of the sutras he will find that this one is variously translated and most of the translations are exceedingly ambiguous. This can be illustrated by giving the translation of Tatya:

"Out of the two trains of self-reproductive thought resulting from the Vyutthana and the Nirodha (respectively), when the former is subdued and the latter is manifested, and, at the moment of manifestation the internal organ (Chitta) is concerned in both of the trains, then such modifications of the internal organ is the modification in the shape of Nirodha."

The others are still more vague, with the exception of Johnston's translation. He gives us the following which throws much light upon the thought involved:

"Out of the ascending degrees is the development of control. First there is the overcoming of the mind-impress of excitation. Then comes the manifestation of the mind-impress of control. Then the perceiving consciousness follows after the moment of control. This is the development of control."

Perhaps the simplest way to understand this thought is to realize that the man in his physical brain is aware of three factors as he attempts to meditate:

1. He is aware of the object of his meditation. This excites or impresses his mind, and throws into activity the "modifications of the thinking principle," or stimulates the tendency of the mind to create thought-forms, and throws the chitta or mind stuff into shapes corresponding to the object seen.

2. He then becomes aware of the necessity to subdue this tendency and so brings in the action of the will and steadies and controls the mind stuff so that it ceases to modify itself and take on shape.

By dint of steady persevering endeavour the sequential nature of these two states of consciousness are gradually offset, and in time they become simultaneous. Recognition of an object and the immediate control of the responsive chitta occur like a flash of lightning. This is the state technically called "nirodha." It must be remembered that (as Vivekananda says):

"If there is a modification which impels the mind to rush out through the senses and the yogi tries to control it, that very control itself will be a modification."

The impress of the will upon the mind will naturally lead to the mind assuming the shape that controls it and it will be thrown into a modification, dependent largely upon the point in evolution the aspirant has reached, the trend of his daily thought, and the extent of his egoic contact. This is not the true and highest form of contemplation. It is but one of the earlier stages, but it is much higher than concentration and meditation with seed as usually understood, for it is inevitably succeeded by the third stage which is one of great interest.

3. He then slips suddenly out of the lower state of consciousness and realizes his identity with the perceiver, with the thinker on his own plane, and because the mind is controlled and the

object seen excites no response, the true identity is able to perceive that which has hitherto been veiled.

It should be made clear, however, that the perceiver on his own plane has always been aware of that which is now recognized. The difference lies in the fact that the instrument, the mind, is now in a state of control, it is therefore possible for the thinker to impress the brain, via the controlled mind, with that which is perceived. Man on the physical plane simultaneously *also* perceives, and true meditation and contemplation for the first time become possible. At first this will only be for a brief second. A flash of intuitive perception, a moment of vision and of illumination and all has gone. The mind begins again to modify itself and is thrown into activity, the vision is lost sight of, the high moment has passed, and the door into the soul-realm seems suddenly to shut. But assurance has been gained; a glimpse of reality has been registered on the brain and the guarantee of future achievement is recognized.

**10.   Through the cultivation of this habit of mind there will eventuate a steadiness of spiritual perception.**

The point of balance between excitation of the mind and control can be achieved with greater frequency by constant repetition, until the habit of stabilizing the mind is acquired. When this is accomplished two things occur:

1. An instantaneous control of mind at will, producing
   a. A still mind, free from thought forms,
   b. A quiescent responsive brain.
2. A downflow into the physical brain of the consciousness of the perceiver, the soul.

This becomes increasingly clearer, more informative and less interrupted as time elapses, until a rhythmic response is set up between the soul and the physical plane man. The mind and brain are completely subdued by the soul.

It should be remembered here that this condition of the mind and brain is a *positive one*, not a negative state.

**11. The establishing of this habit, and the restraining of the mind from its thought-form-making tendency, results eventually in the constant power to contemplate.**

Little need be said in explanation of this sutra owing to its clarity. It is in the nature of a summation of the previous sutras.

The idea conveyed is that of the achievement of a constant state of meditation. Though periods in which definite work is done at certain specific and stated hours are of exceeding value, particularly in the early stages of soul unfoldment, yet the ideal condition is that of being in a state of realization all day every day. The ability at will to draw upon the resources of the ego, the constant recognition that one is a Son of God incarnate upon the physical plane, and the ability to draw down, when needed, the power and the force of the soul, is one which will be eventually achieved by every aspirant! But first, however, the habit of recollection has to be instituted and the instantaneous ability to restrain the modifications of the thinking principle has to precede this desirable state of being.

**12. When mind control and the controlling factor are equally balanced, then comes the condition of one-pointedness.**

The Sanskrit term used is difficult to explain clearly. Such terms as one-pointed, single in intent, fixed, synthesized, perfected concentration, all give some idea of the mind condition under consideration.

The aspirant is now deliberately unconscious of all states of mind relating to the three worlds. His attention is focussed upon a specific object, and primarily upon the reality or subjective life, veiled by the form of the object. He is likewise unconscious of himself, the thinker or knower, and only that which is contemplated is realized in the true sense of the term. This is the negative aspect.

It should be remembered, however, that this is a very active mental state, for the perceiving consciousness is aware of the object in a most comprehensive manner. The sum of its qualities, aspects and vibration is revealed to him, as well as e essential central energy which has called that particular object into manifestation. This is revealed by the illuminating light of the mind being steadily directed upon that object. The perceiving consciousness is also aware of its identification with the reality behind the form. This is the true occult realization, but it is not the realization of the object so much as a realization of unity with, or identification with the life it veils.

This is in itself a dual condition but not in the ordinarily accepted sense. There is, however, a still higher state of consciousness when the unity of the life in *all* forms is realized, and not simply unity with the life in one specific object.

**13. Through this process the aspects of every object are known, their characteristics (or form) their symbolic nature, and their specific use in time-conditions (stage of development) are known and realised.**

It should here be borne in mind that every form of divine manifestation has three aspects and hence is made truly in the image of God with all divine potentialities. In the human kingdom this is recognised. It is equally true of all forms. This triple nature is grasped by the truly concentrated yogi and the three are seen as they exist and yet are recognised as constituting one whole. In his commentary, Johnston gives us a picture of the ideas involved, in the following words:

". . . we get a twofold view of this objec seeing at once all its individual characteristi its essential character, species and genus; we see it in relation to itself and in relation to the Eternal."

In a curious way these three aspects cover the three aspects of the time equation or of the relationship of the object to its environment.

1. *Characteristics of the form.* In this phrase the tangible outward aspects of the form are seen. The matter-side of the manifesting idea is dealt with, and that which can be contacted through the medium of the senses is first considered and dismissed. This form is the result of the past, and the limitations due to the point in evolution are recognised. Every form carries in itself the evidence of the previous cycles and this can be seen in:

a. Its rate of vibration,
b. The nature of its rhythm,
c. The amount of light which it permits to manifest,
d. Its occult colour.

2. *Symbolic nature.* Every object is but the symbol of a reality. The difference in the development of the forms which symbolize or embody that reality is the guarantee that at some future date all the symbols will achieve the fruition of their mission. A symbol is an embodied idea, the working out in objective existence of some life. This is the consciousness aspect and two great revelations are latent in every symbol or form.

a.  The revelation of full consciousness, or the streaming forth of that response to contact which is potential or differing as yet in all forms but which can and will be carried forward to the full flood-tide of awareness.

b.  The revelation of that which the consciousness aspect (the second aspect) is in its turn veiling. The unveiling of the soul leads to the manifestation of the one life. The manifestation of the Son of God leads to a knowledge of the Father. The shining forth of the higher self, through the medium of the lower self, produces the revelation of the divine or spiritual self. The matrix holds the diamond and when the matrix reveals its hidden gem, and the work of cutting and polishing is accomplished, the glory of the jewel will be seen. When the lotus plant has grown to maturity, the flower comes to fruition and in the centre of its petals the "Jewel in the Lotus" (Om mani padme hum) can be seen.

This symbolic aspect of forms is true of all, and whether the symbol is the atom of substance, the mineral, or a tree, an animal or the "form of the Son of God" the jewel of the first aspect will be found hidden. It will make its presence known through the quality of consciousness in one or other of its many states.

3.  *Specific use in time conditions.*  As the yogi one-pointedly concentrates on the form, or object, meditates on its quality (the subjective aspect or symbolic nature), and contemplates the life veiled by the form but testified to by the factor of consciousness, he becomes aware of the *present* stag

[ 266 ]

of development, and thus the future, past and present, stand revealed to his intuition.

It will be apparent therefore to even the casual reader, that if meditation in its three above mentioned stages is carried forward correctly, all knowledge becomes possible to the yogi, the Eternal Now is a realized fact in nature and intelligent cooperation with the evolutionary plan becomes possible. Service is then based on complete understanding.

14. **The characteristics of every object are acquired, manifesting or latent.**

Much the same idea is covered in this sutra as in the previous one. In time and space all characteristics have relative values. The goal is one; the origin is one, but owing to the differing rates of vibration of the seven great breaths or streams of divine energy, every life borne forth upon them differs and is distinctive. The stage of development of the seven Lords of the Rays is not equal. The unfoldment of the life of the various planetary Logoi, or of the seven Spirits before the Throne of God, is not uniform and the atoms in Their bodies, or the monads who constitute Their vehicles are therefore not uniform in unfoldment.

This is a vast subject and cannot be more than touched upon here. Students will find it of interest to search for information given in the different presentations of the one truth anent the great Lives in whom we "live, and move and have

our being." They can be studied under the following names:

1. The seven Rays,
2. The seven Spirits before the Throne,
3. The seven planetary Logoi,
4. The seven great Lords,
5. The seven Aeons,
6. The seven Emanations,
7. The seven Prajapatis,

and other less known terms, and much light will
be forthcoming.

In the characteristic form (taking into consideration its specific point in development, and
its lack of development) is revealed to the
knower:

a. The sum total of acquirement. That which
the *past* has given. This is the total chord which
the soul of that object is as yet capable of sounding.

b. The particular range of qualities out of
that total acquisition which the life is manifesting
through any specific form. This is the *present*
note in the acquired chord which the soul of the
object has chosen to sound.

c. That which is latent and possible. This
knowledge will be dual, revealing first, the latent
possibilities to be unfolded through the medium
of the form contemplated, and secondly, the latent
possibilities capable of unfoldment in the present
world cycle through various forms. This covers
*future* developments. This will give the yogi
the completed chord when the great evolutionary
cycle has run its course.

**15.  The stage of development is responsible for the various modifications of the versatile psychic nature and of the thinking principle.**

This is a very general paraphrase of the idea involved and is in the nature of a summing up of the rather abstruse ideas of the text.  The sutras following upon this one deal (for the remainder of Book III) with the results of meditation.  The preceding sutras have considered the hindrances and difficulties that have to be overcome before true meditation becomes possible.  The key to that overcoming and the difference between aspirants to the path is made apparent in this sutra.  The ascertaining of one's approximate place upon the ladder of evolution, the summing up of one's assets and debits is one of the most useful activities the would-be aspirant can undertake.  An understanding of the stage reached and of the next step to be taken is essential for all true progress.

Johnston translates this sutra in the words: "Difference in stage is the cause of difference in development," and goes on to say: "The first stage is the sapling, the caterpillar, the animal.  The second stage is the growing tree, the chrysalis, the man.  The third is the splendid pine, the butterfly, the angel . . ."

**16.  Through concentrated meditation upon the triple nature of every form, comes the revelation of that which has been and of that which will be.**

The sutra which we are considering sums the

preceding ideas and it is interesting to note how this first great result of meditation takes one right back to the true facts anent divine manifestation and emphasizes the three aspects through which every life (from an atom of substance to a solar Logos) expresses itself. The great Law of Cause and Effect and the entire process of evolutionary unfoldment are recognized and that which is, is seen to be the result of that which has been. Similarly that which will later eventuate is recognized to be the working out of causes set in motion in the present, and thus the cycle of development is seen to be one process existing in three stages.

These three stages in the three worlds of human unfoldment correspond to the three dimensions, and students will find it interesting to work out these analogies of the various triplicities, remembering that the third aspect (intelligent substance), the Holy Ghost or Brahma aspects, corresponds to the past (hence a hint as to the nature of evil). The second aspect (consciousness) or the Christ or Vishnu aspect relates to the present, whilst only the future will reveal the nature of spirit, the highest or Father aspect. This line of thought, through concentrated meditation will become clear, and a sense of proportion and a sense of just values as to the present point in time will grow. A recognition also of the relation of all lives to each other will be developed and the life of the aspirant will be stabilized and adjusted so that past karma will be adjusted and possible future karma negated and the process of liberation will proceed with rapidity.

**17. The Sound (or word), that which it denotes (the object) and the embodied spiritual essence (or idea) are usually confused in the mind of the perceiver. By concentrated meditation on these three aspects comes an (intuitive) comprehension of the sound uttered by all forms of life.**

This is one of the most important sutras in the book, and holds the key to the object of the entire meditation process. This is to reveal or to unveil to the perceiver or spiritual man, the true nature of the self, the second aspect, and the correspondence to the second aspect in all forms of sub-human life, as well as to put him en rapport with the second aspect in all superhuman forms. Thus it concerns the subjective side of all manifestation and deals with those forces which in every form constitute the consciousness aspect, which concern the Christ or buddhic principle and which are the direct cause of objective manifestation and the revelation of spirit through the medium of form.

This is the AUM. First the breath, then the word and all that is, appeared.

Just as long as the great Existence who is the sum total of all forms and of all states of consciousness continues to sound the cosmic AUM, just so long will the objective tangible solar system persist.

The following synonyms in connection with this sutra must be borne in mind if clarity of thought is to be achieved:

## BOOK III

| I. *Spiritual Essence.* | II. *The Sound or Word.* | III. *The Object.* |
|---|---|---|
| 1. Spirit. | 1. The Soul. | 1. Body. |
| 2. Pneuma. | 2. The Psyche. | 2. Form. |
| 3. The Father. Shiva. | 3. The Son. Vishnu. | 3. The Holy Spirit. Brahma. |
| 4. The Monad. The One. | 4. The cosmic Christ. | 4. The vehicle of life and of incarnation. |
| 5. The eternal Will or Purpose. | 5. Eternal Love-Wisdom. | 5. Eternal activity and intelligence. |
| 6. One great Breath. | 6. The AUM. | 6. The Worlds. |
| 7. Life. | 7. Consciousness Aspect. | 7. Activity Aspect. |
| 8. Synthesising Energy. | 8. Attractive Force. | 8. Matter. |
| 9. First Aspect. | 9. Second Aspect. | 9. Third Aspect. |

In the mind of man these three aspects are confused and that which is outward and objective is usually recognized as reality. This is the great maya or illusion and can only be dissipated when the perceiver can distinguish the three great aspects in every form, his own included. When the second aspect, the soul, the middle or mediating principle is known, the nature of the form is also known, and the essential nature of spirit can be inferred. The immediate field of knowledge, however, which the yogi has to master is that of the second aspect. He must arrive at the Sound or Word which brought every form into manifestation, and which is the result of the breath, the essence or spirit.

"In the beginning was the Word and the Word

was with God and the Word was God. All things were made by Him. . . ." (John I. 1:2.)

Here, in the Christian Bible, is the substance of the entire teaching, and in the significance of the three letters of the Sacred Word, AUM, lies the clue to the entire cosmic process. The meditation process when duly and correctly carried out reveals therefore the second or soul aspect, and the Sound, or Word (the Voice of the Silence) can then be heard.

Once heard and the work carried steadily forward, the realm of consciousness is revealed and the yogi is en rapport with the second aspect of his own nature and with the second aspect in every form. This is the basis of the whole science of the soul and leads a man to know his own soul or psyche and the psyche in every form of divine life. It is the foundation for the entire science of psychism, both in its higher and lower aspects.

When a man is a lower psychic he is aware of, and responds to the soul aspect of the material forms and the third or Brahma aspect (the body), dominates, for every atom of matter has a soul. This concerns all that is subhuman.

When he responds to the higher correspondence of this, to the reality of which the lower is but the shadow, he is in touch with the Christ consciousness, with the soul of his being which is one with the soul in all the superhuman kingdoms.

In connection with this, two things must be remembered. If he is a lower psychic he is in touch with the second aspect of the lower man, the astral body, the middle principle in the lower

[ 273 ]

man, linking the mental body and the etheric. He is, therefore, en rapport with all that can be contacted on that plane.

If, however, he is a higher psychic he is en rapport with the second aspect of divine manifestation, the ego or soul on its own plane, mediating between and linking the monad with the personality, spirit with the body.

It is interesting here to note that a clue to the truth of this can be found in the manifestations of lower psychism such as are seen in the average mediumistic seance and the ordinary type of spiritualism. Contact with the astral plane is made through that great centre, the solar plexus which links the higher three centres and the lower. It accounts also for the fact that flowers are such a feature in materializations at seances, for the vegetable kingdom is the middle kingdom of the three subhuman kingdoms, mineral, vegetable, and animal. The explanation as to the prevalence of Indian guides is also found here, for they are the shells and powerful thought-forms left by the second of the three strictly human races, Lemurian, Atlantean and Aryan. No Lemurian shells or thought-forms are left now, but many Atlantean shells are still to be found preserved through the use of certain forms of Atlantean magic.

By concentrated meditation upon the distinction between these aspects there will eventually come a hearing of the Voice of the Silence and contact with a man's own second aspect. He will know himself as the "Word made flesh" and will recognize himself as the AUM.

When this is the case he will then hear the word in other units of the human family, and will awaken to a recognition of the sound, as it is emanated by all forms in all the kingdoms of nature. The realm of the soul will stand open to him and this, when it includes recognition of the sound in all the four kingdoms, will lead him to know himself as Master. Soul knowledge and the power to work with the soul of all things in the three worlds is the distinctive mark of the Adept

18. **Knowledge of previous incarnations becomes available when the power to see thought-images is acquired.**

The significance of this sutra is very great, for it gives the basis for the regaining of a knowledge of past experience. This basis is strictly mental, and only those mentally polarised and with the mind under control can regain this knowledge if they so wish. The power to see thought-images only comes through mind control, and the mind can only be controlled by the real or spiritual man. Therefore only egoically centred people can truly acquire this knowledge. It might be asked here what therefore do those people see who are emotional and *not* mental, when they claim to know who they are, and to relate the past lives of their friends? They are reading the akashic records and because their mental control and equipment are not adequate, they cannot discriminate nor ascertain accurately what they see.

The akashic record is like an immense photographic film, registering all the desires and earth experiences of our planet. Those who perceive it will see pictured thereon:

1. The life experiences of every human being since time began,

2. The reactions to experience of the entire animal kingdom,

3. The aggregation of the thought-forms of a kamic nature (based on desire) of every human unit throughout time. Herein lies the great deception of the records. Only a trained occultist can distinguish between actual experience and those astral pictures created by imagination and keen desire.

4. The planetary "Dweller on the Threshold" with all that appertains to that term and all the aggregations of forms which are to be found in its environment.

The trained seer has learnt to dissociate that which pertains to his own aura and the aura of the planet (which is in actuality the akashic record). He can distinguish between those records which are:

a. Planetary,

b. Hierarchical or pertaining to the work of the twelve Creative Hierarchies as they bring to concretion the plan of the Logos.

c. Imaginative forms, the result of the desire-thought activity of the myriads of men, animated by desire for some form of experience or other.

d. The historical record pertaining to races, nations, groups and families in their two great divisions on the physical plane and on the astral.

It should be borne in mind that every human being belongs to a *physical* family which constitutes his link with the animal kingdom, and also belongs to an astral family. Through that affiliation on the upward arc he is linked with his egoic group and on the downward arc with the vegetable kingdom.

e. The astrological record, or the forms taken on the astral plane under the influence of the planetary forces. These are in two great groups.

1. Those forms or pictures in the akasha produced by the inflow of solar force via the planets.

2. Those forms or pictures which are produced by the inflow of cosmic force from one or other of the signs of the zodiac, that is, from their corresponding constellations.

These points are enumerated to show how impossible it is that the majority of the claims regarding past incarnations can be true. They are the result of a vivid imagination and the assumption that the flashes of astral sight which reveal glimpses of the akashic film give that which pertains to the one who sees. This is not the case any more than the people and activities seen out of any window in a big city reveal to the onlooker his own relatives, friends and pursuits.

The knowledge referred to in the sutra comes in three ways:

1. Direct ability to see the records if so desired. This form of acquiring knowledge is seldom employed except by initiates and adepts in connection with their pledged disciples.

[ 277 ]

2.   Through direct knowledge of the group activities and relations of a man's own ego.   This, however, only covers that cycle of time which began when a man stepped upon the probationary path.   Experiences prior to that are relatively of no more vital importance than is a second in the life of an old man as he passes in retrospect his long life.   All that stands out are events and happenings and not the individual hours and seconds.

3.   Through the instinctual life.   This is based on *memory*, on acquired faculty and capacity and on the possession of those qualities which go to the equipment of the ego.   The ego knows that the possession of the power to do thus and so in the three worlds, is the direct result of past experience, and knows too that certain effects are only to be achieved through certain causes.   These he arrives at through concentrated meditation.

The thought images he becomes aware of are:

1.   Those in his aura at the time of his meditation,

2.   Those in his immediate environment,

3.   Those of his present family, group and race,

4.   Those of his present life cycle,

5.   Those of his egoic group.

Thus through the process of elimination he gradually works his way through grade after grade of thought images until he arrives at the particular layer of thought impression which deals with the cycle about which he is concerning himself.   This is not therefore simply a perception of certain aspects of the records, but a definitely

scientific process, known only to the trained occultist.

**19. Through concentrated meditation, the
thought images in the minds of other people
become apparent.**

It should be remembered that the result of the
eight means of yoga is to produce a yogi or trained
knower. He is, therefore, one who concerns
himself with causes and not with effects. He perceives that which causes the tangible to appear,
that is the thoughts which start into motion the
forces of substance and eventually produce the
concretion of that substance.

The use of this power to read the minds of
others is only permitted to the yogi in those cases
where it is necessary for him to understand the
*causes,* lying back of certain events, and this only
in order to work out intelligently the plans of the
Hierarchy and of evolution. The power here is
analogous to that of telepathy but it is not identical. Telepathy entails the tuning in of one mind
with another, and necessitates their being en rapport. This faculty of the trained seer is more
in the nature of *an act of the will* and the manipulation of certain forces whereby he can instantly
see what he wants in any aura at any time.

The subject of his investigation may be attuned
to him or not; through intense meditation and
the use of the will faculty thought images stand
revealed. This power is a dangerous one to use
and is only permitted to trained disciples.

**20. As however the object of those thoughts is not apparent to the perceiver, he sees only the thought and not the object. His meditation excludes the tangible.**

All that he is "awake" to in his meditation is thought substance, his own chitta (or mind-stuff) and that of others.

It is the inherent activity of this chitta which is the cause of the eventual appearing of forms, tangible and objective, on the physical plane.

Everything that *appears* is the result of a subjective happening. All that is exists in the mind of the thinker, not in the sense that is usually understood but in the sense that *thought* sets in motion certain currents of force. These currents of force gradually sweep into shape forms which correspond to the thinker's idea and those forms persist as long as the mind of the thinker is on them and disappear when he "takes his mind off" them.

It is the nature of the thought force or current which is perceived through concentrated meditation. The form which will be ultimately produced does not interest the seer. He knows from the cause what the inevitable effect will be.

**21. By concentrated meditation upon the distinction between form and body, those properties of the body which make it visible to the human eye are negated (or withdrawn) and the yogi can render himself invisible.**

This is one of the most difficult of the sutras to the western thinker for it involves certain recognitions which are foreign to the occident. It involves primarily the recognition of the etheric or vital body and its functions as the attractive force holding the dense physical vehicle in shape. Through this etheric substratum the physical body is realized as a coherent whole and its objectivity is observable. This vital body is the true form from the standpoint of the occultist and not the dense tangible sheath.

The yogi, through concentration and meditation, has acquired the power to center his consciousness in the true or spiritual man and to control the thinking principle. It is an occult law that "as a man thinketh, so is he" and it is equally true occultly that "where a man thinketh there is he." At will the trained seer can withdraw his consciousness from the physical plane and center it on the mental. At will he can "shut off the light" and when that is the case visibility is negated and (from the standpoint of the human eye) he disappears. He also becomes intangible from the point of view of touch, and inaudible from the standpoint of hearing. It is this fact that demonstrates the reality of the hypothesis that there is nothing but energy of some form or other, and that that energy is triple; in the East they call the nature of energy sattvic, rajasic, or tamasic. That is translated as follows:

| Sattva | rhythm | spirit | life |
| Rajas | mobility | soul | light |
| Tamas | inertia | body | substance |

All are differentiations in time and space of the one eternal primordial spirit-essence. It may

be suggested that the modern western correspondences are to be found in the terms:

| | | |
|---|---|---|
| Energy | spirit | life |
| Force | soul | light |
| Matter | form | substance |

The outstanding characteristic of spirit (or
energy) is the life-principle, that mysterious
something which causes all things to be and to
persist. The outstanding characteristic of the
soul (or of force) is light. It brings into visibility that which exists.

The outstanding characteristic of living matter
is that it is that which "sub-stands" or is found
back of the objective body; and provides the true
form. It should be remembered here that the
basis of all occult teaching and of all phenomena
is to be found in the words:

"Matter is the vehicle for the manifestation of soul on
this plane of existence; and soul is the vehicle on a higher
turn of the spiral for the manifestation of spirit." (*Secret
Doctrine* I. 80.)

When the soul (or force) withdraws itself out
of the matter aspect (the tangible objective
form), that form is no longer to be seen. It disappears, and temporarily is dissipated. At present this can be adequately accomplished by the
seer through a concentration of his consciousness
in the ego, the spiritual man or soul, and (through
the use of the thinking principle and an act of
the will) his withdrawal of the etheric body from
the dense physical. This is covered by the word
"abstraction" and entails:

[ 282 ]

## BOOK III

1. A gathering together of the life or vital forces of the body into the physical plane nerve centres up the spine,

2. Their direction up the spine to the head,

3. Their concentration there and subsequent abstraction along the thread or sutratma, via the pineal gland and the brahmarandra,

4. The seer then stands in his true form, the etheric body, which is invisible to the human eye. As etheric vision develops in the race this will necessitate a further abstraction, then the seer will likewise withdraw the vital and luminous principles (the qualities of sattva and of rajas) out of the etheric body and stand in his kamic or astral body and thus be also etherically invisible. However, that time is still distant.

W. Q. Judge, in his commentary, makes certain interesting remarks, as follows:

"Another great difference between this philosophy and modern science is here indicated. The schools of today lay down the rule that if there is a healthy eye in line with the rays of light reflected from an object—such as a human body—the latter will be seen, and that no action of the mind of the person looked at can inhibit the functions of the optic nerves and retina of the onlooker. But the ancient Hindus held that all things are seen by reason of that differentiation of Satwa—one of the three great qualities composing all things—which is manifested as luminosity, operating in conjunction with the eye, which is also a manifestation of Satwa in another aspect. The two must conjoin; the absence of luminosity or its being disconnected from the seer's eye will cause a disappearance. And as the quality of luminosity is completely under the control of the ascetic, he can, by the process laid down, check it, and thus cut off from the eye of the other an essential element in the seeing of any object."

This entire process is only possible as the result of concentrated and one pointed meditation, and hence is impossible to the man who has not passed through the long discipline and training involved in the work of gaining control of the thinking principle and setting up that direct alignment and functioning which is possible when the thinker on his own plane, the mind, and the brain, are all aligned and coordinated via the sutratma, thread or magnetic silver cord.

**22. Karma (or effects) are of two kinds: immediate karma or future karma. By perfectly concentrated meditation on these, the yogi knows the term of his experience in the three worlds. This knowledge comes also from signs.**

This sutra can be somewhat elucidated if read in connection with Sutra 18 of Book III. The karma referred to here deals primarily with the present life of the aspirant or seer. He knows that every event in that life is the effect of a previous cause, initiated by himself in an early incarnation; he knows also that every act of the present life must produce an effect (to be worked

out in another life) unless it is done in such a
way that:

1. The effect is immediate and culminates
within the scope of the present life time,

2. The effect involves no Karma, for the
act has been done from a selfless motive and carried out with complete detachment. He then
produces the effect desired in accordance with the
law but it carries no consequences for himself.

When the seer enters into incarnation in a life
wherein only a few more effects remain to be
worked out, and when all that he initiates is freed
from karma, then he can set a term to his life
experience and he knows that the day of liberation
is at hand. Through meditation and ability to
function as the ego he can arrive at the world of
causes, and he knows therefore what acts must
be performed to release the few remaining effects.
Through strict attention to the motive underlying
every act of the present life he obviates the necessity for their effects to tie him in any way to the
wheel of rebirth. Thus he consciously and intelligently nears his goal and every deed, act and
thought is governed by direct knowledge, and in
no way chains him.

The signs or portents referred to, relate primarily to the mental world, where the real man
dwells. Through an understanding of three
things:

a. Numbers,
b. Colours,
c. Vibrations,

the seer becomes aware of the freedom of his

aura from "death producing" effects. He knows there is nothing more written, symbolically, in the records which can bring him back to the three worlds, and therefore "by signs" his path is seen to be clear.

This has been expressed for us in the ancient writings found in the Masters' archives as follows:

"When the star with five points shines with clarity and no forms are seen within its points, the way is clear.

When the triangle encloses naught but light, the path is freed for the passing of the pilgrim.

When within the aura of the pilgrim the many forms die out and colours three are seen, then the road is freed from that which might obstruct.

When thoughts call not to forms and when no shadows are reflected, the thread provides a way direct from the circle to the center."

From that point of rest, no return is possible. The term of necessary experience in the three worlds is at an end. No karma then can draw the freed spirit back to earth for further lessons, or the working out of prior causes. He may, however, continue or resume his work of service in the three worlds, without ever really leaving his true home in the subtler realms and higher spheres of consciousness.

**23. Union with others is to be gained through one-pointed meditation upon the three states of feeling—compassion, tenderness and dispassion.**

Some understanding of this will come if the student will compare this sutra with one in the first book (Sutra 33). The union here dealt with marks a step further than the previous attainment. In that, the nature of the aspirant is being trained to harmonious peaceful association with all around him. In this, he is taught to identify himself with all other selves through concentration upon what are sometimes called the "three states of feeling." These are:

a. *Compassion,* the antithesis of passion which is selfish and grasping,

b. *Tenderness,* the antithesis of self-centredness, which is always hard and self-absorbed,

c. *Dispassion,* the antithesis of lust or desire.

These three states of feeling when understood and entered into, put a man en rapport with the soul of all men.

Through compassion, he is no longer occupied with his own selfish interests but enters into and suffers with his brother; he can adapt his vibration so that it responds to his brother's need; he is enabled to share in all that is taking place in his brother's heart. This he does through the keying up of his own vibration to respond to the love nature of his own ego, and through that unifying principle all hearts everywhere are open to him.

Through tenderness, that compassionate understanding works out into practical expression. His activities are no longer in-going and self-centred but are out-going and inspired by an unselfish heartfelt desire to serve and aid. This state of feeling is sometimes called mercy, and characterall the servers of the race. It involves active help, unselfish intent, wise judgment and loving activity. It is free from any wish for reward or recognition. This has been beautifully covered by H. P. Blavatsky in *The Voice of the Silence* in the following words:

"Let thy Soul lend its ear to every cry of pain like as the lotus bares its heart to drink the morning sun.

Let not the fierce sun dry one tear of pain before thyself hast wiped it from the sufferer's eye.

But let each burning human tear drop on thy heart and there remain; nor ever brush it off until the pain that caused it is removed.

These tears, O thou of heart most merciful, these are the streams that irrigate the fields of charity immortal."

Through dispassion, the aspirant and server stands free from the karmic results of his activity on behalf of others. It is, as we know, our own desire which binds us to the three worlds and to others. "Binding to" is of a different nature to "union with." One is full of desire and causes obligation and effects; the other is free from desire, produces "identification with" and has no binding effects in the three worlds. Dispassion has more of a mental quality than the other two. It might be noted that dispassion brings in the quality of lower mind, tenderness is the emotional result of dispassionate compassion and involves the kamic or astral principle, whilst compassion concerns also the physical plane for it is the working out into physical manifestation of the two other states. It is the practical ability to identify oneself with another in all the three world conditions.

This union is the result of the egoic one-

brought down into full activity in the three worlds through meditation.

> **24. Meditation, one-pointedly centred upon the power of the elephant, will awaken that force or light.**

This sutra has given rise to much discussion and its usual interpretation has given the idea that meditation upon the elephant will give the strength of the elephant. Many commentators infer from these words, that meditation upon other animals will give their characteristics.

It should be remembered that this is a scientific text-book, having for its objective the following:

1. Training the aspirant so that he can enter into subtler realms.

2. Giving him power over the mind, so that it is his instrument to use as he will as an organ of vision into the higher worlds and as a transmitter or intermediary between the soul and the brain.

3. Awakening the light in the head so that the aspirant can become a radiant centre of light and illumine all problems, and through its light see light everywhere.

4. Arousing the fires of the body so that the centres become active, luminous, connected and coordinated.

5. Producing a coordination between:

a. The ego or soul on its own plane,

b. The brain via the mind,

c. The centres. By an act of the will they can  all be thrown into uniform activity.

6. This effected, the fire at the base of the spine, dormant hitherto, will be aroused and can proceed upward with security, blending ultimately with the fire or light in the head, and so pass out, having "burned out all dross, and left all channels clear" for the use of the ego.

7. Developing thus the powers of the soul, the siddhis, higher and lower, so that an efficient server of the race is produced.

When these seven points are borne in mind, it is interesting to note that the symbol of the centre at the base of the spine, the muladhara centre, is the elephant. It is the symbol of strength, of concentrated power, of the great moving force, which once aroused, carries all before it. It is for our fifth root race, the symbol of the most powerful and mighty of the animal kingdom. It is a picture of the transmutation or sublimation of the animal nature, for at the base of the spine is the elephant and in the head is the thousand petalled lotus hiding Vishnu, seated in the centre. Thus is the animal nature carried upward into heaven.

By meditation upon this "elephant force," the power of the third aspect, the energy of matter itself and therefore of God the Holy Ghost or of Brahma, is aroused and conjoined to that of the second or consciousness aspect, to soul energy, that of Vishnu, the second aspect, the Christ force. This produces the perfect at-one-ment, or union between soul and body, which is the true goal Raja Yoga.

Will the students of this science remember h

however, that these forms of one-pointed meditation are only permitted after the eight means of yoga (dealt with in Book II) have been followed.

**25. Perfectly concentrated meditation upon the awakened light will produce the consciousness of that which is subtle, hidden or remote.**

Throughout all teachings of an occult or mystical nature reference is found frequently to what is called the *"Light."* The Bible has many such passages as have all the Scriptures of the world. Many terms are applied to this but space only permits us to consider those to be found in the various translations of the *Yoga Sutras of Patanjali*. They might be enumerated as follows:

a. The awakened inner Light (Johnston),
b. The Light in the head (Johnston),
c. The Light of immediate cognition (intuitive knowledge) (Tatya),
d. That effulgent Light (Vivekananda),
e. The Light from the top of the head (Vivekananda),
f. The coronal Light (Ganganatha Jha),
g. The Light of the luminous disposition (Ganganatha Jha),
h. The inner Light (Dvivedi),
i. The mind, full of Light (Dvivedi),
j. The radiance in the head (Woods),
k. The luminosity of the central organ (Rama ·asad),

The Light of the higher sense-activity ma Prasad).

·om a study of these terms it will be apparent

that within the physical vehicle there is to be found a point of luminosity which (when contacted) will pour the light of the spirit upon the path of the disciple, thus illuminating the way, revealing the solution of all problems, and enabling him to stand as a light bearer to others.

This light is in the nature of an internal radiance, its position is in the head, in the neighborhood of the pineal gland, and it is produced by the activity of the soul.

A good deal of discussion has been aroused, by the term "central organ" associated with this light. Some commentators refer this to the heart, others to the head. Technically neither of them are entirely right, for to the trained adept the "central organ" is the causal vehicle, the *karana sarira*, the body of the ego, the sheath of the soul. This is the middle of the "three periodical vehicles" which the divine Son of God discovers and utilizes in the course of his long pilgrimage. These find their analogies in the three temples found in the Christian Bible:

1. The transitory ephemeral tabernacle in the wilderness, typical of the soul in physical incarnation, persisting for one life.

2. The more permanent and beautiful temple of Solomon, typical of the soul body or causal vehicle, of longer duration and persisting for aeons, and increasingly revealed in its beaut' upon the Path up to the third initiation.

3. The, as yet, unrevealed and inconceivab' beautiful, temple of Ezekiel, the symbol of sheath of the spirit, the home of the Father,

of the "many mansions," the "auric egg" of the occultist.

In the science of yoga, which has to be wrought out and mastered in the physical body the term "central organ" is applied to the head or the heart, and the distinction is one of time primarily. The heart in the earlier stages of unfoldment upon the Path is the central organ; later it is the organ in the head where the true light has its abiding place.

In the process cf unfoldment, heart development precedes head development. The emotional nature and the senses unfold prior to the mind, as can be seen if we study humanity as a whole. The heart centre opens before the head centre. Love must ever be developed before power can be safely used. Therefore the light of love must be functioning before the light of life can be consciously employed.

As the lotus centre of the heart opens and reveals the love of God, through meditation a synchronous unfoldment takes place within the head. The twelve petalled lotus in the head (which is the higher correspondence of the heart centre, and the intermediary between the twelve petalled egoic lotus on its own plane and the head centre) awakens. The pineal gland is gradually brought from a state of atrophy to full functioning activity and the centre of consciousness is transferred out of the emotional nature into the illuminated mind consciousness. This marks the transition which the mystic has to make onto the path of the occultist, keeping, as he always does, his mystical

[ 293 ]

knowledge and awareness but adding to it the intellectual knowledge and conscious power of the trained occultist and yogi.

From the point of power in the head the yogi directs all his affairs and undertakings, throwing upon all events, circumstances and problems the "awakened inner light." In this he is guided by the love, insight and wisdom which is his through the transmutation of his love nature, the awakening of his heart centre and the transference of the fires of the solar plexus to the heart.

It might be asked very pertinently here how this junction between head and heart, producing the luminosity of the central organ and the emission of the inner radiance can be brought about. Briefly stated, it is produced as follows:

1. *Through the subjugation of the lower nature* which transfers the activity of all the life below the solar plexus and including the solar plexus, into the three centres above the diaphragm, the head, heart and throat. This is done through life, love and service, not through breathing exercise and sitting for development.

2. *Through the practice of love,* the focussing of the attention upon the heart life and service, and the realization that the heart centre is the reflection in man of the soul, and that this soul should guide the heart issues from the throne or the seat between the eyebrows.

3. *Through a knowledge of meditatio* Through meditation, which is the exemplificati of the basic yoga aphorism "energy follⁿ thought," all the unfoldments and developmⁿ

which the aspirant desires are brought about. Through meditation, the heart centre, which in undeveloped man is pictured as a closed lotus *turned downwards,* is reversed, turned upwards and unfolded. At its heart is the light of love. The radiance of this light, being turned upwards, illumines the path to God, but is not the Path, except in the sense that as we tread upon that which the heart desires (in a lower sense) that path leads us on to the Path itself.

Perhaps clarity will come if we realize that part of the path is within ourselves and this the heart reveals. It leads us to the head, where we find the first portal of the Path proper and enter upon that part of the path of life which conducts us away from the body-life, to the fullest liberation from experience in the flesh and in the three worlds.

It is all one path, but the Path of Initiation has to be trodden consciously by the thinker functioning through the central organ in the head, and from there intelligently traversing the Path which leads through the three worlds to the realm or kingdom of the soul. It might be stated here that the awakening of the heart centre leads a man to consciousness of the source of the heart centre within the head. This in turn leads a man to the twelve-petalled lotus, the egoic centre on the higher levels of the mental plane. The path from the heart centre to the head, when followed, s the reflection in the body of the building of e antaskarana on the mental plane. "As above, below."

4. *Through perfectly concentrated meditation in the head.* This carries on automatically the increased stimulation and awakening of the centres up the spine, five in number, arouses the sixth centre, the one between the eyebrows, and in time reveals to the aspirant, the exit at the top of the head, which can be seen as a radiant circle of pure white light. This begins as a mere pin point and passes through various stages of increasing glory and radiant light until the Portal itself stands revealed. More along this line is not permissible.

This light in the head is the great revealer, the great purifier, and the medium whereby the disciple fulfills the command of the Christ, "Let your light shine." It is the "path of the just which shineth ever more and more until the perfect day." It is that which produces the halo or circle of light seen around the heads of all the sons of God who have come or are coming into their heritage.

Through this light, as Patanjali here points out, we become conscious of that which is subtle, or of those things which can only be known through a conscious use of our subtle bodies. These subtle bodies are the means whereby we function upon the inner planes, such as the emotional or astral plane and the mental. At present the majority of us function on these planes unconsciously. Through this light we also become conscious of that which is hidden or as yet unrevealed. The Mysteries are revealed to the man whose light is shining and he becomes a knower

That which is remote or the future is likewise unfolded to him.

**26. Through meditation, one-pointedly fixed upon the sun, will come a consciousness (or knowledge) of the seven worlds.**

This passage has been commented upon at length by many writers for many centuries. Simply for the sake of clarity let us modernize the statement and reduce its terms to those of modern occultism.

"By constant steady meditation upon the emanating cause of our solar system will come a realization of the seven states of being."

The various terms used here serve frequently to confuse the student and it might be wise if we used only two sets of terms, one conveying the orthodox oriental terminology as found in the best commentaries, and the other the one most easily recognizable by the western investigator. Using Woods' translation we find the following:

Svar
- Brahma
  - 7. Satya.......the world of those Gods who are unmanifest.
  - 6. Tapas......the world of the self-luminous Gods.
  - 5. Jana.........the lowest of the Brahma world.
- 4. Mahar Prajapatya....the great world.
- 3. Mahendra............the home of the Agnishvattas (the Egos).

2. Antariksa............the intermediate space.
1. Bhu............the earth world.

This differentiation of the world into seven

great divisions is also interesting in so far as it demonstrates the equal accuracy of the fivefold division which some of the commentators hold.

These seven worlds correspond to the modern occult division of our solar system into seven planes embodying seven states of consciousness and enfolding seven great types of living beings. The analogy will be seen as follows:

1. Physical Plane..Bhu..........................Earth world.
   Physical conscious-
   ness.
2. Astral Plane......Antariksa..............World of the emotions.
   Kamic or desire con-
   sciousness.
3. Mental Plane....Mahendra..............World of the mind and
   of the soul.
   Mind consciousness.
4. Buddhic Plane..Mahar Prajapatya..Christ world.
   Intuitional or Christ
   consciousness.
   Group consciousness.
5. Atmic Plane......Jana.........................Spiritual world.
   Planetary conscious-
   ness.
   World of the third
   aspect.
6. Monadic Plane..Tapas....................Divine world.
   God-consciousness.
   World of the second
   aspect.
7. Logoic Plane....Tatya......................World of the emanating cause.
   Absolute conscious-
   ness.
   World of the first
   aspect.

[ 298 ]

## BOOK III

It is interesting to note certain comments of Vyasa on this differentiation, for they blend in with modern Theosophical thought.

The earth plane is described by him as "supported respectively by solid matter, by water, by fire, by wind, by air and by darkness . . . wherein living creatures, having been allotted a long and grievous length-of-life, feeling the misery incurred as the result of their own karma, are born." Comment here is needless.

In connection with the second plane, the astral, reference is made to the fact that the stars (the lives), on that plane are "driven by the wind as cows are driven by the ploughman in a circle around the threshing floor" and that they are "regulated by the steady impulsion of the wind." We have here a wonderful picture of how all lives are driven by the force of their desires on the wheel of rebirth.

Vyasa notes that the mind world is peopled by six groups of Gods (the six groups of egos and their six rays, the six subrays of the one synthetic ray, which is apparently inferred). These are the sons of mind, the Agnishvattas (referred to at length in the *Secret Doctrine* and in *A Treatise on Cosmic Fire*) and they are portrayed as:

1. Fulfilling their desires, therefore driven by desire to incarnate,

2. Endowed with atomisation and other powers, therefore able to create their vehicles of manifestation,

3. Living for a mundane period, therefore in incarnation during a world period,

4. Goodly to behold, for the sons of God **are** luminous, radiant and full of beauty,

5. Delighting in love, for love is the characteristic of the soul, and all sons of God, or sons of Mind reveal the love of the Father,

6. Possessing bodies of their own "not caused by parents," that body "not made by hands, eternal in the heavens" mentioned by St. Paul.

In connection with the fourth world, Vyasa notes that it is the world of mastery, therefore the home of the Masters, and all liberated souls whose "food is contemplation" and whose lives are "for a thousand mundane periods," therefore who have immortality.

Then he describes the three highest planes, with the great existences who are the lives of those planes and in whom we "live and move and have our being." These correspond to the three planes of the Trinity and of these existences in their various groups, the following comments by Vyasa are illuminating. He states:

1. "Their lives are chaste," *i. e.*, free from impurity, or the limitations of the lower forms.

2. "Upwards there is no impediment to their thinking and in regions below there is no object obscure to their thought." They know all things within the solar system.

3. "By them no laying down of foundations for a dwelling is made," therefore they have no dense bodies.

4. "They are grounded in themselves . . . and live as long as there are creations." They are the great lives back of all sentient existence.

5. They delight in contemplation of varying kinds. Our worlds are but the reflection of God's thought and they are the sum total of the mind of God.

The ancient commentator sums up by making two basic statements which should be noted by the student. He says:

"This whole well-founded configuration stretches out in the midmost part of the (World) Egg. And the Egg is a minute fragment of the primary cause, like a firefly in the sky."

This means that our solar system is but a cosmic atom and is itself only a part of a still greater spheroidal whole. Then he states:

"By performing constraint upon the door of the sun, the yogin should directly perceive all this." Constraint is a term frequently used in translating phrases which mean "the harnessing or restraining of the modifications of the thinking principle;" in other words, perfect one-pointed meditation. By meditation upon the door of the sun full knowledge can be achieved. This means very briefly that through a knowledge of the sun within one's own heart and, through the light emanating from that sun, having found the portal of the path, one enters into relationship with the sun which is at the heart of our solar system and eventually finds that portal which admits a man to the sevenfold cosmic path. Of this no more need be said, as the object of Raja Yoga is to enable a man to find the light within himself and in that light see light. It enables him also to find the door to life and subsequently to tread the path.

Only one more point need be touched upon. Esoterically the sun is regarded as triple:

1. The physical sun ....................body .......intelligent form.
2. The heart of the sun.................soul..........love.
3. The central spiritual sun........spirit ......life or power.

In man, the microcosm, the correspondences are:

1. The personal physical man.... body........intelligent form.
2. The ego or Christ......................soul..........love.
3. The monad ..................................spirit ......life or power.

### 27. A knowledge of all lunar forms arises through one-pointed meditation upon the moon.

There are two translations permissible here, the above and the following:

"A knowledge of the astral world comes to him who can meditate upon the moon." Either is correct and probably a true understanding of the Sanskrit is only arrived at through combining the two. It might suffice here to give a simple English paraphrase which will give the essence of the significance of this sutra:

"One-pointed concentration upon the mother of forms (the moon) will reveal to the aspirant the nature and purpose of form."

If the student will remember that the moon is the symbol of matter, whereas the sun in its aspect of light is the symbol of the soul, he will have no difficulty in ascertaining the meaning of the two sutras we have just considered. One deals with the soul and the various states of consciousness; the other deals with the body, the vehicle of consciousness. One concerns the body incorruptible, not made with hands, eternal in the heavens. The other deals with the "lunar mansions" (as one translator calls it) and with the home of the soul in the three worlds of human endeavour.

We must be careful however to remember that the moon aspect is the governing one in all the kingdoms below the human, whilst the sun aspect should dominate in the human.

A knowledge of the lunar mansions or of forms would give an understanding of the physical body, of the astral or desire vehicle and of the mental sheath.

**28. Concentration upon the Pole-Star will give knowledge of the orbits of the planets and the stars.**

This sutra is of small significance to the ordinary student, but is of profound use to the initiate or pledged disciple. Suffice it here to say that this sutra forms the background for all astrological investigation and from an appreciation of its meaning will eventuate an understanding of:

1. The relation of our solar system to the other six constellations which (with ours) form the seven force centres of which the seven great spiritual influences of our system are the reflections and agents.

2. The path of our sun in the Heavens and the twelve signs of the Zodiac through which our sun apparently passes. Therefore it will be apparent that this sutra is the key to the purpose of the

[ 303 ]

seven and the twelve upon which all our creative processes are built.

3. The meaning of the twelve labours of Hercules in their relation to man, the microcosm.

4. The purpose of our planet, gained by the adept through an understanding of the triplicity formed by:

a. The Pole Star,

b. Our Earth Planet,

c. The Great Bear.

Other meanings are available to those who hold the key, but the above will suffice to show the deep, though esoteric significance attached to these brief words.

**29. By concentrated attention upon the centre called the solar plexus, comes perfected knowledge as to the condition of the body.**

In the commentary upon Book I Sutra 36, the various centres were enumerated and their qualities given. In this section of the book, five of these centres are mentioned and they are the five which most closely concern the aspirant, and which are the most dominant in the fifth or Aryan race, being awakened but not unfolded in the fourth race. These are:

1. The centre at the base of the spine................4 petals,
2. The solar plexus centre...........................10 petals,
3. The heart centre..................................12 petals,
4. The throat centre.................................16 petals,
5. The head centre................................1000 petals.

With these five, the aspirant is primarily concerned. The centre called the spleen was dominant in Lemurian days but is now relegated to the domain of the fully functioning and therefore automatic centres, and has sunk below the threshold of consciousness. The centre between the eyebrows is the one through which the light in the head is cast upon things "subtle, obscure, hidden or remote" and is a result of the unfolding of the head and heart.

The three major centres are so powerful in the most unevolved person even in their unopened state that they have produced physical correspondences or glands. Their vibration is such that already in all men they *sound,* and through sounding attract and consequently produce a form. In the disciple or initiate these three centres not only sound but *form words*; they therefore command the building of vital forces and take the entire man under control.

The glands corresponding to the three centres are:

1. The pineal gland and pituitary body..... Head centre,
2. The thyroid gland........................................ Throat centre,
3. The spleen..................................................... Heart centre.

"Out of the heart are the issues of life"; from it the current of the life blood circulates; from its development in the Atlantean race and the consequent coordination and growth of the astral or emotional body, the heart centre has become the most important in the body. Its activity and development has been paralleled by the spleen, which is the organ of vitality, of prana or physical sun force, in the body.

## BOOK III

There are other glands having a close relation to the various centres but the subject is too vast to be more than hinted at here. There is not, however, the same close relation existing between the glands associated with the centres below the diaphragm as with those connected with the major centres, situated above the diaphragm.

In the sutra under consideration we are dealing with one of the five most important centres, and this for the reason that:

1. It is situated in the centre of the trunk. It is therefore a correspondence of the middle principle. In man in Atlantean days the three major centres for that race were:

a. The Head..............................Father or spiritual aspect,
b. The Solar Plexus..................The Son or soul aspect,
c. The Base of the Spine........The Holy Ghost or matter aspect.

The soul was not then so individualized as it is now. The animal soul controlled, and consequently full contact with the anima mundi was the dominant factor. As time elapsed, the soul became more individualized in each human being, and more and more separative, as the mind aspect (the great dividing factor) dominated. At the close of this race, the three main centres will be the head, the heart, and the base of the spine. In the sixth race we shall have, the head, the heart, and the throat.

In the final race of the illuminated sons of God, the seventh, we shall have as the centres through which they work:

a. The thousand petalled head center....life or spiritual
aspect,
b. The centre between the eyebrows........Son or consciousness aspect,
c. The throat................................................The Holy Ghost
or creative as-
pect.

Through the first, spiritual life will pour in from the monad; through the second, the Christ principle, the light of the world, the soul will work, pouring light and life on all things, and using it as the great organ of awareness. Through the last, the work of creation will be carried on, and the creative word sent forth.

This general view is given so as to present to the student the vision of what lies ahead. It is, however, of no present value; most aspirants are concerned with the solar plexus and hence the necessity of our present consideration.

2. It is the organ of the astral nature, of the emotions, moods, desires and feelings and hence is most active in all. It is through it that the lower bodily functions are aroused—desire to eat, to drink, and to procreate, and through it the lower centres are contacted and work with them is carried forward. In the disciple, the heart supersedes the solar plexus; in the Master, the head. All the centres, however, are the expression of the life and love of God, and in their totality and perfection express the Christ life.

3. It is the centre wherein is carried forward the great work of transmuting all the lower and animal desires into the higher. Through it liter-

ally must be passed the forces of the lower nature. It gathers up the forces of the body below the diaphragm and directs them upward.

4. In the solar plexus, the animal soul becomes merged in the soul of man, and the Christ consciousness is seen in germ. Taking the analogy of the antenatal state and the germinating of the Christ in each human being, students who have their intuition developed will see the correspondence between the activity of the solar plexus and its function, and the first three and one-half months of the antenatal period. Then comes what is called the "quickening" and life makes itself felt. A rising up takes place, and the correspondence can then be seen between the natural physiological process and the birth of the Christ in the cave of the heart. Herein lies the deep mystery of initiation, and it is only revealed to those who tread the Path of Discipleship to the end.

We are told in this sutra that knowledge as to the condition of the body comes through meditation upon this centre. The reason is this: when man arrives at an understanding of his emotional body and of the force centre through which it functions upon the physical plane, he finds that all that he is (physically and etherically) is the result of desire, of kama, and that it is his desires which chain him upon the wheel of rebirth. Hence the emphasis laid by the yogi upon that basic *discrimination* through which a man develops the capacity to choose between the real and the unreal and which cultivates in him a just sense of values. Then follows *dispassion* which, when developed, gives him a distaste for the life of sensuous perception.

When the aspirant can grasp the place that desire plays in his life, when he realizes that it is his emotional or astral body which produces the greater part of the trouble in his lower nature, and when he can grasp the technical side of the process which desire-energy follows, then the work of the solar plexus is understood and he can begin the great dual work of transference and transmutation. He has to transfer the energy of the centres below the diaphragm into those above, and in the process transmute and change the energy. The centres are to be found up the spine, but it aids the student considerably if he can grasp the idea of the relative localities in the body which are energized and affected by these centres. All these centres have physical plane organs which are the result of the response of dense substance to their vibration.

### The Three Major Centres.

1. Head centre.............brain, pineal gland and pituitary body,
2. Throat.......................larynx, vocal cords and palate, thyroid gland,
3. Heart.........................pericardium, ventricles, auricles with spleen affected.

### The Four Minor Centres.

4. Solar plexus.............stomach,
5. Spleen.......................spleen,
6. Sacral........................generative organs,
7. Base of spine...........eliminative organs, kidneys, bladder.

These physical organs are results or effects; the centres are their physical cause and they are produced through the activity of the etheric centres.

These details have been given and the above information collated, owing to the importance of the solar plexus in this fourth round of the fourth creative Hierarchy (the Hierarchy of human monads or spirits), the fourth centre in man whether considered upward or downward. One more technical point might here be given. In the process of transmutation the student should remember that:

a. The energy at the base of the spine must go to the head,

b. The energy of the sacral centre must go to the throat,

c. The energy of the solar plexus must go to the heart. Splenic energy concerns solely the physical body. It goes to all the centres.

**30-31. By fixing the attention upon the throat centre, the cessation of hunger and thirst will ensue. By fixing the attention upon the tube or nerve below the throat centre, equilib·rium is achieved.**

It should be remembered that all the sutras which deal with psychic powers are capable of a lower and a higher interpretation. This is nowhere more apparent than in this sutra. Through an understanding of the nature of the throat centre and a steady meditation upon it, the yogi can arrest the pangs of hunger and of thirst and thus do without food indefinitely, whilst through directing energy to that portion of the great nerve in the throat which lies just below the throat centre (found in the well or pit of the throat) he can achieve absolute immobility and rigidity of the human form. Similarly through concentration upon the solar plexus he can become aware in full consciousness of every part of his physical body. But these concern the lower siddhis or powers and with these the student of Raja Yoga is not concerned, regarding them as the secondary effects of soul development. He knows them to be the result of the correct following of the eight means of yoga, and therefore automatic and inevitable results. He knows too the danger to the physical organism when their lower or physical aspect is emphasized.

The true significance of the above sutras which are here bracketed together, grows out of an understanding of the transmutative process and the transference which is effected in the solar plexus.

The energy of the sacral centre which feeds the generative organs is in due course of time transferred into the throat centre. The creative process is then carried on by thought, sound and the spoken Word. Hunger and thirst are the two aspects of desire, the one, hunger, being positive, masculine and grasping; the other, thirst, being negative, feminine and receptive. Those two words are but symbols of the two great impulses underlying the sex impulse. When these impulses are dominated and controlled, then the energy of the centre lying behind the organs concerned, can be carried upward to the throat, and hunger and thirst are arrested in the esoteric sense. It should be borne in mind here that these two words are the physical plane analogies to the great pairs of opposites which the yogi has to balance and which he does balance when the solar plexus is performing its highest function.

On the astral or desire plane, within the astral body of the aspirant, must this balancing process be wrought out to completion. This is the great battleground, symbolized so beautifully for us in the human body, with its three higher centres, its lower energy focal points and that great middle centre, the solar plexus, typifying the astral plane and its work. It will now be apparent why the two sutras are read as one, for they cover one completed work.

After achieving some measure of equilibrium, the aspirant learns to perfect that balancing process and gains the power to stand firm and immovable, preserving an unshakable equilibrium between the pairs of opposites. The nerve, called "kurma-nadi" or the "tortoise tube" is the physical correspondence to the point the aspirant has reached. He stands erect and unshaken before the entrance to the path; he is at the point in his evolution where he can "escape upward" and function in the head.

The tortoise has from the earliest ages been th symbol of the slow creative process, and of t long evolutionary road travelled by the spi Hence the appropriateness of this term, as ap to what is considered the lowest of the three r

centres, and the one which represents the Creator
or Brahma aspect of divinity, of God, the Holy
Ghost, with His function as the energizer of matter or body.

**32. Those who have attained self-mastery
can be seen and contacted through focussing
the light in the head. This power is developed
in one-pointed meditation.**

This is a paraphrase of a very general nature,
but gives the exact sense of the terms employed.
In the twenty-fifth sutra we considered the nature
of the light in the head. Here it might briefly be
stated that when the aspirant is aware of the light
in the head, and can utilize it at will, turning its
radiance upon all that he seeks to know, the time
comes when he can not only turn it *outward* on to
the field of knowledge wherein he functions in the
three worlds, but can turn it inward and direct
it upward into those realms wherein the saints of
God, the great "Cloud of Witnesses" walk. He
can, therefore, through its medium, become aware
of the world of the Masters, Adepts and Initiates
and thus contact them in full waking consciousness, registering those contacts with his physical
brain apparatus.

Hence the necessity of becoming aware of one's
wn light, of trimming one's lamp and of using
e light that is in one, to the full. By use and
·e, the power of the spiritual light grows and
·es and develops a dual function.

ιe aspirant becomes a light or lamp set in a

dark place and illumines the way for others. Only thus can the light within be fanned to a flame. This process of lighting others and being a lamp must always precede that wonderful experience wherein the mystic turns his lamp and light into other realms and finds the "way of escape" into those worlds where the Masters work and walk.

This point needs emphasis for there is too strong an inclination among students to search for the Masters or some Guru or Teacher who will "give" them light. They can only be found by the one who has lit his own light, trimmed his own lamp and thus provided himself with the means of penetrating into Their world. The more technical side of this matter has been well covered in the words of W. Q. Judge:

"There are two inferences here which have nothing to correspond to them in modern thought. One is, that there is a light in the head; and the other, that there are divine beings who may be seen by those who thus concentrate upon the 'light in the head.' It is held that a certain nerve, or psychic current, called Brahmarandhra-nadi, passes out through the brain near the top of the head. In this there collects more of the luminous principle in nature than elsewhere in the body and it is called jyotis—the light in the head. And, as every result is to be brought about by the use of appropriate means, the seeing of divine beings can be accomplished by concentration upon the part of the body more nearly connected with them. This point—the end of Brahmarand nadi—is also the place where the connection is made between man and the solar forces."

It is this light which causes the "face to shine" and is responsible for the halo depicted around the head of all saints and Masters and which is seen by those with clairvoyant vision around the head of all advanced aspirants and disciples.

Dvivedi also gives the same teaching in the following words:

"The light in the head is explained to be that collective flow of the light of sattva which is seen at the Brahmarandhra which is variously supposed to be somewhere near the coronal artery, the pineal gland, or over the medulla oblongata. Just as the light of a lamp burning within the four walls of a house presents a luminous appearance at the keyhole, so even does the light of sattva show itself at the crown of the head. This light is very familiar to all acquainted even slightly with Yoga practices and is seen even by concentration on the space between the eyebrows. By Samyama (meditation) on this light the class of beings called siddhas—popularly known in theosophic circles as Mahatmas or high adepts— able to walk through space unseen, are immediately brought to view, notwithstanding obstacles of space and time."

**33. All things can be known in the vivid light of the intuition.**

There are three aspects of knowledge associ- with the light in the head.

rst, there is that knowledge which the ordinary man can possess, which perhaps is best expressed in the word *theoretical*. It makes a man aware of certain hypotheses, possibilities and explanations. It gives to him an understanding of ways, means and methods, and enables him to take the first step towards correct ascertainment and achievement. This is true of that knowledge which Patanjali deals with. By acting upon this knowledge and by conforming to the requirements of the intended investigation or development, the aspirant becomes aware of the light in the head.

Secondly, discriminative knowledge is the next type utilized by the aspirant. The light having been contacted, is used, and the result is that the pairs of opposites become apparent, duality is known, and the question of choice comes in. The light of God is cast upon either side of the razor edged path the aspirant is endeavouring to tread, and at first this "noble middle" path is not so apparent as that which lies on either side. By the addition of dispassion or non-attachment to discriminative knowledge, hindrances are worn away, the veil which hides the light becomes increasingly thin until eventually the third or highest light is touched.

Thirdly, the "light of the intuition" is one of the terms which can be applied to this type of illuminative knowledge. It results from the treading of the path and the overcoming of the pairs of opposites, and is the forerunner of comple illumination and the full light of day. Gan natha Jha in his brief commentary touches or these three. He says:

## BOOK III

"Intelligence is the emancipator—the forerunner of discriminative knowledge, as the dawn is of sunrise. On the production of intuitional insight, the yogi comes to know everything."

These flashes of intuition are at first simply vivid flashes of illumination, breaking forth into the mind consciousness and disappearing almost instantaneously. But they come with increasing frequency as the habit of meditation is cultivated and persist for increasingly long periods as stability of the mind is achieved. Gradually the light shines forth in a continuous stream until the aspirant walks in the full light of day. When the intuition begins to function, the aspirant has to learn to utilize it by turning the light which is in him upon all matters "obscure, subtle and remote," and thus enlarging his horizon, solving his problems, and increasing his efficiency. What he sees and contacts through the use of this spiritual light has then to be registered, understood and adapted for use by the man upon the physical plane, through the medium of the brain. Here is where the rational mind plays its part, interpreting, formulating and transmitting to the brain that which the true spiritual man on his own plane knows, sees, and understands. Thus this knowledge becomes available in full waking consciousness to the incarnated son of God, the man the physical plane.

Another side of this, equally true and necessary, is pictured for us by Charles Johnston on 123 of his edition. He says:

his divining power of intuition is the power

which lies above and behind the so-called rational
mind; the rational mind formulates a question
and lays it before the intuition, which gives a real
answer, often immediately distorted by the rational mind, yet always embodying a kernel of
truth. It is by this process, through which the
rational mind brings questions to the intuition for
solution, that the truths of science are reached,
the flashes of discovery and genius. But this
higher power need not work in subordination to
the so-called rational mind, it may act directly, as
full illumination, 'the vision and the faculty
divine.' "

**34. Understanding of the mind-conscious-
ness comes from one-pointed meditation upon
the heart centre.**

The sons of men are distinguished from the animal kingdom by the possession of intelligence, of
the rational reasoning mind. Hence in the Ageless Wisdom, the Secret Doctrine of the world,
human beings are frequently called "sons of
mind." It is this which gives them their sense of
individuality, of their separate identity; it is this
which makes them egos.

In the centre of the brain, seated in the pineal
gland, we are told is the home of the soul, an out
post of the life of God, a spark of pure spiritual
fire. This is the lowest point which pure spirit
life, direct from the Monad, our Father in Heav-
en, contacts or reaches. It is the termination
the sutratma, or thread which links and con

the various sheaths and passes from the monad on
its own high plane, via the soul body on the
higher levels of the mental plane down into the
physical vehicle. This life of God is triple and
combines the energy of the Father, the Son and
the Holy Ghost, and is therefore responsible for
the full functioning of all the parts of man's
nature on all planes, and for all states of consciousness. One strand of this triple thread or
path, the first, is the giver of life, of spirit, of
energy. Another, the second, is responsible for
the consciousness or intelligence aspect, for the
power of spirit to respond to contact and to evolve
response. The third concerns the life of the matter or body aspect.

The first aspect via the monad reaches to the
pineal gland—the point where spirit resides in
man. The second or consciousness aspect, via the
ego, makes a point of contact with the heart centre, whilst the third aspect or third part of the
sutratma links up with the centre at the base of
the spine, which is the main source of the personality or bodily activity.

Through concentration, therefore, on the light
in the head, knowledge of the spiritual worlds and
of those pure spirits who work and walk in them
is achieved, for Atma or spirit shines there.
Similarly through concentrated meditation upon
the heart, knowledge of the second aspect, of the
conscious intelligent principle which makes a man
son of God, is gained.

Through the development of the head and the
of the head centre, the will is brought into

functioning activity. It is the characteristic of spirit, and demonstrates purpose and control. Through the unfolding and use of the heart centre the love-wisdom aspect is similarly brought into use and the love of God is seen working out in a man's life and work. For the mind of God is love, and the love of God is intelligence, and these two aspects of one great quality are brought into play for the working out of His will and purpose. Of this the Christ was the outstanding example to the Occident, as Krishna was to India, and this has to be reflected and manifested also in every man.

**35. Experience (of the pairs of opposites) comes from the inability of the soul to distinguish between the personal self and the purusa (or spirit). The objective forms exist for the use (and experience) of the spiritual man. By meditation upon this, arises the intuitive perception of the spiritual nature.**

Again we have quite a loose paraphrase of the original text, but one which nevertheless conveys the correct interpretation.

We have seen in the preceding sutras that the narrow path to be trodden between the pairs of opposites (through the practice of discrimination and dispassion) is the path of equilibrium, or balance, the noble middle path. This sutra is in the nature of a comment upon this stage of the soul's experience and points out the following lessons:

[ 320 ]

First, that the reason we are confronted by the pairs of opposites, and so frequently choose that line of activity or attitude of mind which produces in us pleasure or pain, is because we fail to distinguish between the lower nature and the higher, between the personal self (functioning as a physical, an emotional, and a mental unit) and the divine spirit to be found in each of us. We identify ourselves with the form aspect, and not with the spirit. We regard ourselves as the not-self, for aeons of time and forget our sonship, our unity with the father and the fact that we are, in reality, the indwelling self.

Second, that the purpose of form is simply to enable the self to contact worlds otherwise closed to it, and to develop full awareness in all parts of the Father's kingdom, and thus demonstrate as a fully conscious son of God. Through the form, experience is gained, consciousness awakened, faculty is developed and powers are unfolded.

Third, that as this fact is grasped intellectually and meditated upon interiorly, awareness of one's identity with the spiritual nature and one's distinction from the form is developed. One knows oneself in truth to be, not the form but the indweller, not the material self but the spiritual, not the differentiated aspects but the One alone, and thus the great process of liberation is carried forward. One becomes what one is, and one accomplishes this through meditation on the intelligent soul, the middle aspect, the Christ principle which links the Father (spirit) and the Mother (matter).

Thus the great triplicity is again to be seen:

1.   The Father, or spirit, the one who manifests, who creates, who indwells,

2.   The Son who reveals, meditates and links the highest aspect with the lower,

3.   The Holy Ghost, overshadowing the Mother, intelligent material substance providing the forms through which experience and development are gained.

The one who experiences, who incarnates and who achieves divine expression through the medium of form is the soul, the self, the spiritual conscious man, the Christ within.   When through this experience he has achieved maturity, he reveals the Father or spirit and so fulfills the words of Christ, when He said (in reply to Philip's question "Lord, show us the Father"), "He that hath seen me hath seen the Father" (John XIV.).

**36.   As the result of this experience and meditation, the higher hearing, touch, sight, taste and smell are developed, producing intuitional knowledge.**

Through meditation the aspirant becomes aware of the counterparts of the five senses as they are found in the subtler realms, and through their awakening and conscious use he becomes able to function as freely on the inner planes he does on the physical.   He can then serve intelligently in those realms and cooperate with great evolutionary scheme.

The senses may be defined as those

whereby man becomes aware of his surroundings. In the animal these five senses exist, but the thinking correlating faculty is lacking. They demonstrate as group faculty, analogous to a racial instinct in the human kingdom.

Each of these five senses has a definite connection with one or other of the seven planes of manifestation, and has also a correspondence on all the planes.

| | *Plane* | *Sense* |
|---|---|---|
| 1. | Physical | Hearing |
| 2. | Astral | Touch or feeling |
| 3. | Mental | Sight |
| 4. | Buddhic | Taste |
| 5. | Atmic | Smell |

A further tabulation taken from *A Treatise on Cosmic Fire* will serve to make clear the five different aspects of the five senses on the five planes, and for further information, the student is referred to that *Treatise* pages 186-202.

MICROCOSMIC SENSORY EVOLUTION

| *Plane* | *Sense* | | *Subplane* |
|---|---|---|---|
| Physical | 1. Hearing | 5th | gaseous |
| | 2. Touch, feeling | 4th | first etheric |
| | 3. Sight | 3rd | super-etheric |
| | 4. Taste | 2nd | sub-atomic |
| | 5. Smell | 1st | atomic |
| Astral | 1. Clairaudience | 5th | |
| | 2. Psychometry | 4th | |
| | 3. Clairvoyance | 3rd | |
| | 4. Imagination | 2nd | |
| | 5. Emotional idealism | 1st | |

Mental......1. Higher clairaudience ..........7th ⎫
        2. Planetary psychometry........6th ⎬ Form
        3. Higher clairvoyance ............5th ⎭
        4. Discrimination .....................4th
        5. Spiritual discernment..........3rd ⎫
           Response to group
             vibration ...........................2nd ⎬ Formless
           Spiritual telepathy...............1st ⎭

Buddhic....1. Comprehension ....................7th
        2. Healing ................................6th
        3. Divine vision .......................5th
        4. Intuition ..............................4th
        5. Idealism ..............................3rd

Atmic.......1. Beatitude ............................7th
        2. Active service ......................6th
        3. Realisation ..........................5th
        4. Perfection ...........................4th
        5. All knowledge .....................3rd

In the following table the numbers one, two, three, four and five under each sense refer to the planes of manifestation as given in the first tabulation above.

    *a. The First Sense...........Hearing.*
       1. Physical hearing.
       2. Clairaudience.
       3. Higher clairaudience.
       4. Comprehension (of four sounds)
       5. Beatitude.

    *b. The Second Sense...........Touch or feeling.*
       1. Physical touch.
       2. Psychometry.
       3. Planetary psychometry.
       4. Healing.
       5. Active service.

[ 324 ]

    *c. The Third Sense............Sight.*
1. Physical sight.
2. Clairvoyance.
3. Higher clairvoyance.
4. Divine vision.
5. Realisation.

    *d. Fourth Sense..................Taste.*
1. Physical taste.
2. Imagination.
3. Discrimination.
4. Intuition.
5. Perfection.

    *e. The Fifth Sense............Smell.*
1. Physical smell.
2. Emotional idealism.
3. Spiritual discernment.
4. Idealism.
5. All knowledge.

**37. These powers are obstacles to the highest spiritual realisation, but serve as magical powers in the objective worlds.**

One fact continuously emerges in this text book of spiritual development, and that is, that the psychic powers, higher and lower, are hindrances to the highest spiritual state and must be left behind by the man who can function freed from the three worlds altogether. This is a hard lesson for the aspirant to grasp. He is apt to think that a tendency towards clairvoyance or clairaudience is indicative of progress and a sign that the practice of meditation is beginning to take effect. It might prove just the opposite and in-

[ 325 ]

evitably will, should the aspirant be attracted by, or attached to, any of these forms of psychic faculty. An old Hindu writer says in connection with these powers:

"A mind whose mind stuff is emergent thinks highly of these perfections, just as a man born in misery considers even a small bit of wealth a pile of wealth. But a yogin whose mind-stuff is concentrated must avoid these perfections, even when brought near to him. One who longs for the final goal of life, the absolute assuagement of the threefold anguish, how could he have any affection for those perfections which go counter to the attainment of that goal."

Dvivedi says:

"The occult powers described hitherto and to be described hereafter . . . serve as obstacles because they become the cause of distracting the mind by the various feelings they excite. But they are not quite useless inasmuch as they are great powers for good in moments when samadhi is suspended."

It is of value to the aspirant to know what these powers are, how to control them and not be controlled by them, and how to use them in the service of his brother and of the Hierarchy, but they must be regarded as instruments and be relegated to the form side. It must be realised that they are the qualities or capacities of the sheaths or the *form* aspect, otherwise they will assume undue importance, engross undue attention and prov stumbling blocks to the progress of soul unfo ment.

**38. By liberation from the causes of bondage through their weakening, and by an understanding of the mode of transference (withdrawal or entrance), the mind stuff (or chitta) can enter another body.**

This entire science of Raja Yoga is based upon an understanding of the nature, purpose and function of the mind. The basic law of this science can be summed up in the words "energy follows thought" and the sequence of activity might be stated as follows:

The thinker on his own plane formulates a thought embodying some purpose or some desire. The mind vibrates in response to this idea and simultaneously produces a corresponding reaction in the kamic, desire or emotional body. The energy body, the etheric sheath vibrates synchronously, and thereby the brain responds and energises the nerve-system throughout the dense physical body, so that the impulse of the thinker works out into physical plane activity.

There is a close connection between the mind and the nervous system so that we have an interesting triplicity,

1. The mind,
2. The brain,
3. Nervous system,

and this triplicity must be carefully borne in mind by the student of Raja Yoga in the initial stage of his work. Later a second triplicity will engross his attention,

1.   The thinker,
2.   The mind,
3.   The brain,

but this will be during the demonstration side of his work.

It is through an understanding of the method of energising the nerves that the thinker can galvanise its instrument into activity during incarnation, and similarly produce trance, samadhi, or death.   The same basic knowledge enables the adept to raise a dead body, as Christ did in Palestine, or occupy the vehicle of a disciple for purposes of service, as Christ occupied the body of the disciple Jesus.   This knowledge and its use, we are told, is subject to the great law of karma, of cause and effect, and even the Christ Himself may not set the law aside in any case unless there is adequate "weakening" of the cause producing the bondage.

**39.   By subjugation of the upward life (the udana) there is liberation from water, the thorny path, and mire, and the power of ascension is gained.**

Pervading the whole body is that sum total of nervous force, called by the Hindu, prana.   It is controlled by the mind via the brain; it is the vitality which brings into activity the sense-organs and produces the outward-going life of the man; its medium of distribution is the nervous system through certain great distributing centres called plexi, or lotuses. The nerve ganglia known to orthodox medicine, are the reflections or shadows of the more vital plexi. The student will not go far astray if he regards the sum total of prana in the human body as constituting the vital or etheric body. This etheric body is formed entirely of energy currents, and is the substratum of living substance which underlies the dense physical form.

One term applied to this energy is the "vital airs." Prana is fivefold in its manifestation, thus corresponding to the five states of mind, the fifth principle and to the five modifications of the thinking principle. Prana in the solar system works out as the five great states of energy which we call *planes*, the medium of consciousness; these are:

1. The atmic or spiritual plane,
2. The buddhic or intuitional plane,
3. The mental plane,
4. The emotional, astral or kamic plane,
5. The physical plane.

The five differentiations of prana in the human body are:

1. *Prana*, extending from the nose to the heart and having special relation to the mouth and speech, the heart and lungs.

2. *Samana* extends from the heart to the solar plexus; it concerns food and the nourishing of the body through the medium of food and drink and has a special relation to the stomach.

3. *Apana* controls from the solar plexus to the soles of the feet; it concerns the organs of elimination, of rejection and of birth, thus having spe-

[ 329 ]

cial relation to the organs of generation and of elimination.

4. *Udana* is found between the nose and the top of the head; it has a special relation to the brain, the nose and the eyes, and when properly controlled produces the coordination of the vital airs and their correct handling.

5. *Vyana* is the term applied to the sum total of pranic energy as it is distributed evenly throughout the entire body. Its instruments are the thousands of nadis or nerves found in the body, and it has a peculiar definite connection with the blood channels, the veins and arteries.

In this sutra we are told that by mastery of the fourth of these vital airs, certain definite results can be achieved and it will be interesting to note what they are. This mastery only becomes possible as the Raja Yoga system is understood and mastered, for it involves the capacity to function in the head and to control the entire nature from the point within the brain. When a man becomes polarised there, then the nervous force or energy found in the top of the head becomes active and through its correct control and through mastery of it, the right direction of the pranas of the body becomes possible and man reaches liberation; through it, noncontact in the three worlds is brought about. The language used is necessarily symbolic and its meaning must not be lost through a materializing of its real significance. Levitation, the power to walk on water, and ability to withstand the gravitational pull of the earth is its lowest and least important significance.

## BOOK III

**1.** *Freedom from water* is a symbolic way of stating that the astral nature is subjugated and the great waters of illusion can no longer hold the emancipated soul. The energies of the solar plexus no longer dominate.

**2.** *Liberation from the thorny path* refers to the path of physical life, and is nowhere more beautifully referred to than by the Christ in His parable of the Sowers, where some of the seed fell among thorns. The explanation is given that the thorns are the cares and troubles of worldly existence which succeed in choking the spiritual life and in veiling the true man for so long. The thorny path must lead to the northern path and that in turn to the Path of Initiation. In one of the old books in the Archives of the Lodge, are found these words:

"Let the seeker after truth escape from drowning and climb the river's bank. Let him turn towards the northern star and on firm ground stand, his face directed towards the light. Then let the star lead."

**3.** *Liberation from the mire* refers to that mixed nature of kama-manas, desire and lower mind, which causes the unique problem of humanity. It is a symbolic way also of referring to the great illusion which snares the pilgrim for so long. When the aspirant can walk in the light, having found the light (the Shekinah) within himself in the Holy of Holies, then the illusion is dissipated. It is of value to the student to trace the analogy between the three parts of Solomon's Temple, and that of the "Temple of the Holy Spirit," the human frame.

The *outer court* corresponds to those energies and their corresponding organs found below the diaphragm. The *Holy Place* is the centres and organs in the upper part of the body from the throat to the diaphragm. The *Holy of Holies* is the head where is the throne of God, the Mercy Seat, and the overshadowing glory.

When these three aspects of freedom have been gained and the man is no longer dominated by the water, the mire or physical plane life, then "the power of ascension" is gained and he can ascend into heaven at will. The Christ or spiritual man can stand upon the mountain of ascension, having passed through the four crises or points of control from the birth to the crucifixion. Thus the "udana" or upward life becomes the controlling factor and the downward life no longer dominates.

**40. Through subjugation of the samana, the spark becomes the flame.**

This sutra is one of the most beautiful in the book and the translation by Charles Johnston should here be noted: "By mastery of the binding life comes radiance." Another interpretation might be "through control of samana the AUM (the Word of Glory) manifests." Out of the heart are the issues of life, and the vital energy called samana controls the heart and the life breath through the lungs. When the body is purified and its energies rightly directed, and when rhythm is achieved, then a radiant life is seen.

This will work out literally and not simply metaphorically, for when the life currents are directed by the soul upon the throne, through the nerves and the blood channels, then only the purest atoms will be built into the body and the result will be a shining forth of light through the entire man. Not only will the head be radiating light so that the clairvoyant will see a halo or circle of brilliant colors, but all the body will be irradiated by the vibrant centres of electrical force distributed throughout the body.

**41. By the means of one-pointed meditation upon the relationship between the akasha and sound, an organ for spiritual hearing will be developed.**

To understand this sutra, it is essential that certain relationships are comprehended—relationships between matter, the senses and the one who experiences.

The Christian believes that "all things were made by the word of God." The oriental believer holds that sound was the originating factor in the creative process and both teach that this word or sound is descriptive of the second Person of the divine Trinity.

This sound or word threw into peculiar activity the matter of the solar system, and was preceded by the breath of the Father which started the original motion or vibration.

First, therefore, the breath (pneuma or spirit) impinging upon primordial substance and setting up pulsation, a vibration, a rhythm. Then the word or sound, causing the pulsating vibrating substance to take form or shape, and thus bringing about the incarnation of the second Person of the cosmic Trinity, the Son of God, the Macrocosm.

This process eventuated in the seven planes of manifestation, the spheres wherein seven states of consciousness are possible. All of these are characterized by certain qualities and differentiated from each other by specific vibrating capacities and called by certain terms.

The following tabulation may prove useful if the student will bear in mind that the first triplicity of planes are those of divine manifestation and the lower triplicity constitute the reflection of that divine process and are the three planes of our normal experience. These two triplicities of God and man are connected by the middle plane of at-one-ment or union whereon God and man are made one. This is the Christ plane in Christian phraseology, the buddhic plane in the eastern terminology.

### THE DIVINE PLANES.

Plane  I. Logoic
             or divine..The Sea of
                          Fire ...........God the
                                       Father ...........Will.
Plane II. Monadic..The
                          Akasha ......God the Son....Love-
                                                         Wisdo
Plane III. Spiritual
             or atmic..The Æther..God the Holy-
                                       Ghost ..............Act
                                                         tel

# BOOK III

## PLANE OF UNION OR ATONEMENT

Plane IV. Christ or
      buddhic..Air..Union..Harmony..At-one-ment.

## PLANES OF HUMAN ENDEAVOR.

Plane   V. Mental ..Fire ............Reflection of
                       the Sea of
                       Fire ................Human
                                 will.

Plane VI. Emo-
        tional or
        astral ....Astral
                Light ........Reflection of
                        the Akasha......Human
                                 love and
                                 desire.

Plane VII. Physi-
        cal ........Ether ........Reflection of
                        the Æther ......Human
                                   activity.

On all these planes, consciousness manifests and
the senses, exoteric and esoteric, produce contacts.

Plane    I. Fire ............The Breath.
       II. Akasha ......The Sound....Hearing......The Ear.
    III. Æther ........Vibratory-
                    response....Touch..........The Skin.
     IV. Air ..............Vision............Sight..........The Eye.
      V. Fire ............Discrimina-
                    tion............Taste..........The
                                     Tongue.

     VI. Astral
           Light......Desire............Smell..........The Nose.
    VII. The Physical counterparts to all of these.

er method of working these out is as fol-

# BOOK III

|       |                  |            |                |
|-------|------------------|------------|----------------|
| VII.  | Physical Plane   | Smell      | Ether.         |
| VI.   | Astral           | Taste      | Astral Light.  |
| V.    | Mental           | Sight      | Fire.          |
| IV.   | Buddhic          | Touch      | Air.           |
| III.  | Atmic            | Hearing    | Æther.         |
| II.   | Monadic          | Mind       | Akasha.        |
| I.    | Logoic           | Synthesis. |                |

It will be apparent, however, that one gives the microcosmic standpoint, the other gives the macrocosmic, and as the aspirant is one who seeks to function as "free in the macrocosm" and to transcend his microcosmic limitations, it is the first category with which we will concern ourselves.

In considering this sutra and its clarification by an understanding of the nature of the planes, their symbols and substance, it becomes apparent that the man who understands the nature of the word and of the second aspect, arrives at the realization of hearing.

This might also be grasped mystically by the aspirant when he realizes that when the voices of desire (astral voices or vibratory response to the second aspect of the reflection, the three lower planes) are superseded by the Voice of the Silence or of the Christ within, then the word or sound is known and the second aspect of divinity is contacted.

1. The Akasha....The word....The sound...... ..The second pect in m festatic

2. The Astral Light....The voices of desire..The ref of th ond

[ 336 ]

## BOOK III

There are many sounds to be heard on all the planes but on the physical is the greatest diversity. The aspirant has to develop the power to distinguish between:

1. The voices of earth............................................physical,
2. The voices of desire............................................astral,
3. The speech or formulated thoughts of the mind ...................................................................mental,
4. The still small voice of the Christ within.....buddhic,
5. The sounds of the Gods..............The creative
                                           words........atmic,
6. The word or sound........................The AUM...monadic,
7. The breath ...........................................................logoic,

and in these distinctions are symbolically conveyed the problem of correct hearing on the various planes and in the various states of consciousness. Only the true mystic and aspirant will comprehend the nature of these distinctions.

Just as all the substances of our manifested solar system are differentiations of the akasha, the first differentiation of the primordial stuff, so all these distinctions of sound are differentiations of the one sound; all are divine in time and space. But all have to be heard correctly and all lead eventually to and form in their totality the AUM, the Word of Glory, the Macrocosmic Word.

With the student of Raja Yoga, however, there e three main voices or sounds with which he is porarily concerned:

The speech of the Earth, so as to rightly t,

The Voice of the Silence, so as to hear it.
the voice of his own inner God, the Christ,

[ 337 ]

3. The AUM, the Word of the Father, expressed through the Son, which will, when heard, put him in touch with the Word of God, incarnate in all nature.

When speech is rightly used and the sounds of earth can likewise be stilled, then the Voice of the Silence can be heard. It might be noted here that clairaudience is awareness of the voice of the great illusion and gives a man power to hear on the astral plane. This in its right place and when controlled from above through knowledge, opens the ear to certain aspects of divine expression in the three worlds. It is not the divine hearing referred to in the sutra. In Charles Johnston's comments on this sutra, he covers the ground beautifully as follows:

"The transfer of a word by telepathy is the simplest and earliest form of the 'divine hearing' of the spiritual man, as that power grows, and as, through perfectly concentrated meditation, the spiritual man comes into more complete mastery of it, he grows able to hear and clearly distinguish the speech of the great Companions, who counsel and comfort him on his way. They may speak to him either in wordless thoughts, or in perfectly definite words and sentences."

42. By one-pointed meditation upon the relationship existing between the body and the akasha, ascension out of matter (the three worlds) and power to travel in space is gair

The akasha is everywhere. In it we live move and have our being. All is but one stance, and in the human body are found the correspondences to the various differentiations.

When a man knows himself, and is aware of the relationship existing between the energies working through the seven centres and the seven states of matter and consciousness, then he is liberated and free and can contact at will and without time limitations all those states. There is a relation between one of the seven states of matter and one or other of the centres; through each one of the centres is the door to a certain plane of the planetary spheres. When the disciple has worked out into his life in correct realization the various means of yoga dealt with in the previous books, certain keys and knowledge, certain words and formulas, can be entrusted to him which will, through concentrated meditation give him the freedom of the heavens and the right to pass through certain gateways into the Kingdom of God.

**43. When that which veils the light is done away with, then comes the state of being called discarnate (or disembodied), freed from the modification of the thinking principle. This is the state of illumination.**

Again, we have a free, rather than a literal translation, and in this the true sense of the ~~ar~~haic terms used is preserved instead of aca-~~dem~~ic correctness. The reason for this will be ~~appa~~rent if certain well-known translations are ~~used.~~ They are correct translations but demonstrate the ambiguity which is inevitable when a literal translation of the Sanskrit terms is used.

"An outwardly unadjusted fluctuation is the great Discarnate; as a result of this the dwindling of the covering to the brightness." Woods.

"The external modification (of the internal organ) . . . thoughtless is (called) the great incorporeal (modification) ; therefrom (results) the destruction of the obscuration of the illumination (of intellect)." Tatya.

Vivekananda expresses the sutra in the following terms:

"By making sanyama on the real modifications of the mind, which are outside, called great disembodiedness, comes disappearance of the covering of light."

The great difficulties under which all translators labour is apparent from this and hence the frank paraphrasing of this passage.

There are two thoughts seeking expression in this sutra. One refers to the veil or covering which prevents the illumination of the mind, and the other to the state of realization which is achieved when a man has freed himself from this veil. That which covers up the light (the "bushel" referred to by the Christ in the New Testament) is the changing, fluctuating sheaths or bodies When they are transmuted and transcended th light of God (the second divine aspect) can flo the lower man and he knows himself as he Illumination pours in and he knows himsel something different to the forms through v he is functioning. He is no longer centr longer polarized in his forms, but is actually in a condition of disembodiedness. His consciousness is that of the man out of incarnation, of the true man on his own plane, the real discarnate thinker. St. Paul, as has been pointed out by several thinkers, had a touch of this state of being. He referred to it in these words:

"I knew a man in Christ above fourteen years ago (whether in the body I cannot tell, or whether out of the body I cannot tell; God knoweth) ; such an one caught up to the third heaven. And I knew such a man . . . how that he was caught up into paradise, and heard unspeakable words, which it is not lawful for a man to utter." (II Cor. XII.)

This "third heaven" can be understood in two ways: first, as standing for the mental plane on which is the true home of the spiritual man, the thinker, or a more specific state to be understood as that found on the third or highest of the three abstract levels of the mental plane.

**44. One-pointed meditation upon the five forms which every element takes, produces mastery over every element. These five forms are the gross nature, the elemental form, the quality, the pervasiveness and the basic purpose.**

t should be remembered that this will have a reference, to the macrocosm and to the micro-. It can refer to the five planes of monadic ion, or to the five forms which every element takes on each and every plane, bearing in mind that this is the case as regards the mind apprehension and the modifications of the thinking principle, for mind is the fifth principle, and man is the five pointed star and therefore can (as man) achieve only a fivefold illumination. There are, however, two higher forms and two other modes of perception, *i. e.*, the intuitional and spiritual realization. With these, however, the present sutra has not to do. The head centre is dual in itself and is composed of the centre between the eyebrows and the highest chakra, the thousand petalled lotus.

The study and understanding of this sutra would result in the complete equipping of the white occultist for all forms of magical work. Students must remember that this does not refer to the elements as we have them, but has relation to the elemental substance out of which all gross forms are made. According to the Ageless Wisdom there are five grades of substance having certain qualities. These five grades of substance form the five planes of monadic evolution; they compose the five vibratory spheres in which man and superhuman man are found. These five planes have each an outstanding quality, of which the five physical senses are the correspondence

| Plane | Nature | Sense | Centre |
|-------|--------|-------|--------|
| Earth | Physical | Smell | Base of s |
| Astral | Emotional | Taste | Solar Ple |
| Manasic | Mental | Sight | Head |
| Buddhic | Intuitional | Touch | Heart |
| Atmic | Spiritual | Sound | Throat |

# BOOK III

As pointed out in *A Treatise on Cosmic Fire*, these senses and their correspondences are dependent upon the point in evolution of the man, just as H. P. Blavatsky stated in connection with the enumeration of the principles.

The above sutra therefore can be applied to the mastery of each plane as well as to the mastery of elements composing that plane. It has reference to the mastery and utilization of all the subtler sheaths through which a man contacts a plane or peculiar rate of vibration.

Ganganatha Jha in his able commentary says: "The specific qualities, sound and the rest belonging to the earth, together with the properties of shape and the rest, are named 'gross.' This is the first form of the elements. The second form is their respective generic characteristic: Shape for the earth, viscidity for the water, heat for fire, velocity for air and omnipresence for the akasa. The specific forms for these generic ones are sound and the rest." He gives a translation of this forty-fourth sutra which is analogous to all the others with the exception of Johnston's, and which runs as follows:

"Mastery over the elements, from the sanyama with the reference to grossness, character, subtlety, concomitance and usefulness."

1. Grossness, gross nature.

Sound and the other senses as they show forth n the physical plane. We must bear in mind at this plane is the gross summation of all the ers. Spirit is matter at its lowest point.

. Character, elemental form.

The nature of the specific characteristics of the elements.

3. Subtlety, or quality.

The basic atomic substance of any one element. That which produces its phenomenal effect. It is that which lies back of all sense perception, and of all the five senses. Another word for this "subtle" form is tanmatra.

4. Concomitance, or pervasiveness.

This is the all-pervasive nature of every element; its inherence. It is the sum total of the three gunas, tamas, rajas and sattva. Every element according to its place in the manifested scheme is characterised by inertia, activity or rhythm. It is inherent in substance. Only the rate of vibration differs. There is the correspondence to every element on every plane.

5. Usefulness, or basic purpose.

This is the right use of every element in the great work of evolution. It is literally the power hidden in every atom of substance which drives it on (through all the kingdoms of Nature) to self expression, and enables it to perform its work in time and space and to proceed towards eventual fruition.

When, through concentrated meditation upon the five distinctive forms of all the elements, the knower has arrived at a knowledge of all their qualities, characteristics and nature, he can then cooperate intelligently in the plan and become a white magician. For the majority it is as yet only possible for us to arrive at three of the forms and this is touched upon in Light on the Path the words: "Inquire of the earth, the air and the water, of the secrets they hold for you. The development of your inner sense will enable you to do this."

**45. Through this mastery, minuteness and the other siddhis (or powers) are attained, likewise bodily perfection and freedom from all hindrances.**

Towards the close of each of these three books on Raja Yoga, there comes a sutra summing up results and giving a vision of that which is possible to the faithful intelligent aspirant. They are as follows:

"Thus his realization extends from the infinitely small to the infinitely great, and from annu (the atom or speck) to atma (or spirit) his knowledge is perfected."   (Book I. Sutra 40.)

"As a result of these means there follows the complete subjugation of the sense organs."   (Book II. Sutra 55.)

"Through this mastery minuteness and the other siddhis (or powers) are attained, likewise bodily perfection and freedom from all hindrances."   (Book III. Sutra 45.)

It will be seen from this how, first there is the attaining of the vision and the inner realization of God; then the complete subjugation of the lower nature and the control of the senses and their organs so that the realization becomes fact in physical plane experience, and there comes the manifestation of that control by the display of in powers.

The entire fourth book deals with the great consummation growing out of the three above results, producing:

1. Cessation of sorrow and toil. (Sutra 30.)
2. Attainment of infinite knowledge. (Sutra 31.)
3. Eternity entered. (Sutra 33.)
4. Return of consciousness to its centre. (Sutra 34.)

In connection with the sutra which is our present consideration, the eight siddhis or psychic powers are frequently called the eight perfections and with the two others make up the ten of perfection as it concerns the lower man. These powers are:

1. *Minuteness . . . anima.* This is the power which the yogi possesses to become as small as an atom, to identify himself with the smallest part of the universe, knowing the self in that atom to be one with himself. This is due to the fact that the anima mundi, or soul of the world, is universally spread throughout all aspects of divine life.

2. *Magnitude . . . mahima.* This is the power to expand one's consciousness and thus enter into the greater whole as well as into the lesser part.

3. *Gravity . . . garima.* This concern weight and mass and deals with the law of gravi which is an aspect of the Law of Attraction.

4. *Lightness . . . Laghima.* This is power underlying the phenomenon of levit It is the capacity of the adept to offset the

tive force of the planet and to leave the earth. It is the opposite to the third siddhi.

5. *The attainment of the objective . . . prapti.* This is the capacity of the yogin to achieve his goal, to extend his realization to any locality, to reach anything or any place he desires. It will be apparent that this will have an application on all the planes in the three worlds, as indeed all the siddhis have.

6. *Irresistible will . . . prakamya.* This is sometimes described as sovereignty, and it is that driving irresistible force found in every adept which bring about the fruition of his plans, the attainment of his desires, and the completion of his impulses. It is this quality which is the distinguishing characteristic of the black and the white magician alike. It necessarily demonstrates with greatest force on that plane in the three worlds which reflects the will aspect of divinity, the mental plane. All the elements obey this force of will as used by the yogin.

7. *Creative power . . . isatva.* This concerns the power of the adept to deal with the elements in their five forms and produce with them objective realities, and thus to create on the physical plane.

8. *The power to command . . . vasitva.* The magician as he controls the elemental forces of nature, utilizes this power and it is the basis f mantra yoga, the yoga of sound or of the creative word. Creative power, the seventh siddhi, ncerns the elements and their vitalizing, so that y become "effective causes;" this siddhi, the

eighth, concerns the power of the Word to drive
the building forces of nature into coherent activity so that forms are produced.

When these eight powers are functioning, then
the ninth, bodily perfection, results, for the adept
can construct a vehicle adapted to his need, can
do with it as he will and through its medium attain his objective. Finally, the tenth power will
be seen in full manifestation and no form provides
any hindrances or obstacles to the fruition of the
yogin's will. He is liberated from the form and
its qualities.

46. **Symmetry of form, beauty of colour,
strength and the compactness of the diamond,
constitute bodily perfection.**

Though many commentators, give to this sutra
a purely physical interpretation, a much wider
concept is involved. In it we have pictured for
us in carefully chosen terms (of which the English is but a paraphrase, lacking the expression
fully to convey the idea) the condition of the third
or form aspect through which the second or Christ
aspect is manifesting. This third aspect is itself
triple, yet forms one coherent whole and hence
the use of four terms to express this lower personal self. The occultist never concerns himself
with the dense physical vehicle. He considers the
etheric body to be the true form and the dens-
as simply the material used to fill in the forr
The etheric body is the true substantial form, t
framework, the scaffolding, to which the de-

[ 348 ]

body necessarily conforms. This form must be symmetrical, or built truly according to number and design, and its basic distinction will be the geometrical exactness of its many units. The emotional or astral body is, as is well known, distinguished by its colourfulness, and according to the stage of unfoldment so will the colours be beautiful, clear and translucent, or ugly, dark and cloudy. The astral body of the adept is a thing of radiant loveliness, lacking all the colours of low vibration. Then the highest aspect of the personal self, the mental body will vibrate to the highest aspect of the spirit, which is will, power or strength—any of these words suffice. Strength, beauty and form, the reflections of power, love and activity, these are the characteristics of the body of manifestation of any son of God who has entered into his kingdom. Then the fourth expression conveys the idea of the unity, the coherence of the three, so that they function as a whole and not independently and separately. Man is thus the Three in One and the One in Three, as is his Father in Heaven, being "made in the image of God."

Two words are used by translators to convey this idea of compact cohering force, *i. e.*, the diamond, and the thunderbolt. The human being who has taken the highest of all our planetary initiations is termed "the diamond-souled"—the man who can perfectly transmit the pure white light and yet reflect equally all the colours of the rainbow, the seven colours of the chromatic scale. personality is here called by the same term for it has become a transmitter of the inner light or radiance.

The term "thunderbolt" is equally expressive, conveying as it does the idea of electrical force. All that we can know of God or of man is the quality of his energy as it demonstrates in force and activity, hence in the *Secret Doctrine,* the highest aspect of divinity is called electric fire.

**47. Mastery over the senses is brought about through concentrated meditation upon their nature, peculiar attributes, egoism, pervasiveness and useful purpose.**

Sutra 44, dealt very largely with objectivity and the nature of the five forms which every element assumes. This sutra concerns itself with that which is subjective, and with the subtle apparatus through which forms are contacted and likewise turned to specific purposes. We are dealing here with the indriyas, or senses, which are usually divided by Hindu philosophers into ten instead of five. They divide the five senses into two groups, those which we call the organs of sense, such as the eye, the nose, etc., and then the faculty which makes it possible for the eye to see and the nose to smell.

In considering the senses, the student studies them, therefore, in five connections and this likewise in relation to their counterparts on the astral and mental planes. The five divisions are as follows:

1. *Their nature* He studies each sense in twofold condition, that of the external instrur

and the internal capacity of that instrument to respond to certain vibratory impacts. He knows why, for instance, the organ of sense called the eye vibrates to those impacts which produce the condition of sight, but fails to respond to those impacts which cause scent or smell. He discriminates therefore between the senses and learns thereby to follow a vibratory impulse back to its source along one or other of the five possible lines of approach, and this he does intelligently and not simply blindly.

2. *Their peculiar attributes.* He studies then the quality of the senses, laying the emphasis not so much upon the particular sense concerned (this is covered above) as upon the peculiar attribute of the sense and of that to which it gives the key in the macrocosm.

3. *Egoism,* refers to the "I" making faculty which so predominantly distinguishes the human being and thus brings in the sixth sense, the mind, as the interpreter and synthesizer of the other five. It is the capacity of the human being to say "I see," "I smell,"—a thing the animal cannot do.

4. *Pervasiveness.* All the senses are capable of infinite extension and every sense when consciously followed and utilized can lead a man in three main directions:

    a. To the centre of all things, back to the heart of God,

    b. Into close communication with his fellow man, putting him en rapport with him, when so desired,

    c. Into touch with all forms.

To the average man there is only that which he can hear, touch, see, taste and smell, only five ways in which he can know. There are only five responses possible to him as he contacts vibration of any kind and in our solar system there is naught else but vibrating energy, God in active motion. These five methods put him en rapport with the five elements and when this is realized, the infinite possibilities open to the aspirant, begin to appear. Later to the advanced man another and higher range of vibration opens up when he can use the mind itself, not only as the unifier of all the five senses but as a sixth sense also. This is the object of all Raja Yoga practice. Through the mind, the soul realm is cognized, just as through the senses the objective world was contacted.

5. *Useful purpose.* When the relation of the five senses to the five elements is understood, and the Law of Vibration is studied and mastered, the adept can then turn to useful purposes all the powers of his nature. He not only can enter into communication with all parts of our planetary system but can also use discriminatingly and wisely all those parts of his own nature which are allied to, or correspondences of the nature of God as shown in the macrocosm.

**48. As a result of this perfection, there comes rapidity of action like that of mind, perception independent of the organs, and mastery over root substance.**

We have been considering the many results o

the meditation process when carried forward to perfection and we are now reaching a climax. The seer has achieved the consummation of the alignment process. His triple personal self has been purified, adjusted and controlled. Each of the three bodies is vibrating in tune with the note of the ego or higher self, which in turn is in process of synchronizing with the Monad or divine self, the spirit on its own plane. The great "Son of Mind," the thinker on the higher levels of the mental plane, is the dominating factor now, and the result of this domination is triple, each effect manifesting on all planes yet primarily on one or another. These results are:

1. *Rapidity of action like that of the mind.* The term "swift as a thought" is frequently used when an expression of the intensest rapidity is required. In the yogin his acts on the physical plane are so synchronized with his thought processes, his decisions are so instantaneous and his ends so swiftly achieved that his physical plane life is characterized by a most startling activity and most amazing results Of him it can be said in degree as is said of the Creator: "God meditated, visualized, spoke, and the worlds were made."

2. *Perception independent of organs.* The adept is not dependent upon the organs of sense for the acquiring of knowledge, nor is he dependent upon the sixth sense, the mind.

With him, the intuition has been developed into a usable instrument, and direct apprehension of all knowledge, independently of the reasoning faculty or rationalizing mind is his privilege and right. The mind need no longer be used to apprehend reality, the senses need no longer be employed as mediums of contact. He will employ all six but in a different manner. The mind will be utilized as a transmitter to the brain of the wishes, and plans and purposes of the one Master, the Christ within; the five senses will be transmitters of different types of energy to the chosen objectives, and herein opens up a vast field of study for the interested investigator. The eye is one of the most potent transmitters of energy, and it was the knowledge of this in the olden days which gave rise to the belief anent the evil eye. There is much to be discovered concerning sight for this study will include not only physical vision, but the development of the third eye, clairvoyance, perfect spiritual vision and on up to that inconceivable mystery covered by the terms the "All-seeing Eye" and the "Eye of Shiva."

The hands are potent factors in all magical work of healing and utilization of the sense of touch is an esoteric science. The sublimation of the sense of hearing and its utilization to hear the Voice of the Silence, or the music of the spheres, is a department of occult teaching of the most profound kind and those adepts who have specialized in the science of sight, and the science of sound are some of the most erudite and advanced in the hierarchy.

The other senses are capable too of profound unfoldments, but they are peculiarly hidden in the mysteries of initiation, and more anent them is not possible here. The three senses of hearing, touch and sight are the three characteristics of the three human races and the three planes in our three worlds.

| | | | | |
|---|---|---|---|---|
| 1. Hearing | Lemurian | Physical plane | Ear | Response to sound. |
| 2. Touch | Atlantean | Astral plane | Skin | Response to touch or vibration. |
| 3. Sight | Aryan | Mental body | Eye | Response to vision. |

This third sense primarily affects our race and hence the word of the prophet "Where there is no vision the people perish." The development of sight and the achievement of spiritual insight is the great objective of our race, and the objective of all Raja Yoga work. This may be called "illumination" by the mystic or "pure vision" by the occultist but it is one and the same thing.

The two other senses are as yet *veiled;* their true significance will be unfolded in the sixth or seventh races which are to succeed ours, and their true relation is to the buddhic or intuitional and the atmic or spiritual planes.

3. *Mastery over root substance.* This root substance is the pradhana and is sometimes called the root of all, primordial substance, and root matter. Rama Prasad in his translation and commentary has these words: "Mastery over the Pradhana means the power of control over all

the modifications of the Prakriti. These three attainments . . . are obtained by conquering the substantive appearance of the five instruments of sensation."

It is interesting to note that these three attainments demonstrate:

a. The inability of matter and form to hold the yogi confined,

b. The powerlessness of substance to prevent the yogi cognizing any aspect of manifestation he desires,

c. The helplessness of matter to withstand the will of the yogi.

These three factors explain how it is that the adept can create at will and his freedom from the limitations of matter forms the basis of all white magic.

It might be noted in conclusion that this capacity is in itself relative, for the adept is freed from limitation in the three worlds of human endeavour. The Master has perfect freedom of action in the three worlds plus the buddhic realm, whilst the Christ and those of similar initiation have this freedom in the five worlds of human evolution.

**49. The man who can discriminate between the soul and the spirit achieves supremacy over all conditions and becomes omniscient.**

The condition of the man who can do this has been well described in the comment of Charles Johnston on this sutra and the beauty of his thought will be seen by the study of his words as follows:

"The spiritual man is enmeshed in the web of the emotions; desire, fear, ambition, passion; and impeded by the mental forms of separateness and materialism. When these meshes are sundered, these obstacles completely overcome, then the spiritual man stands forth in his own wide world, strong, mighty, wise. He uses divine powers, with a divine scope and energy, working together with divine Companions. To such a one it is said: 'Thou art now a disciple, able to stand, able to hear, able to see, able to speak, thou hast conquered desire and attained to self-knowledge, thou hast seen thy soul in its bloom and recognized it, and heard the voice of the silence.'"

The wonderful synthesis of the teaching is nowhere more apparent than in this sutra, for the point reached here is of a higher order again than the one referred to in Book II. Sutra 45, and intermediate to the condition mentioned there and that referred to in Book IV. Sutra 30 to 34.

In Book I. Sutra 4, we find the true man entangled in the meshes of the psychic nature and the light in him veiled and hidden. By learning to discriminate between the true self and the lower personal self he disentangles himself, the light which is in him is seen and he is liberated. Having achieved liberation, developed the soul-powers and attained mastery, there opens up before him a still vaster and wider experience and realization. He can begin to expand his consciousness from the planetary to the solar, and group con-

sciousness can be developed into God consciousness. The first step towards this is stated
in the sutra we are now considering, which is
more fully dealt with and hinted at in the final
book. The rules for this expansion are not given,
for they concern the development of the Master
and the unfoldment of the Christ into that higher
state of being which is for Him possible, but the
fourth book touches on the preparatory stages
and hints at further possibilities. Here the first
basic requirement is touched upon, discrimination between the soul, the Christ within and the
spirit or Father aspect. Intelligent activity has
been demonstrated, based upon an unfoldment of
the love nature. With safety now the spirit or
will aspect can be developed and power delivered
into the hands of the Christ.

Three terms serve to throw light on this process
of unfoldment.

The first great realization which the aspirant
has to achieve is that of *omnipresence;* he has to
realize his unity with all, and the oneness of his
soul with all other souls. He has to find God in
his own heart and in every form of life. Then, as
an initiate, he arrives at *omniscience* or all-knowl-
edge, and the Halls of Learning and of Wisdom
render up to him their secrets. He becomes a
Christ, a knower of all things, knowing what is in
the heart of the Father and in the hearts of men.
Finally, he can eventually achieve *omnipotence* or
all-power, when the keys of Heaven will be handed
to the Son of Man and all power will be his.

**50. By a passionless attitude towards this attainment and towards all soul-powers, the one who is free from the seeds of bondage, attains the condition of isolated unity.**

The isolated unity referred to here is that of complete separation from all form aspects and the achievement of spiritual Oneness. It is aloofness from the material consciousness and a living in the spiritual consciousness. It is harmony with the spirit and disharmony with matter. It involves identification with the Father in Heaven, and a true understanding of the word of the Master of all the Masters, "I and My Father are one."

A proper sense of values has been established and the powers which have been developed, and the perceptions which have been gained are seen as having in them the "seeds of bondage" and therefore with them the true yogin does not concern himself. At will and in service he will perceive that which is needed; at will and in service he will employ the occult powers, but he himself remains detached, and freed from all karmic limitations.

**51. There should be entire rejection of all allurements from all forms of being, even the celestial, for the recurrence of evil contacts remains possible.**

Rama Prasad's translation is illuminating and should be quoted here. It runs as follows:

"When the presiding deities invite, there should

be no attachment and no smile of satisfaction, contact with the undesirable being again possible."

And Dvivedi's interpretation gives still another angle:

"There should be entire distinction of pleasure or pride in the invitations by the powers of various places, for there is possibility of the repetition of evil."

The yogin or disciple has achieved his objective. He has (through dispassion and discrimination) freed himself from the trammels of form and stands free and liberated. But he needs to be on his guard for "Let him that thinketh he standeth take heed lest he fall." Form life ever beckons, and the allurements of the great illusion are ever present. The emancipated soul must turn his eyes away from the invitation of the "presiding deities" (those lives who in the three worlds form the sum total of plane life) and fix them on those more spiritual aspects which constitute the life of God Himself.

Even the realm of the soul itself, and the "Voice of the Gods," as it is called, are seen to have latent in them the seeds of attachment; therefore, turning his back upon all that he has gained, and putting behind him all thought of the perfections achieved and the powers developed, the Son of God, the Christ in manifestation, again presses forward towards a higher goal. At every stage of the path, the injunction sounds forth: "Forgetting the things which are behind, press forward" (Phil: III.), and every new initiation but marks the commencement of a new cycle of endeavour.

Commentators upon this sutra point out that there are four classes of chelas or disciples. These are:

1. Those whom the light is just beginning to illumine. They are called "observant of practice," and are those who are just entering the Path. These are the probationers, the aspirants.

2. Those whose intuition is awakening and who demonstrate a corresponding development of psychic power. This is a stage of great danger for such disciples are apt to be allured by the possibilities of power which the possession of psychic faculty opens up. They are apt to be deluded and to consider that psychic power is an indication of spiritual growth and unfoldment. Such is not the case.

3. Those disciples who have overcome all sense attractions and cannot be deluded by the form aspect in the three worlds. They have conquered the senses and are victors over the form nature.

4. Those who have passed beyond all the above and who stand firm in the true spiritual consciousness. These are the illuminated ones, who have progressed through the seven stages of illumination. See Book II., Sutra 27.

If the student will here study Book III. Sutra 26, and the commentary upon it, he will gain some idea of the nature of these worlds of form and their presiding deities whose voices seek to lure the aspirant off the path into the realm of illusion. He will find it also of interest to contrast and compare the first four classes of spirits enumerated

there with these four types of disciples. Everything in the three worlds is a reflection of that
which is found in the heavenly realms and much
may be gained through a comprehension of the
great Hermetic aphorism, "As above, so below."
That reflection is what constitutes evil; that reverse aspect of reality forms the great illusion,
and with these the sons of God have no concern.
It is evil where they are concerned but in no
other sense. The forms of life in these worlds,
and the lives animating those forms are good and
right in themselves and are pursuing their own
evolutionary path, but their immediate objective
and their state of consciousness is not synchronized with that of the evolving disciple and therefore with them there must be no trafficking.

**52. Intuitive knowledge is developed through
the use of the discriminative faculty when there
is one-pointed concentration upon moments and
their continuous succession.**

It has been said that a complete understanding
of the Law of Cycles would bring man to a high
degree of initiation. This Law of Periodicity
underlies all the processes of nature and its study
would lead a man out of the world of objective
effects into that of subjective causes. It has also
been said that time itself is simply a succession of
states of consciousness and this is true of an
atom, a man or a God. It is this truth which
underlies the great systems of mental science and
Christian Science in the occident, and many of th

oriental philosophies. This sutra gives the key to the relation between matter and mind, or between substance and its informing soul, and this can be realized when the words of a Hindu commentator are considered. He says:

"As an atom is a substance in which minuteness reaches its limit, so a moment is a division of time in which minuteness reaches its limit. Or a moment is that much of time which an atom takes in leaving the position in space it occupies and reaching the next point. The succession of moments is the non-cessation of the glow thereof."

When we can realize that an atom and a moment are one and the same, and that back of these lies the Realizer or Cognizer of both, we have got the clue to all states of consciousness itself, and to the nature of energy. We shall also have reached a true understanding of the Eternal Now, and a just appreciation of the significance of the past, the present, and the future. This, we are told here, can be gained by concentrated meditation upon time and its units.

It might be appropriate here to point out that the various kinds of concentration dealt with in this third book are not applicable or appropriate to all types of aspirants. Men are found to exist in seven main types, with distinguishing characteristics and natures and with definite qualities predisposing them to certain definite aspects of the Path of Return. Certain types with mathematical bent and with a tendency to divine geometry and space and time concepts, will with wisdom follow the method of developing intuitive knowledge, dealt with in this sutra; others will find it of great difficulty and would wisely turn to other forms of concentrated meditation.

**53. From this intuitive knowledge is born the capacity to distinguish (between all beings) and to cognize their genus, qualities and position in space.**

The difficulty of this sutra will be obviated if a free paraphrase is here given.

"Through the development of the intuition there will arise exact knowledge of the sources of the manifested life, of its characteristics or qualities, and of its location within the whole."

Right through the *Yoga Sutras* it has been made apparent that the divine triplicities are everywhere to be found, and that every form ensouling a life (and there is naught else in manifestation) is to be known as:

1. *Life.* The life of God emanates from its source in seven streams, emanations or "breaths," and every form in the objective world is the expression of a life as breathed forth on one or other of these streams. The development of the intuition enables the seer to know the nature of the life atom. This is inferred in the word "genus." The modern occultist might prefer the word "ray," and the Christian "pneuma" or spirit, but the thought is one.

2. *Consciousness* or soul. All these living forms of divine life are conscious, even though all states of consciousness are not the same but range from the life of the atom of substance, limited

and circumscribed as it may be, to that of a solar
Logos. The state of the conscious response of
all forms to their environment, exoteric and unseen, produces the varying characteristics plus
the distinction produced by:

a. Ray,
b. Plane of manifestation,
c. Rate of vibration,
d. Point of development,

and these characteristics form the *quality* referred to in the sutra. This is the subjective
aspect in contradistinction to the objective and
the essential.

3. *Form or body.* This is the exoteric aspect,
that which emerges from the subjective as a result of spiritual urge. The *position in space* is
that part of the body of the Heavenly Man in
which any atom or form has its locale. Here it
should be remembered that according to the occult
student "space is an entity" (*Secret Doctrine* I.
583), and this entity is one and the same as the
cosmic Christ, the "body of Christ," referred to
by St. Paul in I. Cor. XII.

In this sutra, therefore, it is made apparent
that the liberated yogi who has developed the intuition can know all things about all forms of life,
and this involves a knowledge of:

| 1. *Genus.* | 2. *Quality.* | 3. *Position in Space.* |
|---|---|---|
| Ray | Character | Place in body of Heavenly Man. |
| Spirit | Soul | Body. |
| Life aspect | Consciousness | Form. |
| Essence | Subjective nature | Objective form. |

[ 365 ]

Of this knower we can apply the words of the teacher whose works are found in the archives of the Lodge:

"To him, standing before the Spark, the flame and the smoke are equally to be seen.

To him, the shadow veils the reflection and yet the light is seen.

To him, the tangible but demonstrates the intangible, and both reveal the spirit, whilst form, color and number speak aloud the word of God."

**54. This intuitive knowledge, which is the great Deliverer, is omnipresent and omniscient and includes the past, the present and the future in the Eternal Now.**

The only part of this sutra which is not clear even to the superficial reader is the significance of the words Eternal Now, and these it is not possible to comprehend until soul-consciousness is developed. To say that time is a succession of states of consciousness and that the present is lost in the past instantaneously, and merged in the future as it is experienced, is of small avail to the average student. To say that there is a time when sight is lost in vision, when the sum total of life anticipations are realized in a moment of accomplishment and that this persists for ever, and to point to a state of consciousness in which there is no sequence of events and no succession of realizations is to speak in a language of mystery. Yet so it is and will be. When the aspirant has reached his goal he knows the true significance of his immortality and the true nature of his libera tion. Space and time become for him meaningless terms. The only true Reality is seen to be the great central life force, remaining unchanged and unmoved at the centre of the changing evanescent temporal forms.

"I am," says the human unit and regards himself as the self, and identifies himself with the changing form. Time and space are for him the true realities. "I am That," says the aspirant and seeks to know himself as he truly is, a living word, part of a cosmic phrase. For him space no longer exists; he knows himself as omnipresent. "I am That I am," says the freed soul, the liberated man, the Christ. Neither time nor space exist for him, and omniscience and omnipresence are his distinctive qualities.

In his comment upon this sutra, Charles Johnston quotes from St. Columba and says:

"Some there are, though very few, to whom divine grace has granted this: that they can clearly and most distinctly see, at one and the same moment, as though under one ray of the sun, even the entire circuit of the whole world with its surroundings of ocean and sky, the innermost part of their mind being marvellously enlarged."

It might be helpful also if the brief comment of Dvivedi were quoted here as it is well put, and the state of consciousness arrived at concisely summed up:

"In aphorism XXXIII. of this section we have already described the nature of taroka-jnana—the knowledge that saves from the bonds of the world. The discriminative knowledge described

[ 367 ]

here results in taraka, the knowledge which is the
end and aim of yoga. It relates to all objects
from the pradhana (spirit-matter. A.B.) to the
bhutas (elements. forms. A.B.), as also to all conditions of these objects. Moreover it produces
knowledge of all things simultaneously, and is
quite independent of the ordinary rules of cognition. Hence it is the highest knowledge which
can be desired by the yogin, and it is a sure index
of Kaivalya (state of absolute oneness. A. B.) to
be described in the following aphorism as its
result."

**55. When the objective forms and the soul
have reached a condition of equal purity, then
is At-one-ment achieved and liberation results.**

That which veils the light of the soul has been
rendered pure, and thus the light of God streams
forth. That which proved a hindrance and an
obstacle to the full expression of divinity in manifestation has been so dealt with that now it serves
as an adequate expression and means of service.
The soul can now function freely and intelligently
in the three worlds because complete unity has
been reached between the lower and the higher
man.

The soul and its vehicles form a unit and are
at one; complete alignment of the bodies has been
achieved and the Son of God can function freely
on earth. Thus has the great objective been
reached and through a following of the eight
means of yoga the soul can manifest through the

lower threefold man, and in its turn form a medium of expression for the spirit. Matter has been brought into a state where its vibration can synchronise with that of the soul, and the result is that—for the first time—spirit can make its presence felt, for "matter is the vehicle for the manifestation of soul on this plane of experience and the soul is the vehicle for the manifestation of spirit on a higher turn of the spiral. These three are a trinity synthesized by life which pervades them all." To the man who has achieved this there is no rebirth. He is free and liberated, and can say with full conscious realization of the significance of the words:

"My life (the lower physical life) is hid with Christ (the soul life) in God (the spirit)." (Col: III. 3.)

## BOOK IV.

### ILLUMINATION

a. Consciousness and form.
b. Union or at-one-ment.
   Topic: Isolated unity.

# THE YOGA SUTRAS OF PATANJALI

## BOOK IV.

### Illumination

1. The higher and lower siddhis (or powers) are gained by incarnation, or by drugs, words of power, intense desire or by meditation.
2. The transfer of the consciousness from a lower vehicle into a higher is part of the great creative and evolutionary process.
3. The practices and methods are not the true cause of the transfer of consciousness but they serve to remove obstacles, just as the husbandman prepares his ground for sowing.
4. The "I am" consciousness is responsible for the creation of the organs through which the sense of individuality is enjoyed.
5. Consciousness is one, yet produces the varied forms of the many.
6. Among the forms which consciousness assumes, only that which is the result of meditation is free from latent karma.
7. The activities of the liberated soul are free from the pairs of opposites. Those of other people are of three kinds.
8. From these three kinds of karma emerge those forms which are necessary for the fruition of the effects.
9. There is identity of relation between memory and the effect-producing cause, even when separated by species, time and place.
10. Desire to live being eternal, these mind-created forms are without known beginning.

[ 373 ]

11. These forms being created and held together through desire, the basic cause, personality, the effective result, mental vitality or the will to live, and the support of the outward going life or object, when these cease to attract then the forms cease likewise to be.

12. The past and the present exist in reality. The form assumed in the time concept of the present is the result of developed characteristics and holds latent seeds of future quality.

13. The characteristics, whether latent or potent, partake of the nature of the three gunas (qualities of matter).

14. The manifestation of the objective form is due to the one-pointedness of the effect-producing cause (the unification of the modifications of the chitta or mind stuff).

15. These two, consciousness and form, are distinct and separate; though forms may be similar, the consciousness may function on differing levels of being.

16. The many modifications of the one mind produce the diverse forms, which depend for existence upon those many mind impulses.

17. These forms are cognized or not, according to the qualities latent in the perceiving consciousness.

18. The Lord of the mind, the perceiver, is ever aware of the constantly active mind stuff, the effect-producing cause.

19. Because it can be seen or cognised it is apparent that the mind is not the source of illumination.

20. Neither can it know two objects simultaneously, itself and that which is external to itself.

21. If knowledge of the mind (chitta) by a remoter mind is postulated, an infinite number of knowers must be inferred, and the sequence of memory reactions would tend to infinite confusion.

22. When the spiritual intelligence which stands alone and freed from objects, reflects itself in the mind stuff, then comes awareness of the Self.

23. Then the mind stuff, reflecting both the knower and the knowable, becomes omniscient.

24. The mind stuff also, reflecting as it does an infinity of mind impressions, becomes the instrument of the Self and acts as a unifying agent.

25. The state of isolated unity (withdrawn into the true nature of the Self) is the reward of the man who can discriminate between the mind stuff and the Self, or spiritual man.

26. The mind then tends towards discrimination and increasing illumination as to the true nature of the one Self.

27. Through force of habit, however, the mind will reflect other mental impressions and perceive objects of sensuous perception.

28. These reflections are of the nature of hindrances, and the method of their overcoming is the same.

29. The man who develops non-attachment even in his aspiration after illumination and isolated unity, becomes aware, eventually, through practised discrimination, of the overshadowing cloud of spiritual knowledge.

30. When this stage is reached then the hindrances and karma are overcome.

31. When, through the removal of the hindrances and the purification of all the sheaths, the totality of knowledge becomes available, naught further remains for the man to do.

32. The modifications of the mind stuff (or qualities of matter) through the inherent nature of the three gunas come to an end, for they have served their purpose.

33. Time, which is the sequence of the modifications of the mind, likewise terminates, giving place to the Eternal Now.

34. The state of isolated unity becomes possible when the three qualities of matter (the three gunas or potencies of nature) no longer exercise any hold over the Self. The pure spiritual consciousness withdraws into the One.

# THE YOGA SUTRAS OF PATANJALI

## BOOK IV.

### ILLUMINATION

**1. The higher and lower siddhis (or powers) are gained by incarnation, or by drugs, words of power, intense desire or by meditation.**

We have now come to the fourth book in which the powers and the results gained by the practice of Raja Yoga are carried forward into group realization and it is seen that they produce universal consciousness and not simply self-consciousness. It seems the part of wisdom to protest here against the use of the words "cosmic consciousness" as untrue and misleading, for even the highest adept (note this term with care) is only gifted with solar consciousness and has no contact with that which is outside our solar system. The planetary Logoi (the seven Spirits before the Throne), and the Lords of Karma (the "four wheels" of Ezekiel) have a realization beyond that of our solar system. Lesser existences may sense it as a possibility but it is not yet part of their experience.

The powers gained fall into two main groups
called:

    a.  Lower psychic powers, the lower siddhis.

    b.  Spiritual powers or the higher siddhis.

The lower powers are the result of the consciousness of the animal soul in man being en
rapport with the anima mundi or the soul of the
world, the subjective side of all forms in the three
worlds, of all bodies in the four kingdoms of
nature. The higher powers are the result of the
development of group consciousness, of the second
aspect of divinity. They not only include the
lesser powers but put a man en rapport with
those existences and forms of life which are to
be found in the spiritual realms, or, as the occultist would say, on those two planes which are
beyond the three worlds, and which cover the
entire scale of man's evolution, human and superhuman.

The goal of the true aspirant is the unfoldment
of these higher powers which can be covered by
the terms direct knowledge, intuitive perception,
spiritual insight, pure vision, the attainment of
the wisdom. They are different from the lower
powers, for they abrogate them. These latter
are accurately described for us in Book III, Sutra
37:

"These powers are obstacles to the highest
spiritual realization, but serve as magical powers
in the objective worlds."

These higher powers are inclusive and are distinguished by their accuracy and infallibility
when rightly employed. Their working is as in-

stantaneous as a flash of light. The lower powers are fallible, the time element is present in its sequential sense and they are limited in their working. They form part of the great illusion and to the true aspirant constitute a limitation.

In the sutra we are considering, five means are given whereby the psychic powers are developed and it is interesting to note that we have in these words an instance of the fact that the *Yoga Sutras* can still be the study and teaching manual of even such advanced aspirants as the Masters of the Wisdom. These five methods are capable of application upon all the five planes of human evolution, which include the two higher planes whereon initiates of the Mysteries function.

1. Incarnation ............ The physical plane method.
2. Drugs .................... The release of the astral consciousness.
3. Words of Power..... Creation by speech, or the method of the mental plane.
4. Intense desire ........ The sublimation of aspiration or the method of the buddhic plane, the sphere of spiritual love.
5. Meditation ............ The method of the atmic plane, the sphere of spiritual will.

In this enumeration, it might be noted that just as intense desire of a spiritual kind is a sublimation of astral or emotional desire, so meditation, as practised by the initiates, is the sublimation of all the mental processes. Therefore the two final methods given as resulting in the unfoldment of the siddhis are the only ones that are practised by initiates, being the synthesis and sublimation of the realizations achieved on the astral and mental planes.

It might, therefore, be observed that (for the seeker after truth) incarnation, intense desire and meditation are the three permissible methods, and the only ones to be practised; drugs and words of power or mantric incantations are the tools of black magic and concern the lower powers.

The question might here be asked, is it not true that words of power and the use of incense form part of the ceremonies of initiation and therefore are used by initiates and aspirants. Certainly, but not in the sense understood here, or for the purpose of developing psychic powers. The Masters and their disciples use words of power in order to deal with the non-human existences, to invoke the aid of the angels, and to manipulate the building forces of nature, and they employ herbs and incenses in order to purify conditions, eliminate undesirable entities and so make it possible for those higher upon the ladder of evolution to make their presence felt. This is, however, a very different thing to their use in order to become psychic.

It is interesting to note here that the first cause producing the unfoldment of soul powers, whether higher or lower, is the great wheel of rebirth. This must ever be taken into account. Everyone is not yet at the stage where it is possible for him to unfold the powers of the soul. The soul aspect is still dormant for many because full experience and development of the lower nature has not yet

▶een undergone. The forty years' wandering in
he wilderness with the Tabernacle and the conquest of Canaan, had to precede the rule of the
kings and the building of the Temple of Solomon.
Lives must be passed before the body, or the
Mother aspect, is so perfected that the Christ
Child can be formed within the prepared vessel.
It should also be remembered that the possession
of the lower psychic powers is in many cases a
symptom of a low stage of evolution and of the
close association of their owner with the animal
nature. This has to be outgrown before the
higher powers can blossom forth.

It is needless to point out that the use of alco-
hol and of drugs can and does release the astral
consciousness, as also the practice of sex magic,
but this is astralism pure and simple and with this
the true student of Raja Yoga has naught to do.
It is part of unfoldment on the left-hand Path.
The gaining of the soul powers by intense desire
(or fervent aspiration) and by meditation has
been covered in the other books and need not be
enlarged upon here.

**2. The transfer of the consciousness from a
lower vehicle into a higher is part of the great
creative and evolutionary process.**

This is a very free translation but conveys a
clear interpretation of the truth to be grasped.
The evolution of consciousness and the effect of
that evolution upon the vehicles in which the
conscious entity functions, is the sum total of the

processes of nature and from the standpoint of the intelligent human unit, three words cover the process and the result. These words are, transfer, transmutation, and transformation.

One of the basic laws in occult development and in spiritual unfoldment is given in the words "As a man thinketh, so is he," and to it one can link the oriental truism, "Energy follows thought" as an explanation. As a man changes his desires, so he changes himself; as he shifts his consciousness from one objective to another, so he alters himself, and this is true in all realms and states, higher or lower.

The effect of the transference of our conscious thinking state from a low objective to a high one produces a flow of energy of a vibratory quality equivalent to the higher objective. This produces a change or a mutation in the vestures of the thinking entity, and they become transmuted and brought to a condition where they are adequate to the thought or desire of the man. Carried to their conclusion, a transformation is produced, and the words of St. Paul become therefore clear: "Be ye therefore transformed by the renewing of your mind."

Change your line of thought and you will change your nature. Desire that which is true and right, pure and holy, and your consciousness of these things will create out of the old a new vehicle or new man, an "instrument meet for use."

This transfer, transmutation and eventual transformation is due to one of two methods:

## BOOK IV

1. A slow method, that of repeated lives, experiences and physical incarnation until eventually the driving force of the evolutionary process brings a man, stage by stage, up the great ladder of evolution.

2. A more rapid process, wherein through such a system as outlined by Patanjali and as taught by all the custodians of the mysteries of religion, a man definitely takes himself in hand, and through conformity to the rules and the laws laid down, brings himself, by his own effort, to a state of spiritual unfoldment. It might be noted here that these three processes bring a man to that initiation called the Transfiguration.

**3. The practices and methods are not the true cause of the transfer of consciousness, but they serve to remove obstacles, just as the husbandman prepares his ground for sowing.**

This is one of the simplest and clearest of the sutras and needs but little comment.

The practices refer primarily to:

1. The means for removing obstacles. (See Book I. Sutras 29 to 39.) This is affected, we are told earlier, by:
   a. Steady application to a principle,
   b. Sympathy with all beings,
   c. Regulation of the prana or life-breath,
   d. Steadiness of the mind,
   e. Meditation upon light,
   f. Purification of the lower nature,
   g. The understanding of the dream state,

h.   The way of devotion.

2.   The way of eliminating obstructions. (Se
Book II. Sutras 2 to 33.) These obstructions ar
eliminated by:

a.   An opposing mental attitude,

b.   Meditation,

c.   The cultivation of right thought.

They concern more specifically the life prepa
ration for the true training in yoga practice
and when practiced, bring the entire lowe
nature into such a condition that the more
drastic methods can produce rapid effects.

The *methods* refer to the eight means of yoga
or union, enumerated as follows: the commandments, the rules, posture or attitude, right
control of the life force, abstraction, attention,
meditation and contemplation. (See Book II.
Sutras 29 to 54, and Book III. Sutras 1 to 12.)

It might be noted, therefore, that we could
refer the practices more specifically to that
stage in the life of the aspirant in which he is
upon the probationary path, the path of purification, whilst the methods relate to the final
stages of that path, and to the path of discipleship. When the practices and methods are followed they bring about certain changes within the forms occupied by the real or spiritual
man, but are not the main cause of the transfer of his consciousness to the soul aspect
and away from the body aspect. That great
change is the result of certain causes, ex-

traneous to the body-nature, such as the divine origin of the man, the fact that the Christ or the soul consciousness is found latent within those forms, and the urge of the evolutionary process which carries the life of God within all forms onward into ever fuller expression. It should be remembered that as the one Life in Whom we live and move and have our being, moves on to greater achievement, so the cells and atoms in His body are correspondingly influenced, stimulated and developed.

**4. The "I am" consciousness is responsible for the creation of the organs through which the sense of individuality is enjoyed.**

Here we have the key to manifestation itself and the reason for all appearances. Just as long as the consciousness of any entity (solar, planetary or human) is outward going towards objects of desire, towards sentient existence, towards individual experience, and towards the life of sensuous perception and enjoyment, just so long will the vehicles or organs be created whereby desire can be satisfied, materialized existence can be enjoyed, and objects perceived. This is the great illusion by which consciousness is glamoured, and as long as the glamour exerts any power, just so long will the Law of Rebirth bring the outward-going consciousness into manifestation upon the plane of materiality. It is the will-to-be and desire for existence that swings outward into the light both the cosmic Christ, functioning on the material plane through the medium of the solar system, and the individual Christ, functioning through the medium of the human form.

In the early stages the "I am" consciousness creates forms of matter inadequate for the full expression of the divine powers. As evolution proceeds these forms become increasingly suitable until the "organs" created enable the spiritual man to enjoy the sense of individuality. When this stage is arrived at, there comes the great realization of illusion. The consciousness awakes to the fact that in form and sense perception, and in the outward going tendency, lie no real joy or pleasure, and there starts a new effort which is characterized by a gradual withdrawal of the outward-going tendency and an abstraction of the spirit from out of the form.

**5. Consciousness is one, yet produces the varied forms of the many.**

Here Patanjali lays down a basic formula which serves to explain not only the purpose and reason of manifestation itself but covers in one short phrase the state of being of God, man and atom. Behind all forms is found the one Life; within every atom (solar, planetary, human and elemental) is found the one sentient existence; back of objective nature, the sum total of all forms in all the kingdoms of nature is found the subjective reality which is essentially a unified whole or unity, producing the diversified many.

The homogeneous is the cause of the heterogeneous, unity produces diversity, the One is responsible for the many. This the student can appreciate more intelligently if he follows the golden rule which reveals the mystery of creation and studies himself. The microcosm reveals the nature of the macrocosm.

He will find that he, the real or spiritual man, the thinker, or the one life in his tiny system, is responsible for the creation of his mental, emotional and physical bodies, his three lower aspects, the "shadow" of the Trinity, just as his spirit, soul and body are the reflections of the three divine aspects, Father, Son and Holy Spirit. He will find that he is responsible for the formation of all the organs in his body, and for all the cells of which they are composed and as he studies his problem more closely he will become aware that his consciousness and life pervades, and is therefore responsible for, myriads beyond number of tiny infinitesimal lives; that he is the cause of their aggregation into organs and forms, and the reason those forms are held in being. Gradually there dawns on him a true understanding of the significance of the words "made in the image of God." His "consciousness is one and yet has produced the varied forms of the many" within his little cosmos, and what is true of him is true of his great prototype, the Heavenly Man, the planetary Logos, and true again of the prototype of his prototype, the Grand Man of the Heavens, the solar Logos, God in manifestation through the solar system.

**6. Among the forms which consciousness assumes, only that which is the result of meditation is free from latent karma.**

Forms are the result of desire. Meditation of the right kind is a purely mental process and into it desire enters not. Forms are the result of an outward-going urge or tendency. Meditation is the result of an inward-turning tendency, of the capacity to abstract the consciousness from form and substance and to centre it within itself.

Form is an effect produced by the love or desire nature of the conscious one; meditation is a producer of effects and relates to the will or life aspect of the spiritual man.

Desire produces effects, and the organs of sentient consciousness then come inevitably the law of cause and effect, of karma, which governs the relation of form—consciousness. The meditation process, when rightly understood and carried on, necessitates the withdrawal of the consciousness of the spiritual man from all forms in the three worlds, and his abstraction from all sense perception and tendencies. Thus he stands *at the moment of pure meditation* free from that aspect of karma which deals with the producing of effects. Temporarily, he is so abstracted that his thought, perfectly concentrated and having no relation to aught in the three worlds, produces no outward-going vibration, relates to no form, affects no substance. When this concentrated meditation becomes a habit and is the normal daily attitude of his life, then the man becomes free from the law

of karma. He becomes aware then of the effects
still remaining to be worked off, and learns to
avoid the creation of new ones, initiating no actions which will "create organs" in the three
worlds. He dwells on the plane of mind, persists
in meditation, creates by an act of will and not
through the helplessness of desire, and is a "free
soul," a master and a liberated man.

7. **The activities of the liberated soul are
free from the pairs of opposites. Those of other
people are of three kinds.**

This sutra expresses the teaching in connection
with the law of karma in such a strictly oriental
manner as to confuse the western student considerably. An analysis of the significance of these
words and a study of the commentary of the
great teacher Vyasa may serve to elucidate the
meaning. It should also be borne in mind that
in the fourth book we are dealing with the exalted
stages of consciousness reached by those who have
followed the eight means of yoga and have experienced the effects of meditation, detailed in
Book III. The yogi is now a liberated man, freed
from form conditions and focussed in his consciousness outside the bounds of the three worlds
of human endeavor. He has reached the realm
of pure thought and can hold his consciousness
untrammelled and free from desire. Therefore,
though he formulates ideas and though he can
carry on powerful meditations and though he can
direct and control the "modifications of the think-

ing principle," he creates no conditions which can serve to draw him back into the vortex of lower plane existence. He is freed from karma and originates nothing and no effects can serve to attach him to the wheel of rebirth.

Vyasa in his commentary points out that karma (or action) is of four kinds which are expressed for us as follows:

1. That type of activity which is evil, wicked and depraved. This is called *black*. This class of action is the product of the deepest ignorance, of the densest materiality, or of deliberate choice. Where it is the result of ignorance, the development of knowledge will gradually bring about a state of consciousness where this type of karma is no longer known. Where dense materiality produces what we call wrong action, the gradual development of the spiritual consciousness will change darkness to light and karma again is obviated. Where, however, it is the result of deliberate choice, or of preference for wrong action, in spite of knowledge and in defiance of the voice of the spiritual nature, then this type of karma leads to what the oriental occultist called "avitchi" or the eighth sphere,—a term synonymous with the Christian idea of the condition of being a lost soul. These cases are, however, exceedingly rare, and have relation to the left hand path, and the practice of black magic. Though this condition involves the severing of the highest principle (that of pure spirit from its two expressions, the soul and the body, or from the six lower principles), yet the life itself remains, and after the

destruction of the soul in avitchi, a fresh cycle of becoming will again be offered.

2. That type of activity which is neither all good nor all bad, which is spoken of as the *black-white*. It concerns the karmic activity of the average man, who is governed by the pairs of opposites, and whose life experience is characterized by a swinging back and forth between that which is kindly, harmless, and the result of love, and that which is harsh, harmful, and the result of hate. Vyasa says:

"The black-white is brought about by external means, as in this, the vehicle of actions grows by means of causing pain to, or acting kindly towards others."

It becomes apparent therefore that the growth of the human unit and his record are dependent upon his attitude towards others and the effect he has upon them. Thus is the return to group consciousness brought about and thus is karma generated or offset. Thus, also, is the swing of the pendulum between these pairs of opposites gradually adjusted until the point of equilibrium is reached, and man acts rightly because the law of love or of the soul, directs from above, and not because either good or bad desire attract him on either hand.

3. That type of activity which is called white. This is the type of living thought, and work, practised by the aspirant and the disciple. It characterizes the stage of the Path prior to liberation. Vyasa explains it thus:

"The white is of those who resort to the means of improvement, of study and meditation. This is dependent upon the mind alone. It does not depend upon external means, it is not, therefore, brought about by injuring others."

It will be apparent now that these three types of karma have direct reference to:

a. The plane of materiality....................the physical plane.
b. The plane of the pairs of opposites....the astral plane.
c. The plane of one-pointed thought......the mental plane.

Those whose karma is white are those who, having made progress in balancing the pairs of opposites, are now engaged in the process of conscious intelligent emancipation of themselves from the three worlds. This they do through:

a. *Study,* or mental development, through an appreciation of the law of evolution and an understanding of the nature of consciousness and its relation to matter on the one hand and to spirit on the other.

b. *Meditation,* or mind control and thus the creation of that mechanism which renders to the soul the control of the lower vehicles, and makes possible the revelation of the soul realm.

c. *Non-injury.* No word, thought or deed brings harm to any form through which the life of God is expressing itself.

4. The final type of karma is described as *neither black nor white.* No karma of any kind is engendered; no effects are set up through causes initiated by the yogi that can serve to hold him to the form side of manifestation. Acting as he does from the standpoint of non-attachment, de-

siring nothing for himself, his karma is nil, and his acts produce no effects upon himself.

**8. From these three kinds of karma emerge those forms which are necessary for the fruition of effects.**

In every life, as it comes into physical manifestation, are latent those germs or seeds which must bear fruit, and it is these latent seeds which are the efficient cause of the appearance of the form. Those seeds have been sown at some time and must come to fruition. They are the causes or skandas which produce those bodies in which the effects are to work themselves out. They are the desires, impulses and obligations which keep a man upon the great wheel, which ever turning, carries a man down into physical plane existence, there to bring to fruition as many of those seeds, as under the law, he can handle or deal with in any one life. These are the subjective germs which produce the form in which they fructify, mature and come to completion. If the karmic seeds are black, the man will be grossly selfish, material, and inclined to the left hand path; if black-white, they will carry him into a form suitable for the working out of his obligations, of his debts, duties and interests and the fulfilling of his desires; if they are white they tend to build that body which is the final one to be destroyed, the causal body, the temple of Solomon, the karana sarira of the occultist. That body, at the final liberation, is itself destroyed and naught then separates the man from his Father in Heaven, and nothing keeps him linked to the lower material plane.

**9. There is identity of relation between memory and effect producing cause, even when separated by species, time and place.**

A paraphrase of the sutra might serve to elucidate, and might be expressed as follows: No matter what the race may have been, no matter in what continent, past or present, a life may have been passed, and no matter how distant that life may be or how many millenia of years may have elapsed, the memory remains with the ego or soul. In due time, under proper adjustment, every cause then initiated must inevitably work out into effects and those effects will appear, working out in some one life. Nothing can prevent it, nothing can stop it. Charles Johnston expresses it in his commentary in the following words:

"In like manner, the same over-ruling selective power, which is a ray of the Higher Self, gathers together from different births and times and places those mind-images which are conformable, and may be grouped in the frame of a single life or a single event. Through this grouping, visible bodily conditions or outward circumstances are brought about, and by these the soul is taught and trained.

Just as the dynamic mind-images of desire ripen out in bodily conditions and circumstances, so the far more dynamic powers of aspiration,

[ 394 ]

wherein the soul reaches toward the Eternal, have their fruition in a finer world, building the vesture of the spiritual man."

**10. Desire to live being eternal, these mind-created forms are without known beginning.**

Another term which might be used in connection with the words "desire to live" is "the will to experience." Inherent in the informing self-conscious lives of our system (those existences who are superhuman and human) is this desire to be, this longing to become, this urge to contact the unknown and the distant. The explanation of this urge, being cosmic and dependent upon the evolutionary standpoint of that great Life in whom we live and move and have our being and in Whose body every form is but a cell or atom, is impossible for us to comprehend. All that a man can do is to build the mechanism which will make this comprehension possible, and to develop those powers which will enable him to contact and thus be en rapport with that which lies both without and within him. When this becomes possible he awakes to the realization that those desires which drive and impel him to action, those longings which force him into varied activities are something which are not only personal and real, but which are also part of the activity of the whole of which he is a tiny part. He discovers that the stream of desire-impelled mind images which occupy his attention and form the motive power of his life are formulated by himself, but are also part of a stream of cosmic mind images arising in the Universal Mind, as the result of the activity of that cosmic Thinker who functions as the Life of our solar system.

Thus the truth and teaching which has been formulated in the three previous books is lifted from the realm of the personal and the individual, and becomes wider, broader and more general. For the human unit the mind images, the result of desire and of thought action are therefore without known beginning. They surround him on all sides, the stream of their activity beats upon him at all times and draws forth from him that response which bears witness to the existence of desire within himself.

Therefore for him there must come two new activities; first, that of transmuting and transcending those desires and longings for sensuous perception which are found within himself, and secondly the task of insulating himself or isolating himself from the allure and influence of those greater streams of mind images which eternally exist. Thus only can he achieve the "condition of Isolated Unity" described in Book III. Sutra 50.

**11. These forms, being created and held together through desire, the basic cause, personality, the effective result, mental vitality or the will to live, and the support of the outward-going life or object, when these cease to attract, then the forms cease likewise to be.**

This sutra expresses a law of nature, and is so clear that but little explanation is needed. It might be of value, however, if we analyzed briefly the teaching given here.

We learn that four factors contribute to the existence of mind-images, or the forms which come into being as the result of the desire nature.

1. The basic cause................................desire.
2. The effect or result............................personality.
3. The will to live.................................mental vitality.
4. The outward going life......................the object.

When the cause, desire, has produced its effect, the personality or form aspect of man, then as long as the will to live exists, so long will the form persist. It is kept in manifestation through mental vitality. This has been demonstrated time and again in the annals of medicine, for it has been proven that as long as the determination to live persists so will be the probable duration of the physical plane life, but that the moment that will is withdrawn, or the interest of the dweller in the body is no longer centered upon personality manifestation, death ensues and the disintegration of that mind-image, the body, takes place.

It is interesting to note the occult meaning conveyed in the words "the support of the outward going life, or object" for it substantiates the occult teaching that the life stream passes downward from the originating cause and finds its object or final manifestation in the vital or etheric body which is the true substance of every form, and which constitutes the support or scaffold of the dense physical vehicle.

These four factors can be well divided into

two groups or pairs of opposites, the cause and the effect, the will to be and the true form or object.

For a long period in the evolutionary process the object or form-existence is the sole interest of the indweller, and the outward going life becomes the sole centre of attraction.

But as the wheel turns and experience after experience is entered into, the desire nature reaches satiety and is satisfied, and little by little the formulating of mind images and the production of their effects come to an end. Form consequently ceases, objective manifestation is no longer sought after, and liberation from maya or illusion takes place.

**12. The past and the present exist in reality. The form assumed in the time concept of the present is the result of developed characteristics, and holds latent seeds of future quality.**

In this sutra the three aspects of the Eternal Now are formulated for us and it is seen that what we are today is the product of the past, and that what we shall be in the future is dependent upon the seeds either latent and hidden, or sown in the present life. That which has been sown in the past exists and nothing can arrest or stop those seeds from coming to fruition. They must bear fruit in this present life or be concealed until a more favorable soil and more suitable condition can cause them to germinate, unfold, grow and flower forth into the clear light of day. There is nothing hidden or concealed which shall not be revealed nor anything secret which shall not be made known. The sowing of fresh seeds, and the originating of activities which must bear fruit at a later date is, however, a different matter and one more completely under the control of the man. By the practice of dispassion and of non-attachment, and by the strenuous control of the desire nature it becomes possible for the man to re-orient himself so that his attention is no longer attracted outward by the stream of mind-images but is withdrawn, and fixed one-pointedly upon reality.

This is first attempted through the control of the vehicle of thought, the mind, and the conquest of the modifications of the thinking principle, and then the work of using that mechanism and its employment in right directions and for the achieving of knowledge of the soul-realm instead of the matter realm proceeds. Thus again liberation is brought about.

**13. The characteristics, whether latent or potent, partake of the nature of the three gunas (the three qualities of matter).**

The characteristics are in reality the qualities, capacities and faculties which the man is manifesting or can manifest (given the right conditions). These are, as we have seen, the result or the effects of his entire past experience carried over the entire cycle of lives up to date. The product of the contacts, unfoldments and developments which have governed him from the earliest dawn of his individuality until the present life-cycle, produce what he is and has, in the present. It must be borne in mind that all these factors which are summed up under the general title of "characteristics" are concerned with the form and its responsiveness to the indwelling spiritual life.

They are produced just as rapidly as the spiritual Indweller can set his impress upon the substance of those forms, bend them to his will, control and subject them. Form has certain vibratory activities of its own, inherent in its own nature. By identification with the form and utilization of it, the Indweller develops a dual set of characteristics. One set demonstrates in the form of the lower self and concerns the adaptability of the form to inner influence, and to outer environment. The other concerns tendencies, impulses and desires which tend to affect permanently the body of the higher, or causal Self. Hence these characteristics are in both cases concerned with the rhythm or gunas of matter.

It might be said that what we are is the product of the past and shows as the characteristics of the form of the personality. What we shall be in the next incarnation is decided by the ability of the true man to influence that personal self, bend it to the higher ends and raise its rate of vibration. Man is one thing when he enters into incarnation; he is another when he passes out of incarnation, for he is then the product of the past, plus the achievement of the present life, and that achievement under the great evolutionary urge inevitably has carried him forward to-

wards a sattvic or rhythmic, harmonious condition, and away from the tamasic condition of
inertia, of immobility. This is achieved through
the imposition of the characteristics of activity,
the middle guna, and that which predominantly
controls the outward-going activity and drives the
man into sensuous experience.

**14. The manifestation of the objective form
is due to the one-pointedness of the effect-producing cause (the unification of the modifications of the chitta or mind stuff).**

The urge towards involution or towards form
taking is so dominant and so one-pointedly the
result of the egoic thought that it makes objective manifestation inevitable. The chitta or mind
stuff (in the great process of form appropriation)
is so thoroughly unified and the desire to experience through physical plane contacts is so dominant, that the many modifications of the mind
are all turned towards the same object.

When the condition is reversed and the man on
the physical plane effects his own liberation, it is
also by the same method, one-pointedness and unification. The old commentary makes this clear
in certain lines found in relation to the symbolism
of the five-pointed star. They are as follows:

"The plunge is downward into matter. The point
descends, darts through the watery sphere and pierces
into that which looms inert, immobile, darkling, silent
and remote. The point of fire and stone unite, and
harmony and union on the downward path are reached.

"The flight is upward into spirit. The point ascends, lifting the two behind and reaching out the three and four towards that which lies behind the veil. The water fails to quench the point of fire; thus fire meets fire and blends. Harmony, union on the upward arc are reached. Thus shall the sun move northward."

**15. These two, consciousness and form, are distinct and separate; though forms may be similar, the consciousness may function on differing levels of being.**

This sutra should not be considered apart from the succeeding one, which predicates the fact of the one Mind, or the one Life being the potent cause of all differentiated lesser minds and lives. This must ever be realized. Three main thoughts therefore lie involved in this sutra.

First, that there are two main lines of evolution, that which concerns matter and form, and that which concerns the soul, the consciousness aspect, the thinker in manifestation. For each of these the path of progress differs and each pursues its course. As has been noted, for a long period of time, the soul identifies itself with the form aspect and endeavors to follow the "Path of Death" for that is what the dark path is in fact to the thinker. Later, through strenuous effort, this identification ceases; the soul becomes aware of itself, and of its own path, or dharma, and follows then the way of light and of life. It should ever be borne in mind, however, that for the two aspects their own path is the right path and that the impulses which lie hidden in the physical ve-

hicle or in the astral body are not in themselves
wrong. They became wrong from certain angles
when twisted from their right use, and it was this
realization that led the disciple in the Book of
Job to cry out and say "I have perverted that
which was right." The two lines of development
are separate and distinct, and this every aspirant
has to learn.

When this is grasped, he seeks to aid the evolution of his forms in two ways; first by refusing to
identify himself with them, and secondly, by
stimulating them.

Through the bringing in of spiritual force, he
will also realize the point in evolution at which his
brothers stand, and cease to criticize them for
what may be to him wrong action, but which is for
them the natural activity of the form during the
cycle wherein form and soul are identified and
considered the same.

The second main line of thought involved in
Sutra 15 is more difficult to express. It lends
colour and veracity to the contention of many
thinkers that things exist and have form and
activity only in so far as the mind of the thinker
formulates them. In other words, that through
the modifications of our own thinking principle
we build our own world, and create our own environment. The inference, therefore, is that
(given the one basic substance, spirit-matter) we
weave it into forms by our own thought impulses.
Others perceive that which we see, because some
of the modifications of their minds are analogous
to ours and their reactions and impulses are sim-

ilar in some respects. Yet no two people see an object in exactly the same way. "Things" or forms of matter do exist; they are created or in process of creation and for them some mind or minds are responsible. It becomes then a question as to who is responsible for the thought forms by which we are surrounded. Dvivedi's commentary and translation leans more to this second line of thought than does the paraphrase of the Tibetan, and it is of profit to study it, for in the approach of many minds to a problem, its magnitude can be appreciated, idle and light conclusions are avoided, and approximation to truth becomes possible. The synthetic point of view is nearer to universal truth than is the specialized. He says:

"Though things are similar, the cause of mind and things is distinct in consequence of the difference of minds."

"The preceding considerations establish, in an indirect manner, the existence of things as objects external to the mind. The Vijnanavadi-Buddhas who maintain that things are but the reflections of our thinking principle, would object to such a position. The objection could not bear examination, for the existence of things apart from the thinking principle is certain. Though there is, indeed, complete similarity among objects of the same class, still the way in which the objects affect the mind, and the way in which the mind is affected by them, are entirely distinct. Hence objects exist out of the thinking principle. Though objects are similar they are not presented to different minds in the same light, which shows that they are apart from the mind. Again, we often hear more than one person saying that he has seen the same object as is seen by another. This would prove that though the object is one, the cognizers are many. This circumstance proves the distinction of the object and the mind. Again the seer and the sight, *i. e.*, the mind and the object or the instrument of knowledge and the object of knowledge cannot be one and the same, for then all distinctive knowledge will be impossible, which, however, is absurd. To attempt a solution of this difficulty by saying that eternal vasana of the form of external objects is the cause of all our distinctive knowledge is useless, for that which has already spent itself cannot become the cause. Hence objective existence must be granted as independent of the subject. Nor should it be imagined how one substance (viz. Prakriti) could produce in this case all the multifarious differences of our experience, for the three gunas and their various combinations in different degrees are enough to account for all that. In the case of Yogins properly enlightened it is but proper that knowledge having produced in them supreme Vairagya they do not care for the gunas, which also assume a state of equilibrium and produce no effect."

The third line of thought deals more specifically with the realization aspect, or with the condition of awareness of the indwelling thinker and is therefore of immediate practical value to the student of Raja Yoga. It involves certain questions which might be expressed as follows:

1.   On what level of being or of realization (for the thought is identical to the occult student) do I function?

2.   Do I identify myself with the form or with the soul?

3.   Which path am I following, the high way of the soul, or the low way of matter?

4.   Am I in a transition period, wherein my realization is being transferred from the lower to the higher consciousness?

5.   Though in the body, is it just my instrument, and am I awake on another plane of awareness?

These, and similar questions are of profound value to the aspirant, if asked sincerely and answered truthfully, as in the presence of God and of the Master.

**16.   The many modifications of the one mind produce the diverse forms, which depend for existence upon those many mind impulses.**

In these words, the whole concept is swung out of the realm of the particular into the kingdom of universals.  We are brought face to face with cosmic and solar impulses and the smallness and littleness of our individual problem becomes apparent.  Every form in manifestation is the result of God's thought; every objective vehicle through which the life impulses of the universe flow is produced and kept in objective manifestation through the steady flow of thought currents emanating from one stupendous cosmic thinker.  His mysterious ways, His secret hidden plan, the great purpose towards which He is working in this solar system, is as yet not apparent to man. However, as man's capacity to think in large terms, as his power to visualize the past as a whole, and to unify what knowledge he has of the life of God as it works through the kingdoms of nature, and as his understanding of the nature of consciousness grows, the will of God (based on loving activity) will become apparent.

The clue to the how and the why lies in man's comprehension of his own mental activities. An appreciation of God's great thought form, a solar system and its maintenance, will grow as man comprehends his own thought forms and the way he builds and creates his own environment and colours his own life. He constructs his own worlds by the power of his mental processes and the modifications of that fragment of the universal thinking principle which he has appropriated for his own use.

The solar Logos, God, let it be remembered, is the sum total of every state of consciousness or awareness. Man,—humanity as a whole, or an individual unit—is part of that total. The many minds, from the mind of the atom (recognized by science) to the mind of God Himself, through all grades of thinkers and stages of awareness, are responsible for every form found in our system. As we work from the infinitely small to the infinitely great, from the microcosm to the macrocosm, a gradually expanding state of consciousness and a steadily increasing condition of awareness becomes apparent. In this scale of development three outstanding types of forms are found, as the result of mind;

1. The form of the atom, the true microcosm.
2. The form of man, the macrocosm for all the subhuman kingdom.
3. The form of God, a solar system, the macrocosm for man and all the superhuman stages.

All these forms, with all intermediate forms are dependent upon some life, endowed with the capacity to think, and through thought impulse to modify and influence sentient substance, and build it into forms.

**17. These forms are cognized or not, according to the qualities latent in the perceiving consciousness.**

This has been translated most ably by Charles Johnston in the words:

"An object is perceived or it is not perceived, according as the mind is, or is not, tinged with the colour of the object."

We see what we are ourselves; we become aware of that in other forms which is developed in ourselves. We fail to see aspects of life because as yet in ourselves, those aspects are undeveloped and latent. To illustrate: we fail to see the divine in our brother because as yet the divine in ourselves is uncontacted and unknown; the form aspect and its limitations are developed in us and the soul is so hidden that we only become aware of the form of our brother, and fail to see his soul. The moment we contact our own soul and live by its light we see the soul of our brother, become aware of his light and our entire approach to him is changed.

Herein lies the clue to our limitations. Herein lies the promise of our success. Latent faculty, when developed, will reveal to us a new world. The hidden powers of the soul when brought to full expression will make us aware of a new world and reveal to us a scheme of life and a kingdom of being hitherto negated by us, because not seen. Hence the need for every investigator of the mysteries of existence to bring to his search his full equipment, and hence the necessity therefore for this process of soul unfoldment to be carried forward and potential faculties to be developed if the truth in its fullness is ever to be realized.

**18. The Lord of the mind, the perceiver, is ever aware of the constantly active mind stuff, the effect-producing cause.**

We have in this sutra a statement which is the key to effective and safe meditation work. The one who meditates is the soul, the ego, and his work is a positive activity, not a negative state or condition. Much of the work done under the name of meditation is dangerous and useless, because that which seeks control is the man on the physical plane, and his endeavour is concentrated on the attainment of brain stillness. He seeks to quiet the brain cells, and render them negative, quiescent and receptive. True meditation, however, concerns the soul and the mind; the receptivity of the brain is an automatic reaction to the higher condition. In Raja Yoga, therefore, contact with the true man, the ego, and the power to "still the modifications of the thinking principle" must precede all brain activity and responsiveness. The Lord of the mind is ever awake, ever aware of the tendency of the mind to respond to force currents, produced by thought or desire; he therefore watches every emanation of force issuing from him, and controls every thought and impulse so that only those streams of energy and those impulses originate with him which are in line with the purpose held constantly in view, and in pursuance of the group plan.

It must never be forgotten that all egos work in group formation and under the direct control of those Thinkers who embody the divine logoic thought. The work every aspirant, therefore, seeks to do is to bring the brain consciousness in line with that thought which reaches him via his own soul-consciousness, and in the consummation of this, the divine plan is gradually worked out into manifestation on the physical plane.

As each son of God brings the active mind stuff for which he is responsible into such a condition that it becomes responsive to divine thought, then will the plan of the ages be carried to a conclusion. No man need despair because of his seeming incompetence or apparent littleness for to each of us is entrusted some part of the plan and we must work it out; without our cooperation there comes delay and confusion. Sometimes there comes much trouble when a tiny part of a big mechanism refuses to function correctly. Frequently much adjustment is needed before the complete machine can go forward successfully in its work, and in the realm of human cooperation an analogous situation is apt to occur.

The constantly active mind stuff can respond to the lower vibration, emanating from the threefold lower man and to the higher impulse, issuing from the soul, as the intermediary between spirit and matter. The soul is ever aware of this condition; man on the physical plane is blind to it or just awaking to the dual possibility. The work of the aspirant to union is to swing the mind stuff gradually and increasingly under the higher impulse and away from the lower vibration, until the responsiveness to the higher becomes a stable condition and the vibratory activity of the lower man fades and dies out.

**19. Because it can be seen or cognized, it is apparent that the mind is not the source of illumination.**

This sutra and the two following give us a typical oriental approach to a very difficult problem, and this method of reasoning is not an easy one for western minds to grasp. In the six schools of Hindu philosophy this whole problem of the source of creation and of the nature of the mind is dissected and discussed and so completely covered that practically all our modern schools can be regarded as outgrowths or logical sequential results of the varied Hindu positions. The clue to the diversity of opinions on these two points may perhaps be found in the six types into which all human beings fall, for the seventh is but the synthesis of them all and inclusive, not exclusive.

In the *Yoga Sutras,* the mind is relegated simply to the position of an instrument, of an intermediary, of a sensitive plate, registering either that which pours into it from above or that which affects it from below. It has no personality of its own; it has no life or light of its own, except that which is inherent in all substance and therefore to be found in the atoms which constitute the mind stuff. These latter, being along the same evolutionary line as the rest of the lower nature, swell the tide of material forces which seeks to hold the soul prisoner, and constitute the great illusion.

The mind, therefore, can be cognized in two directions: first, it can be known, recognized and seen by the thinker, the soul on its own plane, and secondly, it can be seen and known as a vehicle of the man on the physical plane. For a long time man became that with which he identified himself to the exclusion of the true spiritual man, who can be known, contacted and obeyed once the mind is relegated to its rightful place as an instrument of knowledge.

A physical plane analogy may help here. The eye is one of our major senses, that whereby we acquire knowledge, a medium through which we see. We, however, do not make the mistake of regarding the eye itself as a source of light and as that which produces revelation. We know it as an instrument which is responding to certain light vibrations whereby certain information is conveyed anent the physical plane to our brain,

at great receiving plate upon the physical plane.
o the soul, the mind acts also as an eye or a
indow through which information comes, but is
ot itself the source of light or illumination.

It is interesting here to note that as the brain
nd the mind became coordinated, (as was first
he case in Lemurian days) the sense of sight was
imultaneously developed. As evolution proceeds,
a higher coordination takes place, and the soul
and the mind become at-oned. Then, that organ
of subtle vision (the third eye) begins to function,
and instead of mind, brain, and two eyes, another
triplicity supersedes and we have soul, mind and
the third eye. The brain, therefore, is not the
source of illumination but becomes aware of the
light of the soul and of what it reveals in the
realm of the soul. The third eye simultaneously
develops and admits its possessor into the secrets
of the subtler realms in the three worlds, so that
the brain receives illumination, information and
knowledge from two directions; from the soul
via the mind, and from the subtler planes in the
three worlds via the third eye. It should be remembered here that the third eye reveals primarily the light to be found in the heart of every
form of divine manifestation.

20. **Neither can it know two objects simultaneously, itself and that which is external to
itself.**

None of the sheaths through which the soul
functions has self-knowledge; they are only the
channels through which knowledge is gained and

life experience undergone. The mind does not know itself, for that would predicate self-consciousness, and therefore not having individual consciousness it is unable to say "this is I, myself, and this is external to me, and consequently the not-self." It is simply another sense whereby information is gained and a further field of knowledge revealed. It is naught but an instrument, as said before, capable of a dual function, registering contacts from one of two directions and transmitting that knowledge to the brain from the soul or to the soul from the lower man. This must be meditated upon and the whole trend of one's endeavor be to bring that instrument into such a condition that it can be used to the best possible advantage. This is what the three last means of yoga seek to do. As this has been covered earlier it is needless to enlarge upon this here.

**21. If knowledge of the mind (chitta) by a remoter mind is postulated, an infinite number of knowers must be inferred, and the sequence of memory reactions would tend to infinite confusion.**

One of the explanations of the functions of the mind is to predicate its capacity to detach itself from itself and view itself as a thing apart. In this way, it becomes a confusion of detached parts, remote from each other and leading (as the idea is carried forward to a logical conclusion) to a chaotic condition. All this has risen from the refusal of orthodox thinkers along philosophical and mental lines to admit the possibility of there being an entity, detached and apart from the mind who simply seeks to use it as a means to knowledge. The problem has arisen very largely from the fact that this thinker cannot be *known* until the mind is developed; he can be sensed and felt by the mystic and the devotee but knowledge of him (in the usual significance of the term) is not available until the instrument of knowledge, the mind, has been developed. Here is where Eastern knowledge comes in and clarifies the work so marvellously done by the mental and Christian scientists. They have emphasized the fact of mind, individual and universal, and our debt to them is great. The nature of mind, its purpose, control, its problems and processes are subjects of common discussion today whereas one hundred years ago this was not the case. But with it all, much confusion remains as the result of our modern tendency to deify the mind and to regard it as the one important factor. Eastern science comes to our rescue and says to us that back of the mind is the thinker, back of perception, the perceiver is to be found, and behind the object of observation lies the one who observes. This perceiver, thinker and observer is the immortal imperishable ego, the soul in contemplation.

**22. When the spiritual intelligence, which stands alone and freed from objects, reflects itself in the mind stuff, then comes awareness of the self.**

This spiritual intelligence, which is the real

man, the Son of God, eternal in the Heavens, is known by many and varied names, according to the school of thought. The appended list of synonyms is of value to the student, for it gives him a broader vision and an inclusive understanding, revealing to him the fact that the Sons of God, revealed or unrevealed, are everywhere to be found.

| | | |
|---|---|---|
| The spiritual Intelligence. | The inner Ruler. | The Word made Flesh. |
| The Soul. | The second aspect. | The AUM. |
| The self-conscious Entity. | The second Person. | The Thinker. |
| The Christ. | God in incarnation. | The Observer, Perceiver. |
| The Self. | The Son of Mind. | The Form builder. |
| The higher Self. | The divine Manasaputra. | Force. |
| The Son of God. | The Agnishvattva. | The Dweller in the body. |

These and many other terms will be found scattered throughout the scriptures and literature of the world. In no book, however, is the nature of the soul, whether macrocosmic (the cosmic Christ), or microcosmic (the individual Christ), so wonderfully portrayed as in the *Bhagavad Gita* and in the three books, the *Bhagavad Gita,* the *New Testament* and the *Yoga Sutras* is contained a complete picture of the soul and its unfoldment.

23. **Then the mind stuff, reflecting both the knower and the knowable, becomes omniscient.**

This sutra is in the nature of a summation and emphasizes the fact that the mind, being stilled and quiescent through the practise of concentra-

ion and meditation, becomes the reflector of "that
which is above and of that which lies below." It
s the transmitter of the knowledge of the self to
the physical brain of the man in incarnation, and
the transmitter also of all that which the self
knows and perceives. The field of knowledge is
seen and known. The knower is also perceived,
and the "perception of all objects" becomes possible. It becomes literally true, therefore, that for
the yogin nothing remains hidden or unknown.
Information on all subjects becomes possible to
him, for he has an instrument which he can use
to ascertain that which the soul knows concerning the Kingdom of God, the realm of spiritual
truth. He can also enter into communication and
convey to the soul that which is known to the man
in physical incarnation. Thus the knower, the
field of knowledge and knowledge itself are
brought into conjunction and the medium of this
union is the mind.

This is one great stage upon the path of return,
and though in due time the intuition will supersede the mind, and direct spiritual perception
take the place of mental perception, yet this stage
is an advanced and important one, and opens the
door to direct illumination. Nothing need now
hinder the downflow of spiritual force and wisdom
into the brain, for the entire lower threefold man
has been purified and dominated, and the physical,
emotional and mental bodies form simply a
channel for the divine light, and constitute the
vehicle through which the life and love of God
may manifest.

**24.** **The mind stuff also, reflecting as it does an infinity of mind impressions, becomes the instrument of the Self and acts as a unifying agent.**

Nothing remains for the spiritual man to do in connection with this purified lower self but to learn to use his instrument, the mind, and through it the other two bodies are directed, controlled and utilized. Through the eight means of yoga his instrument has been discovered, developed and mastered and must now be brought into active use, and employed in three ways.

1. As a vehicle for the life of the soul.
2. In the service of the Hierarchy.
3. In cooperation with the plan of evolution.

In Book I. Sutra 41, we find these words: "To him whose Vrittis (modifications of the substance of the mind) are entirely controlled there eventuates a state of identity with, and similarity to, that which is realized. The knower, knowledge and the field of knowledge become one, just as the crystal takes to itself the colours of that which is reflected in it." This gives us a picture of what happens to the man who has mastered his instrument. He registers in his brain, via the mind, that which is true and real; he becomes aware of the nature of the ideal and bends every power which he possesses to the work of bringing that ideal into objective manifestation; he sees the vision of the kingdom of God as it will be in the latter days, and all that he has and is he renders up in order that the vision may be seen by all;

he knows the plan, for it is revealed to him in the "secret place upon the Mount of God," and he cooperates with it intelligently upon the physical plane; he hears the Voice of the Silence and obeys its injunction, working steadily at the task of spiritual living in a world consecrated to things material.

All this is possible to the man who has stilled the versatile psychic nature and has mastered the kingly science of Raja Yoga.

In the hidden literature of the adepts the following stanzas sum up the state of the man who has achieved, who is master and not servant, conqueror and not slave:

"The fivefold one hath entered into peace, yet walks our sphere. That which is dense and dark now shineth with a clear pure light, and radiance poureth from the seven sacred lotuses. He lighteneth the world, and irradiateth the nethermost place with fire divine.

That which hath hitherto been restless, wild as the ocean, turgid as the stormy sea, lies quiet and still. Limpid the waters of the lower life and fit to offer to the thirsty ones who, groping, cry of thirst.

That which hath slain and veiled the Real for many lengthy aeons is itself slain, and with its death the separated life is ended. The One is seen. The Voice is heard. The Real is known, the Vision glimpsed. The fire of God leaps upward into a flame.

The darkest place receives the light. The dawn appears on earth. The dayspring from on high, sheds its bright beams in hell itself, and all is light and life."

Then before the liberated yogi a choice is placed. He faces a spiritual problem and its nature has been conveyed to us in the following fragment of an old esoteric catechism:

"What dost thou see, Oh! liberated one? Many who
suffer, Master, who weep and cry for help.

What will thou do, Oh! man of peace? Return from
whence I came.

Whence comest thou, Pilgrim divine? From the
lowest depths of darkness, thence upwards into light.

Where goest thou, Oh! Traveller upon the upward
way? Back to the depths of darkness, away from the
light of day.

Wherefore this step, Oh! Son of God? To gather those
who stumble in the darkness and light their steps upon
the path.

When is the term of service, Oh! Saviour of men?
I know not, save that whilst one suffers I stay behind
and serve."

**25. The state of isolated unity (withdrawn
into the true nature of the Self) is the reward
of the man who can discriminate between the
mind stuff and the Self, or spiritual man.**

This state of isolated unity must be regarded as
the result of the attainment of a particular state
of mind, rather than as a separative reaction.

All meditation work, all moments of reflection,
all affirmative exercises, all hours of recollection
of one's true nature are means employed to detach
the mind from the lower reactions and tendencies,
and build in the habit of a constant realization of one's true divine nature. When this realization is achieved, the need for such exercises
ceases and one enters into one's heritage. The
isolation referred to is the detachment of the self
from the field of knowledge, the involving of the
refusal of the self to seek outward-going sensu-

ous experience and its standing firm in the state of spiritual being.

The man becomes conscious of himself as the knower and is no longer primarily concerned with the field of knowledge, as in the early stages of his unfoldment; neither is he engaged with knowledge itself, as during the stage of mental development either as an advanced man or as a disciple. He can discriminate between all three, and identifies himself henceforth neither with the field of knowledge, life in the three worlds through the medium of his three vehicles, and the five senses plus the mind, nor with the knowledge gained nor the experience undergone. He knows the self; he identifies himself with the true knower, and thus sees things as they are, dissociating himself entirely from the world of sensuous perception.

He does this, however, whilst functioning as a human being on earth. He participates in earth experience; he involves himself in human activities; he walks among men, eating and sleeping, working and living. Yet all the time he "is in the world, yet not of the world," and of him it can be said as it was said of the Christ,

"Who, being in the form of God, thought it not robbery to be equal with God:

But made himself of no reputation, and took upon him the form of a servant, and was made in the likeness of men:

And being found in fashion as a man, he humbled himself, and became obedient unto death, even the death of the cross." (Phil. II. 6. 7. 8.)

He is at-one with the soul of all, but isolated off, separated from all that concerns the form or material nature. The next three sutras should be read as one, giving as they do a picture of the gradual growth of the spiritual nature in the man who has arrived at the state of discriminating detachment, and through utter dispassion, knows the meaning of isolated unity.

**26, 27, 28. The mind then tends towards discrimination and increasing illumination as to the true nature of the one Self. Through force of habit, however, the mind will reflect other mental impressions and perceive objects of sensuous perception. These reflections are of the nature of hindrances and the method of their overcoming is the same.**

The right tendencies and rhythm having been set up, it becomes simply a question of steady perseverance, common sense and endurance. Unless the utmost vigilance is exerted, the old habits of mind will very easily reassert themselves, and even until the final initiation the aspirant must "watch and pray."

The rules which govern victory, the practices which bring success are the same for the advanced expert warrior and initiate as they are for the humblest neophyte. In Book II. the methods whereby the hindrances and obstacles could be overcome and negated are most carefully given and from the moment of stepping upon the probationary path until that high moment when the last great initiation has been experienced, and the liberated man stands forth in the full light of day, these methods and modes of disciplined living must be adhered to unswervingly. This involves patience, the capacity to go on after failure, to persevere when success seems far away. This was well known to the great initiate, Paul, and was the cause of his injunction to the disciples he sought to help. "Stand therefore . . . and having done all, stand." James gives us the same thought where he says "Behold we count them happy that endure."

It is the going on when the point of exhaustion has been reached, the taking of another step when the strength to do so seems gone, the holding steady when there seems nothing but defeat ahead, and the determination to endure whatever may be coming, when endurance has been taxed to the limit, which is the hallmark of disciples of every degree. To them goes out the clarion call of Paul:

"Stand therefore, having your loins girt about with truth, and having on the breastplate of righteousness;
And your feet shod with the preparation of the gospel of peace;
Above all, taking the shield of faith, wherewith ye shall be able to quench all the fiery darts of the wicked.
And take the helmet of salvation, and the word of the Spirit, which is the word of God." (Eph. VI. 14. 15. 16. 17.)

The equally clear command of Krishna to Arjuna sounds out also:

"Having regard to thy duty, deign not to shrink back. For nothing is better for a warrior than a righteous

battle. And such a battle has come to thee of its own
accord, a very door of heaven will be opened; happy the
warriors . . . who find such a fight as this. . . . Therefore, arise, determined to do battle. Making equal good
and ill fortune, gain and loss, victory and defeat, gird
thyself for the fight." (Gita II. 31. 32. 38. 37.)

**29. The man who develops non-attachment
even in his aspiration after illumination and
isolated unity becomes aware, eventually, of the
overshadowing cloud of spiritual knowledge.**

It is difficult for the neophyte to be impersonal
where his own spiritual unfoldment is concerned.
Yet the very earnestness of his aspiration may
serve as a hindrance, and one of the first things
he has to learn is to go forward along the path,
adhering to the rules, following the practices,
employing the means and steadily fulfilling the
law and at the same time to be occupied with the
vision and with service and not with himself.
It is so easy to be the victim of high desire and
so busy with the reactions and emotions of the
aspiring lower man that rapidly one is enmeshed
afresh in the toils of the versatile psychic nature.

Non-attachment to all forms of sensuous perception, the high as well as the low, has to be
developed.

Many people, when they are transferring from
the path of feeling and the devotional heart approach (the mystic line) on to the path of intellectual control,—the approach via the head,
the occult method,—complain that the old moments of joy and bliss, experienced in meditation,

have gone. The system now followed seems arid, dry and unsatisfactory. But joy and peace are registrations of the emotional nature and in no way affect reality. It is immaterial from the standpoint of the soul whether its reflection, man in incarnation, is happy or not, blissful or sad, contented or in trouble. Only one thing matters, the attainment of soul contact, the arriving at union (conscious and intelligent) with the One. This union may work out in the physical plane consciousness as a sense of peace and joy; it *must* work out in increased capacity to serve the race and to serve it more efficiently. The feelings of the disciple are of small moment; his understanding and usefulness as a channel for spiritual force are of importance. It should be remembered that on the path neither our virtues nor our vices count (except in so far as we escape from the pairs of opposites). That alone counts which impels us forward on that path which "shineth more and more until the day be with us."

When a man can detach his eyes from all that concerns the physical, emotional and mental, and will raise his eyes and direct them away from himself, he will become aware of "the overshadowing cloud of spiritual knowledge," or of the "rain-cloud of knowable things," as it has also been translated.

Here we have, esoterically, and symbolically given, the indication that there lies before the initiate (advanced as he is) a still further progress, another veil to be penetrated. He has made a great at-one-ment and has unified soul and body. He stands (as regards the three worlds) at the stage called that of isolated unity. But another union becomes possible, that of the soul, with the spirit. The Master must become the Christ and to do this the raincloud of spiritual knowledge must be reached, used and penetrated. What lies on the other side of that veil which hides the Father it is needless for us to consider. In our *New Testament,* when the Father communicated with the Christ, the voice issued out of a cloud. (See Matt. XVII.)

**30. When this stage is reached then the hindrances and karma are overcome.**

The two verses we have just studied have carried the aspirant on from the stage of adept to that of the Christ.

All that hindered, veiled or prevented the full expression of the divine life has been overcome; all barriers are down, all obstacles removed. The wheel of rebirth has served its purpose and the spiritual unit which has entered into form, carrying with it potential powers and latent possibilities, has developed them to their full extent and unfolded the full flower of the soul. The law of cause and effect as it functions in the three worlds no longer controls the liberated soul; his individual karma comes to an end, and though he may still be subservient to group karma (planetary or solar), he himself has nothing to work out nor does he initiate anything which can serve to bind him, by the chains of desire, to the three worlds. His state is summed up for us in the next sutra.

**31. When, through the removal of hindrances and the purifications of the sheaths, the totality of knowledge becomes available, naught further remains for the man to do.**

The dual work is accomplished. Those hindrances which are the result of ignorance, blindness, environment and activity have been done away with; the grossness of the sheaths has been corrected and because of this, and through following the means of yoga, all knowledge becomes available. The yogi is now aware of his essential omnipresence or that his soul is one with all souls and part therefore of the one essential unity, the one all-pervading life, the boundless immutable principle which is the cause of all manifestation. He is likewise omniscient, for all knowledge is his and all avenues of knowledge are open to him. He stands free of the field of knowledge, yet can function in it; he can utilize the instrument of knowledge and ascertain all that he seeks to know, but is himself centered in the consciousness of the knower. Neither space nor time can hold him, nor can the material form imprison him, and there comes for him the grand consummation given to us by Patanjali in his three concluding sutras:

[ 427 ]

"Sutra 32. The modifications of the mind stuff (or qualities of matter), through the inherent nature of the three gunas come to an end, for they have served their purpose.

Sutra 33. Time, which is the sequence of the modifications of the mind, likewise terminates, giving place to the Eternal Now.

Sutra 34. The state of isolated unity becomes possible when the three qualities of matter (the three gunas or potencies of nature) no longer exercise any hold over the Self. The pure spiritual consciousness withdraws into the One."

# THE GREAT INVOCATION

From the point of Light within the Mind of God
Let light stream forth into the minds of men.
Let Light descend on Earth.

From the point of Love within the Heart of God
Let love stream forth into the hearts of men.
May Christ return to Earth.

From the centre where the Will of God is known
Let purpose guide the little wills of men—
The purpose which the Masters know and serve.

From the centre which we call the race of men
Let the Plan of Love and Light work out
And may it seal the door where evil dwells.

Let Light and Love and Power restore the Plan on Earth.

"The above Invocation or Prayer does not belong to any person or group but to all Humanity. The beauty and the strength of this Invocation lies in its simplicity, and in its expression of certain central truths which all men, innately and normally, accept—the truth of the existence of a basic Intelligence to Whom we vaguely give the name of God; the truth that behind all outer seeming, the motivating power of the universe is Love; the truth that a great Individuality came to earth, called by Christians, the Christ, and embodied that love so that we could understand; the truth that both love and intelligence are effects of what is called the Will of God; and finally the self-evident truth that only through *humanity* itself can the Divine Plan work out."—ALICE A. BAILEY.

Training for new age
discipleship is provided
by the *Arcane School.*
The principles of the
Ageless Wisdom are
presented through esoteric
meditation, study and
service as a *way of life.*

*Write to the publishers*
*for information.*

# INDEX

## A

...lute principle, 99
...raction—
  spirit out of form, 386
...ocess, 282-283
  *e also* Yoga, means.
...on—
  ...pidity, 352, 353
  ...ga of, 119-125
...vity—
  ...tribute, 32, 148-149
  *...e also* Gunas.
...pt—
  ...eative work, 96, 196, 348
  ...stinctive mark, 275
  ...ee of attachment, 138
  ...ee of limitations, 356
  ...erm of all knowledge, 49
  ...hysical vehicle, 147
  ...ower, 196
  ...Christ, process, 426
  ...ration of devotee, 135
  ...ishvattas, portrayal, 299-300
  ...mkara principle, 128, 158-159
  ..., purification by, 208
  ...a centre, 81, 83, 305
...sha—
  ...ature of, 338-339
  ...elation to body, 338-339
  ...elation to sound, meditation on,
    333
...vidya concerned, 140
...ashic records—
  ...escription, 275-276
  ...eading, 275, 276-279
...cohol, use, 381
...ignment—
...of bodies, 226, 232, 368
...of thinker, mind, and brain, 284
...process, consummation, 338-339,
    353
...l—
...knowledge, germ, expansion, 49-
    51

plan or purpose, knowledge of,
    34
  that is, existence for sake of
    soul, 164
All-self, one with, 177
All-soul, knowledge and oneness
  with, 35
Alone with himself, 135-136
Alta-major centre, activation, 69
Analogy, law, 89
Angel—
  of the Presence, 40
  Solar, 40, 48-49
Angels, aid, invocation, 380
Anima mundi, 378
Annu to atma, 88-89, 345
Antaskarana, building, 295
Anxieties, concerns, 149-150
Apana, concern, 329-330
Appearance, relation to subjective
  happening, 280
Appearances, all, reason for, 385
Archetype of Plan, 41
Archives, Masters', quotation, 286
Army of the Voice, 96
Aryan—
  disciple, task, 215
  initiation, 14
  line of contact, 43
  unfoldment, 304-310
  Word, 56
  work, 56
  yogas, x, xi, 214
Ascension out of matter, 338-339
Aspect, second, functioning in, 19
Aspiration, fiery, 119-125, 187,
    189-190, 208-209
Astral—
  body—
    colours, 349
    coordination and growth, 305
    mystery concerned, 216
    purification, results, 205, 206
    responsiveness to two types of
      energy, 216

431